ASSESSMENT AND INTERVENTION IN SOCIAL WORK

CHRIS BECKETT

ASSESSMENT AND INTERVENTION IN SOCIAL WORK

Preparing for Practice

$SAGE

Los Angeles | London | New Delhi
Singapore | Washington DC

First published 2010

SAGE Publications Ltd
1 Oliver's Yard
55 City Road
London EC1Y 1SP

SAGE Publications Inc.
2455 Teller Road
Thousand Oaks, California 91320

SAGE Publications India Pvt Ltd
B 1/I 1 Mohan Cooperative Industrial Area
Mathura Road
New Delhi 110 044

SAGE Publications Asia-Pacific Pte Ltd
33 Pekin Street #02-01
Far East Square
Singapore 048763

Library of Congress Control Number: 2010926585

British Library Cataloguing in Publication data

A catalogue record for this book is available from
the British Library

ISBN 978-1-84860-130-7
ISBN 978-1-84860-131-4 (pbk)

Typeset by C&M Digitals (P) Ltd, Chennai, India
Printed and bound in Great Britain by TJ International Ltd, Padstow, Cornwall
Printed on paper from sustainable resources

Mixed Sources
Product group from well-managed
forests and other controlled sources
www.fsc.org Cert no. SGS-COC-2482
© 1996 Forest Stewardship Council
FSC

CONTENTS

LIST OF TABLES

LIST OF FIGURES

LIST OF PLACEMENT QUESTIONS

LIST OF CASE EXAMPLES

1 INTRODUCTION

- The nature of social work
- Recognising our limits
- Using this book

This book is about how we come to make judgements about what needs addressing in a given situation (assessment), and about providing a service (intervention). It is about how you decide what needs doing, in other words, and what you actually do. Since these two activities arguably encompass most of the job of a social worker, the book could almost just have been called 'Doing Social Work'.

The book is aimed in particular at social work students who are on placement, or are writing about their placements. This book does not offer a comprehensive 'how to do it' guide, and does not pretend to offer comprehensive cover of all the literature, but I hope it will help you to think about what you are seeing and doing, and support you in using your own eyes, ears and critical faculties. Part of being a good social worker is being awake to what is around you, thinking for yourself, and not just repeating formulas provided for you by others, whether those others be your employers, your teachers, your colleagues or even your service users.

As I will mention more than once in the course of this book, social work intrudes into the personal sphere and involves interactions with human beings that can sometimes completely transform their lives, for better or for worse. This places a heavy obligation on social workers to think as clearly as possible about what they are doing and why. (The fact that social work deals with people who are relatively marginalised in society – physically frail old people, children, people with disabilities, young offenders, people with mental health problems – increases this obligation.) What makes social work particularly challenging, though, is that it combines this potential for transforming lives (think of a child being removed from a parent and placed for adoption, to give one extreme example) with an absence of a precise science to guide it, or even anything approximating to a precise science. This means that in trying to decide how best to approach a problem we cannot fall back on certainty and cannot rely on formulas. We can often only do the best we can, trying to be as clear-headed as possible about the implications of what we are doing.

It is my belief that a book is more interesting to read if the writer invests something of himself in it, and is prepared to express his own views. I therefore offer here a particular perspective. Mine is of course only one person's perspective, with all of the blind spots and limitations that implies, but I think the most useful thing I can do is to try to present that perspective honestly – to try to be honest about how I see things – rather than to try to offer some sort of bland consensual view. The reader is of course most welcome to disagree with me.

THE NATURE OF SOCIAL WORK

My grandmother disapproved of social work. She felt that the sort of work that social workers do ought to be left to family, neighbours, churches, volunteers, not done as a job for pay, not professionalised, but carried out as a basic moral duty, an expression of being human, as she believed had happened in the past.

Actually I don't believe there was ever a time, prior to the advent of organised professional social work, in which everyone was wonderfully looked after by these informal networks. If you read novels from the eighteenth and nineteenth centuries (look at Defoe's *Moll Flanders*, Charlotte Brontë's *Jane Eyre*, Dickens' *Nicholas Nickleby*) you encounter a world in which mentally ill people could be locked away out of sight in institutions or in back rooms in their own homes, children could endure abuse alone with no one to turn to for help and people who could not support themselves could end up in the workhouse. We should be really under no illusions that a golden idyll of mutual care existed in the past into which social work intruded, like a bossy and unwelcome guest at a happy party. Nor does such an idyll prevail, as far as I know, in those present-day societies where professional social work (at least as it is understood in Europe and North America) still does not exist, though it *is* true that people from developing countries are often shocked by the way in which (for instance) white British people allow strangers to care for their elderly relatives.

The fact remains, though, that social work *does* intrude into the personal area of life, into family relationships, into people's homes. And social work *can* be an unwelcome and sometimes bossy guest, not only offering but also sometimes even *imposing* alternatives to the informal networks of family and neighbourhood. My grandmother's unease about the whole enterprise is still widely shared, as is demonstrated by the prevalence of various negative stereotypes of social workers as 'interfering busy-bodies', as 'do-gooders', as bureaucratic tyrants imposing 'politically correct' dogma, or as 'bleeding hearts' making excuses for bad behaviour. And, while no social worker likes these labels, I think many social workers actually to some extent share the underlying unease. Any good social worker will at some point wonder if they are making things worse for people rather than better.

RECOGNISING OUR LIMITS

Intrusion into the personal sphere feels uncomfortable – and so it should do – but it can quite properly be justified in many instances where vulnerable people would otherwise suffer hardship, oppression and even sometimes death without outside help. What I think social work should be careful not to do, though, is to *colonise* the personal, to claim for itself as its own special territory the functions of caring for others, or of advocating for the excluded, or of supporting the vulnerable. You do not need a degree in social work to be caring and empathic, or to be helpful, or to be supportive and encouraging, or to stand up against injustice. It would be a sorry world if you did.

For this reason I am a bit suspicious of sweeping statements about social work's mission, like the often-quoted International Federation of Social Workers (IFSW) definition of social work, which includes 'The social work profession promotes social change, problem solving in human relationships and the empowerment and liberation of people to enhance well-being … etc.' (IFSW, 2000). It's not that I disagree that social workers should try to empower and liberate people; it is just that I don't think that is particularly the job of social workers any more than it is the job of school-teachers, or doctors – or indeed of anyone else, not least the recipients of social work services themselves. (Anne Wilson and Peter Beresford, 2000, make what I think is a related point when they point out the paradox of 'anti-oppressive practice' being claimed as an expert specialism by social work academics.) It seems to me that if we really believed that it was *uniquely* our role to right wrongs, challenge injustices and empower the powerless, then we would be in danger of becoming precisely the bossy, interfering busy-bodies that the jokes and stereotypes portray. We know from history that those who set themselves up as liberators can very easily become tyrants.

I think it is important to remind ourselves that what social workers do in their daily work is to perform certain rather specific and (we hope) useful functions. Some social workers try to help physically frail elderly people to cope in their own homes, others try to prevent children from being abused or neglected by their carers, others work with disabled people to maximise their ability to participate fully in society … and so on. In my view, it is only when we look at social work in these specific local terms that we can start to really think about what is entailed in doing it well.

It can be difficult, after all, for social workers to perform even these relatively modest tasks well, given the inevitable constraints that are imposed by limited resources, by organisational structures, by politics, by competing principles and competing claims, not to mention our own personal limitations. It is often all too easy to make things worse, to become part of the problem instead of part of the solution. That being so, I do not think it is necessarily helpful to be bombarded with sweeping generalisations about a reified, mythical, idealised 'social work', or about what social workers ought to do, *if only* they could operate without any of those boring everyday constraints that actually exist. In fact that kind of advice is often about as helpful as the advice given to the apocryphal traveller who asked a local for directions and was told 'Oh I wouldn't start from here.' Certainly I found it very difficult when I was a newly qualified social worker to be clear about what was my job and what was not, because my head was full of grand ideas about how I ought somehow to be able to fix *everything* (and that at a time when I had hardly learned to lead my own life!). I have no doubt I confused many service users as a result.

It is often easier and more fun to construct elaborate castles in the air, than to engage in the struggle that is typically involved in building even quite modest structures in the real world. But I think we have a duty (Beckett and Maynard, 2005: 97–101; Beckett, 2007a), not only as social workers but also as human beings, to try to deal with the world as it actually is, not the world as we might like it. After all, if the world was perfect, there would be no need of social work, so social workers, of all people, really should not expect ideal conditions in which to work.

When you consider the work of the agency where you are placed, or reflect on your own work, you need to think not only about what people in that agency would like to do, or would like to think they do, or would do if only they had the time, or even what they *say* they do, but also about what they really do in practice. What is important to the recipients of a social work service is *what is actually delivered*, not the good intentions and noble sentiments of the agency and its staff.

USING THIS BOOK

This book is written (I hope) so that it can be read through from cover to cover without being too tedious, but each chapter also makes sense on its own, so the book can be dipped into, as students normally do with textbooks, or read in any order. I have grouped my material under single-word chapter titles, each covering a topic that seems to me central either to how we come to make judgements about human situations (assessment), or to how we respond to them (intervention), or both. So, while there are chapters headed 'assessment' and 'intervention', which give an overview of these subjects, all the chapters should be relevant to one or other, or both, of these two topics of the book.

'Placement questions' inserted in boxes are intended to provide you with a prompt to relate the discussion to what you are seeing and doing in practice. I hope they may help you too when you have to write about your placement. In some chapters there are also 'Case examples' in which (as in my other books) I offer fictional illustrations intended to illustrate the point I am making. Of course the amount of information given in these examples is much less than you would want to have if dealing with real-life people, and it has to be acknowledged that in this respect they are not realistic, but I hope they give at least a sense of the kinds of issues that real-life situations raise.

Each chapter begins with a list of main headings and (except for this short introductory chapter) ends with a summary of the discussion for quick reference.

FURTHER READING

The following is a forthcoming book on this subject to which I have also contributed:

Walker, S. with Beckett, C. (2011) *Social Work Assessment and Intervention* (2nd edn). Lyme Regis: Russell House.

I would recommend the following as a general introduction to social work assessment:

Milner, J. and O'Byrne, P. (2009) *Assessment in Social Work* (3rd edn). Basingstoke: Palgrave.

For further thoughts on methods of intervention, I would strongly advise the reader to seek out books that are specific to the particular area of work that they engage in (if you are on placement in an agency that works with people with physical disabilities, for instance, then seek out books about this area of work). But for a general overview, books on social work theory are useful and I would recommend that this book is read in conjunction with such books. Payne's is probably the most comprehensive text in this area. I have written a shorter text which is (unsurprisingly) more similar in style to the present book.

Beckett, C. (2006) *Essential Theory for Social Work Practice*. London: Sage.
Payne, M. (2005) *Modern Social Work Theory* (3rd edn). Basingstoke: Palgrave.

2 CONTEXT

- Mandate
- Competing principles
- Resources
- Politics

Social work is not all one thing, but a collection of different activities, and what makes sense in one context may make no sense at all in another. This is a point that is not always recognised in writing about social work, as Karen Healy observes:

> Social workers are well aware of the importance of context in service users' lives. Indeed, understanding, and responding to, the 'person in their environment' is a guiding credo of modern professional social work. However, less attention has been paid to how we might understand and respond to our practice environment … [and] … theories for professional practice are often written about, and taught, as though the social worker's institutional context were minimally relevant, or even something to overcome, in practising social work. (Healy, 2005: 2)

As Healy goes on to say, 'our institutional contexts must be understood as integral to how we practice' (2005: 2). Each agency that employs social workers is set up with a specific purpose, and this purpose has an important influence on the overall character of the agency's work. An agency set up with the sole purpose of protecting children from maltreatment, for example, will operate in a very different way, provide different kinds of services, and have a different working relationship with the recipients of its service than an agency set up with the sole purpose of providing services for older people with personal care and mobility problems. Some general principles will undoubtedly apply across both contexts and some difficulties and challenges will also crop up in both: for example the difficulties involved in assessing and balancing risks, or the challenge of deciding when the duty to protect the vulnerable overrides the duty to allow people to run their own lives. But there are many aspects of working in one of these contexts which are not relevant to the other one.

Similarly, a state social work agency, whose duties and powers are defined by law, will have a very different character from a voluntary or independent agency set up to meet the needs of a specific group in the community. And voluntary agencies themselves can differ from one another as much as they differ from state agencies. For example the NSPCC (National Society for the Prevention of Cruelty to Children) is a large organisation with a nationwide structure, which has specific powers conferred upon it by law and operates 180 community projects in the UK (NSPCC, 2009). Other charities may have only a single base in a single town.

Even *within* a single agency, different teams and units may present very different challenges for those working in them, and may have very different working relationships with their service users. In a children's social care agency, for instance, there may be residential establishments, where the staff eat with, watch TV with, go on outings with, and periodically spend the night under the same roof as, a small group of service users who they get to know very well. On the other hand the same agency may also have 'intake' fieldwork teams, who have a fairly limited number of contacts with children and parents in the office and in their own homes, and fostering teams which don't work with service users but which recruit and support foster-parents who are themselves part of the service provided by the agency.

Many social workers, too, work in a context which is not a social work agency at all. Some are attached to schools or medical practices (student social workers are likewise sometimes placed in these kinds of non-social work contexts). Some work in multi-disciplinary teams, with nurses or teachers or police officers as their closest colleagues. These are very different working environments to purely social work agencies in which all the staff have a similar training and professional ethos.

If we attempted to confine our thinking about social work to general principles that applied equally to all of these different contexts, then we would have to restrict ourselves to some rather broad and general statements, which might be little more than platitudes. To think about what constitutes good social work practice, we need to think about the particular issues and dilemmas that arise in the particular context under discussion. So I will spend the remainder of this chapter looking at a few of the ways (there are of course many others) in which each context will be different and unique.

MANDATE

The term 'service user', and quite often still the older word 'client', are both typically used to describe all of the people towards whom social work services are directed, the people into whose lives social workers are attempting to bring some kind of change or opportunity. The term 'service user' is thought by some to be less stigmatising than 'client', though as Stephen Cowden and Gurnam Singh (2007) point out (referring to work by Gupta and Blewett, 2005), the word 'user' itself has negative connotations and is not always appreciated by those it is applied to:

> The families they worked with actually rejected the term 'User' entirely, firstly because they felt it had the implication of someone who used illegal drugs and secondly because they wanted to be seen as people 'who give something back' rather than people who just use. (Cowden and Singh, 2007: 16)

But, leaving aside the question of the right word to use, what I want to draw attention to here is that, just as there are many kinds of social work, so there are also many ways of being a 'service user'/'client', depending on the nature of the mandate under which the social worker is operating.

I will explain what precisely I mean by 'mandate' presently. For the moment, suppose you are a YOT (Youth Offending Team) worker who is working with a young person – 'Susan' – who has received a supervision order from a criminal court as a result of offences to do with stealing and driving away cars. (For more on YOTs, see Youth Justice Board, 2009.) Susan has no choice but to work with you, assuming she doesn't want to be taken back to court. She also cannot determine the overall direction of your work. Whether Susan wants it or not, your aim will be to try to reduce the chances of further offending (though in working towards this aim, you may well want to allow Susan some choice as to how to go about it, and you may negotiate with her about other areas to work on). The word 'service user' does not fit terribly comfortably in this case, since your work is imposed on Susan, and she herself may not necessarily see it *either* as a 'service' *or* as something she finds useful, though you will of course try to make it so. And indeed your work is not solely aimed at enhancing Susan's well-being, but rather at preventing Susan behaving in a way that harms and endangers other people. The word 'client' doesn't fit very well either.

But now suppose you are working for a voluntary agency which provides advocacy services for people with physical disabilities. Here your service users will come to you of their own free will, presumably because they anticipate finding your service useful. Imagine that 'Stephen', who has mobility problems as a result of cerebral palsy, seeks your help in negotiating for additional help from the local authority. It seems quite natural to describe him as a 'service user' or indeed as a 'client', just as the people who make use of solicitors are usually described as their 'clients'. Some might argue that Stephen's working relationship with you is that of a 'customer', but unless Stephen is paying for the service himself, his situation is not quite the same as that of a customer in the commercial sense. Arguably whoever is *paying* for the service is actually the customer.

Now here is a third case. Suppose you are a social worker in a state-funded team for elderly people and you are working with an elderly person – 'David' – who is suffering from severe dementia caused by Alzheimer's disease. David has very little understanding any more as to where he is or who anyone around him is, and he is placing himself at serious risk by doing things like turning on the gas rings on his cooker and leaving them unlit, accosting strangers in the street and offering them money, and wandering around the city in a state of undress in the middle of the night. Here the aim of the social worker *is* to provide a service to the old person – the social worker seeks to take actions that will improve David's quality of life and reduce the risk of harm coming to him – but the social worker cannot necessarily take her instructions solely from David himself, as David may well lack the mental capacity to understand his situation. Thus, while the word 'service' still seems appropriate, the word 'user' seems less so, since that would imply that David is actively seeking a specific service, whereas in fact he may not even be able to understand who you are.

There are some distinctions to be made here. But even the very important distinction that is often made between 'involuntary' and 'voluntary' clients/service users (Rooney, 1992; Trotter, 2007) does not entirely clear things up, because although Stephen is a voluntary client, and Susan and David are both involuntary ones, Susan's and David's relationships with their social workers are not the same. They are not involuntary in the same way.

As noted earlier, in the social work literature, the expressions 'service user' or (particularly in older texts) 'client' are both used across the board, to describe people whose working relationship with social work agencies may be like that of Stephen, Susan or David with their respective social workers. There have been many debates about what word to use (see for instance, McLaughlin, 2009) but one trouble with using *any* particular one word is that it implies that essentially the same working relationship exists, or ought to exist, in all situations, whereas in fact what applies to people in Stephen's position does not necessarily apply to those in Susan's or David's.

For example when we talk about the desirability of 'service user-led' services or 'user involvement', we tend to be thinking in particular of people in Stephen's sort of situation (and much of the service user movement tends to be led by people whose relationship with agencies is, *or at least could be*, like Stephen's: particularly people with disabilities and people with mental health needs). In principle, why shouldn't people in situations like Stephen's be given their own budget and commission their own services rather than have a social worker do it for them (the idea behind what are called Individual Budgets in the UK [DH, 2009])? I can see no reason at all, if that is what they want (although, as Peter Scourfield [2007] notes, we should not assume that everyone does). But it would not be feasible for dementia services to be commissioned by people with dementia, or services for under-fives to be commissioned by preschool children, and it would not be in their own interests (which is not to say that both groups should not be respectfully listened to). Nor would it be appropriate for services aimed at assessing the risk from offenders to be run by offenders, because it would not be in the interests of potential victims of those offenders (though again, this is not to say that offenders should not be carefully listened to, treated with the respect due to them as human beings and consulted about what they find helpful). Cowden and Singh make a similar point as follows:

> Progressive rhetoric about the value of the service user's perspective sits uncomfortably alongside the expectations that Social Workers will impose their own professional understandings when the time is right to do so. This is not to suggest that they [social workers] should not do this, but rather to note the incoherence of the importation of a business/consumer model into a complex profession like social work. (Cowden and Singh, 2007: 15)

Think for instance of the media and political upheaval in the UK in 2008 surrounding the 'Baby Peter' case (originally just referred to as 'Baby P') in the London Borough of Haringey (see for instance, Glendinning and Jones, 2008). No one would argue that social workers should have taken more of a lead from Baby Peter's mother (who concealed from them and other professionals the abuse to which Baby Peter was being subjected). On the contrary, no one could seriously disagree that it would have been better if they had challenged, questioned and been sceptical about what she told them to a much greater extent.

In spite of the awkwardness and vagueness of the terms 'service user' and 'client' I will use them interchangeably in this book in the same way that they are normally used in contemporary social work texts, to describe *all* of those people who are the focus of the efforts of social workers: the people whose lives social workers are seeking in some way to change. But I do want to emphasise here that, when thinking about your own work and the work of your placement agency, it is important to distinguish between the very different kinds of working relationship that social workers have with service users:

- People like Stephen receive social work services at their own request, based on their own belief that those services may be useful to them. As I noted above, the relationship that people in Stephen's position have with social work agencies is a bit like that of a customer, except that 'customer' has commercial implications which are not applicable and can be misleading. (He is like a customer in the sense that he does not have to receive any service that he does not actually request and want. He is unlike a customer in that he is not paying for the service and the resources available are determined by people other than himself.) For the purposes of this discussion, we will refer to the relationship those in his position have in relation to social work agencies as that of a *service requester*.
- People like Susan are required to work with social workers because of their perceived risk to others (for example: offenders, parents in child protection cases, some people with acute mental health problems, etc.). We might call the relationship that Susan and others in this position have with social work agencies as that of *supervisees*: they are people who are subject to some sort of supervision and control which is not of their own choosing, and which is connected to the concerns of others about their behaviour and its potential to cause harm to others.
- People like David are provided with social work services in the belief that it is in their interests, even though they are not in a position, due to a limited mental capacity or developmental stage, to make the decision themselves (for example: small children, people with severe learning difficulties or severe dementia, people suffering acute psychotic episodes, etc.). We might call the working relationship that David and others in this position have with social work agencies as that of *protectees*: social workers are involved in working with them because of their need for protection, though not necessarily at their own request.

Of course there are many service users whose relationship with social work agencies will fall somewhere in between these categories, or will move at different times from one category to another. A person with a mental health problem may perhaps best be regarded as a 'protectee' during acute psychotic episodes, but as a 'service requester' at other times. A parent with learning disabilities who is thought to be neglecting her child, may best be regarded as a 'service requester' in respect of the help she needs for her disabilities, but as a 'supervisee' in respect of her parenting. An eleven-year-old child in public care may be regarded as something between a 'protectee' and a 'service requester': she ought to have a good deal of say over what happens to her, but the social worker responsible for her also has a duty of care which in some circumstances would require him to set aside her wishes in her own long-term interests, just as a responsible parent would do under the same circumstances. (I would not let my children decide what time they came in at night at the age of 11, for instance.)

I think we ought also to recognise the existence of a *fourth* group of service users, which may in fact be at least as numerous as any of the others. Imagine that Jenny has requested that a social work agency help her with the behaviour of her four-year-old child who is driving her to distraction. The social work agency becomes involved, recruiting the input of a number of other agencies, and offers Jenny a 'package' of services which are supposed to help her manage her child's behaviour problems. Actually, Jenny does not really find the proposed package at all helpful. In truth it seems to her like an additional burden, but she is afraid to say so because she is aware of the power of the social work agency and she is afraid of incurring its displeasure for one or both of two reasons: (a) because she badly needs help, doesn't know where else to turn and doesn't want to offend or alienate the social worker and the agency, and/or (b) because she feels that if she doesn't co-operate she may be seen as a bad mother.

Jenny is ostensibly a 'service requester', requesting and accepting a service of her own free will, and not having a service imposed on her either because of risks she poses to others, or because of a limited mental capacity on her own part. But in fact she *feels* like a 'supervisee' and perhaps she is treated like one too. It seems to me that many social work service users who are ostensibly 'service requesters' are in fact in a position more like that of Jenny, and that this includes not only parents like Jenny herself but also many elderly people and people who need services because they have disabilities or mental health problems. A lot of people feel as if they have to surrender control over their own lives in order to get a service, or that they have no choice but to accept a service that is proposed to them, even though there is technically no legal reason why they should accept anything that they don't want. I will call this fourth group *nominal service requesters.* They may technically be voluntary clients but they don't feel that way. (I think what I mean by 'nominal service requesters' is something close to what Ronald Rooney [1992] means by 'nonvoluntary clients'.) One thing that it is important to notice about this group is that it may not always be obvious to you as a social worker that a service user belongs to it. You may fondly imagine that you are working with someone 'in partnership' (to use that dreadfully overused phrase) on a completely mutual and voluntary basis, even though in fact the service user may be going along with you and your proposals, not because she really wants to, but because she is worried that there will be unpleasant consequences for her if she does not.

It seems to me that one of the dangers of the kind of over-interventionist, 'colonial' approach towards social work I discussed in the previous chapter – an approach that thinks social workers ought to be able to solve everything – is that it is prone to create a lot of Jennys, a lot of nominal service requesters ('semi-captive clients' in William Reid and Laura Epstein's memorable phrase [1972]). It also seems to me that the biggest contribution of the service user movement (see Warren, 2007) in recent years has been to challenge social workers' collusion in the creation of what I have called 'nominal service requesters'. (Jenny should *not* feel she has to accept a service which does not help her with her problem, she should not feel that she has to pretend that she is finding it helpful.) The service user movement also challenges us to question whether every 'protectee' or 'supervisee' of a social work agency actually *needs* to be a protectee or a supervisee, or whether some of them could instead be treated as service requesters, and not have services imposed on them that they do not want.

Let it be quite clear, though, that some people *do* need to be in a protectee or supervisee relationship with social work agencies – the 'service requester' relationship is not necessarily always the right one in every context, even in principle, as I pointed out earlier, mentioning the case of 'Baby P' as an example – and the relationship a social worker should have with protectees and supervisees is appropriately different in important respects to that which a social worker should have with a service requester. This is why it is very important for you as a social worker to be very clear – both in your own mind and with the service user – about the nature of your *mandate* in a given case. By 'mandate' I mean the justification or authority for your involvement. What exactly is it that gives you the right to get involved in the lives of service users?

If the service user himself has requested assistance of a kind your agency is set up to provide, the mandate is fairly straightforward, and uncontentious. The mandate comes from the service user, just as the mandate comes from you when you visit your GP and she looks, at your request, at your sore throat. But what if someone else has requested that you get involved and the service user himself has not requested it? To get involved in someone's life without their requesting it is a serious intrusion (imagine your GP looking at your throat without you asking for it!) and can only be justified if (a) it turns out that the service user, when asked, does indeed want your involvement, or (b) your agency has legal obligations to protect vulnerable people, and there are grounds for thinking that the service user in question poses a risk to himself or others that come within the scope of those obligations (in which case the mandate is provided not by the service user only, but by the legal powers that society has given the social work agency). The two mandates are very different things. It is one thing to enter a person's home at their request, quite another to insist on entry. Both service user and social worker need to be clear about where they stand.

Table 2.1 summarises the different ways I have been discussing in which 'service users'/'clients' may be involved with an agency.

PLACEMENT QUESTIONS 2.1   THE AGENCY'S RELATIONSHIP WITH SERVICE USERS

- What is the nature of the working relationship between your placement agency and the recipients of its services?
- Are agency staff always clear about their mandate for intervention: (a) in their own minds; (b) with service users?
- If the agency has 'protectees' and/or 'supervisees' as well as 'service requesters' is this status always in your view justified? Does the agency exercise control unnecessarily? Or does it fail to exercise control in situations where it ought to do so to protect the vulnerable?
- If an agency has 'protectees' and/or 'supervisees' among its service users, to what extent does this compromise its ability to offer a 'service requester' relationship to any of its service users?
- Do you feel that the agency has a lot of 'nominal service requesters' and what do you think it could do differently in order to make them into 'service requesters'? (That is: what could it do to make people feel that they didn't have to accept services they don't want, and/or feel that they have a genuine say as to the services they do want?)
- What are the strengths and limitations of the kind of working relationship that it is possible to have with service users in the context of this agency?

Table 2.1   Different kinds of 'service user'/ 'client' relationship

'Service User'/ 'Client' relationship with agency	Alternative name	Example given above	Description
'Service requester'	Voluntary client, voluntary service user	Stephen	Receives services at own request, which he or she is fully entitled to refuse.
'Supervisee'	Involuntary client, 'mandated client', involuntary service user	Susan	Is required to accept some form of social work intervention due to the risk of harm to others that is believed to exist.
'Protectee'	Ditto	David	Receives services, not necessarily at own request, due to limited ability to make decisions for self, either due to limited mental capacity or due to being a child.
'Nominal service requester'	'Nonvoluntary client'	Jenny	Receives services ostensibly at own request, or at least with own agreement, and is ostensibly entitled to refuse them, but in fact feels unable to control the intervention.

COMPETING PRINCIPLES

When talking in abstract terms about social work in general, it is possible to list basic principles that social workers should honour at all costs. In specific contexts, though, these matters are often less clear cut. One important principle, or one important way of looking at things, may need to be balanced with another principle, or another way of looking at things. The 'social model' of disability, for instance, is often seen as a corner-stone of good anti-oppressive practice, but, as Tom Shakespeare (2006) argues with some force, the 'social model' may be too simple to encapsulate all facets of the experience of being disabled and having impairments. Shakespeare does not dispute that the social model of disability (that is: the idea that disability is essentially a problem created by society rather than a problem of the individual person) was necessary as a corrective to the purely 'medical model'. But he argues that the social model itself has its limitations. For example, if your impairment causes you pain, then it hurts, and this isn't a problem created by society.

Slogans and simple models may serve important political functions but, when it comes down to day-to-day practice and specific human situations, slogans, broad aspirations and noble ideals remain important, but they cannot be used as a substitute for examining the situation on its own merits: 'judgements about how to improve individual situations are complex, and should be based on evidence, not ideology' (Shakespeare, 2006: 62).

The 'social model of disability' is one example. Another example might be the idea that services should be led by their users. This is a valuable idea, which challenges the paternalistic assumption that professionals and experts know better than the actual users of services, but there are in practice other competing principles that may set limits to the applicability of the idea of 'user-led' services: for example the need to ensure that resources are distributed as fairly as possible, or the need to protect the vulnerable.

But giving priority to protecting the vulnerable is another example again. While obviously an important principle this cannot necessarily be taken as the sole guide to action in every situation, because it also competes with other important principles. What about the principle of respecting privacy and confidentiality for example? Should child protection agencies be entitled to demand whatever information they like, on the basis that it might be useful for child protection purposes? Or should a mental health agency, say, be able to tell a child protection agency that it cannot automatically disclose personal information given to it in confidence, because that would be a breach of trust, and because it would prevent people who needed help from coming forward in the future?

You are bound to come across ethical dilemmas of this kind in any area of social work, but you may notice that, depending on the context, different ethical dilemmas will predominate. Sometimes, coming in from outside, you may also notice that people within an agency have lost any sense that there *is* an ethical dilemma, or that there are other important principles which go against the ones that they hold dear. Child protection social workers, for example, sometimes find it hard to understand why other agencies insist on confidentiality. Agencies that work with vulnerable adults sometimes find it equally hard to understand why child protection workers think it important to separate out the needs of a child from the needs of his parent. (The fact that it would exacerbate his mother's mental health problems, for instance, is not necessarily a reason for not taking a child into care if the child would otherwise be placed at risk of serious harm.) Workers in voluntary agencies sometimes find it hard to understand how workers in statutory agencies can in all conscience ration and restrict access to their services, and cannot see that this may sometimes be the fairest thing to do when an agency is simply incapable of responding to all the demands made on it. Workers in statutory agencies, for their part, sometimes find it hard to see how much the business of rationing has taken over their thinking and prevented them from being able to respond in an open and undefensive way to requests for help.

PLACEMENT QUESTIONS 2.2   CONFLICTING PRINCIPLES

- Can you see instances in your placement agency of generally recognised social work principles being disregarded or set aside? Why is this happening? What competing principles are at play and are they valid ones?

- Do you notice workers in your placement agency being blinkered in the way they seem to see things? Do you notice them having difficulty in being able to see things from other perspectives than their own? If so, what instances have you noticed, and why do you think this is happening?
- Typically in social work, there are tensions between the aspiration to support, empower and emancipate people, and requirements to control and evaluate people, arising out of legal duties to protect. How is this played out in your agency?

RESOURCES

One of the most important aspects of the context in which social work is practised is the resource context: the time, the skills, the money, the space that is available to the agency to meet the demands made on it. And one of the things that social work students tend to notice on placements is the shortage of resources in many social work agencies. In statutory agencies, they become aware that many needs that are referred to the agency are not actually met, or are met only with minimal or even tokenistic responses. They become aware that social work activity is often directed towards filtering and prioritising requests for a service. They notice that social workers are often under pressure to close cases quickly so as to make space to take on new ones. In voluntary agencies, the external demands on the agency may not seem so overwhelming, but students may notice that the service itself seems to run on a shoestring and perhaps is never sure from one year to the next how it will be funded. It may be heavily reliant on volunteer workers, or on unqualified staff on very low wages.

Different kinds of service will have different resource regimes, in terms of the amount of time and money they have available, the degree to which they can turn down requests for services, the degree to which they have to engage in screening or rationing, and the freedom they have to choose what kind of work they take on and what they don't. These will be linked to how the agency is funded, and what its brief is, and they are among the most important determinants of the character of an agency and even of the nature of its relationship with service users.

RATIONING

If a hairdresser becomes popular in her area and gets a lot of custom, then that will generate income for her and place her in the position of being able to expand her business if she wishes to do so. Alternatively, she can just tell potential customers that she is fully booked and suggest they try somewhere else.

But now imagine a hairdresser who was *not* paid by her customers but received a fixed salary from the state for providing hairdressing services to everyone who lived in a given area. Faced with increased demand, she would have to resort to measures like trying to cut everyone's hair more quickly, or only offering the most basic kinds of haircut, or making rules about how many haircuts she would offer each customer in a given year. It would be a completely different situation from the one she would face as an independent business-woman and it would be nonsense to suggest that she should be able to deliver the same level of service as a hairdresser who was able to charge her customers.

In the UK, public services are frequently compared unfavourably with private businesses, and castigated for not being as responsive to their consumers as private businesses allegedly are. But state social work services, in common with other public services, are in the position of the second hairdresser in my example. The comparison with commercial organisations is unfair and fundamentally flawed. Because of the way they are funded, state social work agencies (like my imaginary state-employed hairdresser, and like other public services) invariably resort to some form of rationing, albeit described as 'targeting' or 'prioritising'. And rationing is in fact the fair, ethical and responsible thing to do when resources are limited. During the Second World War, for instance, food was rationed in the UK because it was scarce. If there had been no rationing, some people would have been able to buy as much food as they wanted and others would not have had enough to eat.

But writers about social work, and commentators on social work practice, often struggle with this. On the one hand there often seems to be a notion that to acknowledge resource limitations, or to assist in the task of rationing, is somehow to collude in oppression. On the other hand there is recognition that planning your work in a responsible way requires that you think about the resource context. Lena Dominelli, for instance, writes disapprovingly about social workers operating within 'a bureau-technological arrangement based on narrowly defined criteria of eligibility' (2002: 32) and about social workers being required to 'separate claimants into "deserving" and "undeserving" ones by applying their discretionary powers to release resources to the former while denying them to the latter' (2002: 28). But later in the same book she says that 'the resources available for meeting a given need' are one of the considerations that need to be taken into account in a piece of work (2002: 87). She does not explain how the agency might determine the resources available to meet a given need without recourse to notions such as eligibility.

In the same way Lord Laming criticised social work agencies for 'devising ways of limiting access to services, and adopting mechanisms to reduce service demand' (2003: 11). But later in the same report he recommended that 'Directors of social services must ensure that no case is allocated to a social worker unless and until his or her manager ensures that he or she has the necessary training, experience and time to deal with it properly' (2003: 377). Again he does not explain how it is possible to protect staff workloads without also limiting the amount of work taken on. (Disappointingly, exactly the same kind of contradictions can be found in his 2009 report, which I will refer to presently.)

None of what I have said so far is meant to imply that social workers should meekly accept whatever resources they are given to work with, or that they should simply turn a blind eye to unmet needs. On the contrary, if the resources available are inadequate to the task, social workers and their organisations would do well to try to challenge this through whatever channels are available. It is in fact in their *own* interest to do so as well as in the interests of their service users, for if they silently attempt to do the impossible, they will be held responsible when things do not work out. Nevertheless, in every given moment, as it responds to day-to-day demands, an agency has to do the best it can with what it has got, and rationing (however it is described) is inevitably part of that. It is part of the context, and assessments that are carried out by state agencies are almost inevitably used in part as tools for rationing.

I should add that the position of voluntary agencies, and of specialist units, may not be the same as that of state fieldwork agencies. For example, imagine a voluntary agency runs a residential unit that works with young sex offenders. It has 20 beds and is funded by state agencies who buy in its services. When the unit is full, it can simply say so, and then not consider any more applications until one of its residents has moved on. The staff of the unit do not have to think of themselves as being involved in rationing, because they do not have to think about what happens to the young people they turn down. In fact of course their service *is* being rationed. It is just that the unit staff are not involved in the rationing process.

FITTING PRACTICE TO THE RESOURCE CONTEXT

When thinking about how to respond to a given situation, or about how to design the service as a whole, it is important to consider the resources available, because what is good advice in one resource context may be bad advice in another, for 'any system only functions when configured to suit local implementation contingencies' (Broadhurst et al., 2010: 365). For the purposes of illustrating this point let us consider the following recommendation from Lord Laming's 2009 report on child protection:

> … Children's Trusts must take appropriate action to ensure:
>
> - all referrals to children's services from other professionals lead to an initial assessment, including direct involvement with the child or young person and their family, and the direct engagement with, and feedback to, the referring professional … (Laming, 2009: 86)

Do you think this recommendation is likely to improve child and family social work practice? I do not think that you can really answer this question unless you know what the resource context is. In some well-resourced contexts this might be a helpful recommendation, which results in children's needs being more thoroughly assessed. But in other contexts it might make things very much worse, as I will now discuss.

The Initial Assesment (IA) process laid down for child and family social work agencies in England and Wales is a time consuming process, not least since (in line with an earlier recommendation of Lord Laming's) every child involved in the assessment is supposed to be 'seen' before the assessment can be considered complete:

> Children are not easy to 'see' under the conditions of initial assessment, for a variety of reasons. First, there is a requirement to see all children, irrespective of ages, but older children can be difficult to track down. Second, 'seeing' should involve talking to the child alone to make an assessment of the child's development and needs, but this is hard to achieve within seven days [the prescribed time limit for Initial Assessments] in a single visit. (Broadhurst et al., 2010: 363)

Children do not tend to open up easily to total strangers. The UK government advises that they 'may need time, and more than one opportunity, to develop sufficient trust to communicate any concerns they may have' (DfES, 2006b: 119). So if 'seeing' children is to mean anything, hours of traveling and interviewing may be entailed just in properly carrying out that one aspect of the assessment process. And it *is* just one aspect, for an IA also involves consultation with parents, schools and other professionals, and the completion of extensive documentation. IAs involve a lot of work.

At the time of writing, social work agencies have some discretion as to whether an IA is required. They have the option to look at a referral and decide whether the concerns raised do warrant an investment of the time that would be involved. If Lord Laming's recommendation was implemented, however, they would no longer have this discretion. This would of course create a substantial amount of extra work.

Now we get to the nub of my point. Where is the extra time going to come from? What is going to be dropped to make it possible? These are the questions that Lord Laming always fails to address with his recommendations. Yet, unless such questions are asked and answered we really can't know whether a change in the rules such as this one will make things better or make things worse, because we won't know whether or not the proposed action will take time away from some other activity that – hour for hour – is likely to protect more children. What we *do* know is that at the moment social work agencies are already struggling to keep up with IAs under currently existing guidelines. So presumably they will struggle even more if they have to complete more IAs.

I will come back to this shortly, but first I want to make the general point that the fact that there are only so many hours in a day is a tedious reality which people such as Lord Laming can if they wish ignore, along with politicians, journalists, academics and those others who are in a position to criticise social work agencies and other public services. But it is a tedious reality which any person required to *implement* policy cannot ignore: they *have* to make choices as to how they use the time available. I think Lord Laming's recommendations, and others like them, are fatally flawed because they do not address this reality at all, they do not acknowledge that the resource context must be taken into account when deciding how to act. I would go further and say that I find this sort of omission morally unacceptable (Beckett, 2007b). Wishlists of recommendations, drawn up with no consideration for the practicalities, may in fact have little benefit other than setting some people up to fail and allowing other people to feel virtuous. They are fundamentally dishonest. But you will often come across them in social work.

CONSEQUENCES OF RESOURCE LIMITATIONS

What actually happens when an agency is required to follow guidelines when its resources are insufficient to the task? Inevitably, something has to give. Either some other task is dropped, or the guidelines themselves are not properly followed. Either way the agency can be blamed, though in fact the problem may not really be the fault of the agency at all, but of those who wrote the unrealistic guidelines or allocated the unrealistic funding. Many examples could be given from all areas of social work, but let us stick, for the purposes of this discussion, to the IA system. Based on their detailed observations of social workers at work in five local authorities, Karen Broadhurst and her colleagues (2010) have shown rather precisely how serious problems can be caused when there is a mismatch between procedures and resources. They suggest that the likelihood of mistakes being made and risks overlooked may as a result be actually *increased* by a system that is purportedly designed to improve efficiency and reduce mistakes, but does not take into account the resource context.

The requirement to complete initial assessments within seven days has, in England and Wales, become a key benchmark against which the performance of local authorities is measured, with the result that workers are under a great deal of pressure from managers to comply with it. Broadhurst et al. found that the pressure to complete these assessments encouraged thinking and behaviour that had the potential to be really dangerous, since 'timescales can create perverse incentives to dispose early on the basis of incomplete information' (2010: 362). One social worker they spoke to described being unable to complete an assessment within the seven days because the health visitor had not yet returned a call. A manager tried to persuade the social worker to come to a decision about the case without hearing from the health visitor, so that the assessment could be 'finished' within the seven days. This pressure to take shortcuts was also reflected in a widespread practice of simply not collecting most of the information that an IA is supposed to cover:

> The IA record requires copious information that is difficult to garner from one home visit and from other professionals; it thus invites workers to discard the majority of its sections as irrelevant. With remarkable consistency, we found an expedient method of 'front and backing' (or 'back-to-back-ing') had spontaneously sprung up across all our sites, wherein middle sections of the document were omitted altogether. (ibid.: 363)

And not surprisingly, the researchers also discovered incorrect information being accidentally entered by social workers working at high speed into a system which makes it difficult to correct incorrect entries after the event:

> The speed with which workers attempted to complete the IA record also meant that errors of recording were common. Whilst workers were aware of these errors, it was difficult to make corrections, as material was often 'locked down' in the system after twenty-four hours, and special permission would be required to make changes. (ibid.: 364)

When thinking about the work of any given agency, one question to ask yourself is whether the agency's practice and thinking seem to be being distorted by demands and expectations which have been designed without due consideration for the resource context. Once you have noticed such things, you may be somewhat more critical of new guidelines and recommendations.

RESOURCES AND RELATIONSHIPS WITH SERVICE USERS

The way the agency is funded, as well as its mandate and the level of demands made upon it, will make a difference to the way that the agency works with its service users and the way that its service users see the agency.

An agency which has many more demands made upon it than it can meet, will find itself in the position of often saying 'no' to requests for a service. (Because it is personally painful and/or politically awkward saying 'no', this may be dressed up in some way – perhaps as 'signposting' to other services – but it will boil down to 'no'.) Even potential service users who *do* meet its eligibility criteria will tend not to be offered much choice as to the services they receive (for it is difficult to give much choice if there is no spare capacity) and will tend to receive less than they felt they really needed. The agency will also have to have some means of screening or prioritising requests for a service, and this will mean that potential service users are likely to have to go through some sort of assessment process to determine whether they receive a service at all (this may feel to them like being made to 'jump through hoops' and perhaps like having hopes raised and then dashed again). If you put all these things together, you can end up with a somewhat uneasy relationship between the agency and the service users, even in a context where all the service users are completely voluntary ('service requesters' in the particular sense I used this term earlier). Service users may feel that they have to battle constantly with the agency to get their needs attended to (ask any parent of a disabled child!). Social workers and other agency staff may become rather defensive, adopting various strategies to distance themselves from the disappointment or distress of service users and would-be service users, and agencies may develop procedures which formalise this defensive distance in various ways.

Notice how the words 'battle', 'defensive' and 'strategies' have been creeping into my account (see Beckett, 2003, for more on military language in social work). Resource difficulties can very easily contribute to an 'us-and-them' relationship which make us reach for metaphors that come from conflict and war. In such a context you may notice social workers hiding behind their organisation, like soldiers behind battlements. They may refuse to take personal responsibility for things, they may constantly refer every little decision to managers, and they may become preoccupied with paperwork, all of which unfortunately is likely to exacerbate further the feeling of distance between them and the service users. The source of the tension lies in the mismatch between resources and the demands that the agency is expected to meet, and it is therefore not possible to completely solve this within the agency itself. This is not to say that good social workers cannot still establish working relationships of respect and trust with their service users in such a context, but it is challenging.

A specialist voluntary agency which is able to concentrate all its efforts on a fixed number of service users, and provide a particular specialist service to them, will not have the same type of problem, and may well align itself with its service users in their 'battle' with the state agencies (to use that military word again). This is fine, though I think voluntary agency workers should bear in mind that their different working relationship with service users is not necessarily the result of their being better workers or more virtuous human beings than those who work in statutory agencies, but simply the result of their being in a different position structurally.

PLACEMENT QUESTIONS 2.3   HONESTY AND CLARITY ABOUT RESOURCE LIMITATIONS

1   Can you identify actions which your placement agency carries out which seem to you disproportionate and which also seem to you to use more resources than seems justified by the benefits obtained? Why do you think this happens?
2   Is your placement agency transparent about the services it is not providing and the requests it is failing to meet? If not how does it conceal these things and why?
3   How does the agency ration (or prioritise, or target) its services? How are social work practitioners involved in this process?
4   To what extent does the need to ration services permeate the thinking and practice of the agency?
5   Does the agency carry out actions in a tokenistic way, in order not to be accused of not doing them, even though it lacks the resources to do them in a way that would actually be meaningful?
6   Does the agency have demands made upon it – for example in the form of legal requirements – which cannot reasonably be met within the resources available?
7   Broadhurst et al. (2010) noted that agencies' staff sometimes used 'deflection strategies' (ways of avoiding taking on work) and questionable 'heuristics' (questionable rules of thumb: for example the idea that referrals about families from neighbours are likely to be malicious) to try to control their workloads. Do you notice any of these?
8   Do you notice 'workarounds' that the agency has had to develop in order to meet targets?
9   Does the agency undertake interventions which it cannot really hope to see through properly with the resources that it has available? Or is it clear about what services it can realistically offer?

POLITICS

Social work is not created solely by social workers, but is the product of society and of a political process. Social workers typically deal with issues in which there is intense political interest: family life, immigration, mental health, anti-social behaviour, etc. State social work agencies, their operating briefs, guidelines, budgets, legal duties, are the product of decisions made by politicians, partly in response (in a democratic society) to pressures and demands from a variety of interest groups. Voluntary social work agencies, though they are not set up by the state, must still operate within the law and are frequently financed largely by public money.

Politics at the level of government – politics at the 'macro' level we might call it – is a process of conflict, negotiation and compromise between different interest groups, resulting in laws, directives, demands, rhetorical gestures. Within a given agency these interact with more local forms of politics, politics at the 'meso' or 'micro' levels, to determine the priorities of an organisation, its working culture, the way it operates in practice.

Most people are rather sceptical about politics in general, but oddly enough social work students are sometimes quite naïve about politics as it applies to social work. Or perhaps it would be more accurate to say that they feel that they are *expected* to be naïve. Thus in student essays I sometimes encounter something along the lines of the following:

... Victoria Climbié died in tragic circumstances but fortunately the Every Child Matters agenda and the Children Act 2004 will ensure that such a thing never happens again ...

I do not by any means suggest that the Every Child Matters agenda (DfES, 2003) and the Children Act 2004, or indeed any other government initiative, should be ignored or dismissed but all such products of government are the result of demands that 'something should be done' about a certain problem, followed by a protracted series of negotiations between various interest groups, with varying degrees of power, about what the 'something' should be. And the political response to a demand that something be done includes gestures and rhetoric as well as substantive acts. Roger Cobb and Marc Howard Ross (1997: 35–37) list a range of ways in which an impression is created for purposes of political expedience that something is being done about a problem, even if in fact nothing much really is. These include creating a committee to study the problem, 'showcasing' or 'tokenism' in which one small aspect of the problem is focused on to give the impression that the whole problem is being addressed, and 'symbolic co-optation' in which language or symbols are adopted from those campaigning for change (like an oil company adopting the 'green' language of the environmental movement). Cowden and Singh, in an article cited earlier in this chapter, point out that the rhetoric of 'user involvement' can be co-opted in this way by politicians and managers to strengthen their own control:

> One of the things that weaken managerial control is the sense that they [managers] do not know what things are like on the front line – hence the ideology of User Involvement can be used by managers to shore up the sense that they are really on the side of the User. User Involvement comes to be very important to managers because the 'User' comes to be seen as embodying a truth, a truth that is simultaneously not available to front-line staff, who are seen as inherently constrained by rules and bureaucracy. This ideology allows managers, and by extension government ministers to appeal directly to Users, over the heads of front-line workers, who in their petty and bureaucratic way do not really understand what Users really want. Yet as we have noted earlier the majority of the so-called Users of services have little or no choice over the matter of how services become organized, resourced or managed. (Cowden and Singh, 2007: 19)

If you look at any new development in social care policy you will see numerous symbolic and rhetorical moves of these kinds. It is important to look behind the new terminology and the rhetoric in order to see what is really taking place.

I do not wish to suggest that students should adopt a stance of complete cynicism towards politics, laws or government guidelines. Far from it: these are among the means by which a society can and does change. (Slavery was abolished by laws. Laws gave women the vote and stopped little children being sent to work underground in mines.) But I do suggest that an effective social worker needs to be cautious about accepting anything of this kind at face value. Cynicism is destructive but scepticism is vital. Guidance from government, and the activity that takes place within a given agency, serve many agendas other than the ostensible one of providing the best possible service to the public.

And there are often unintended consequences of new policy initiatives. In early 2008 it came to light, for instance, that some hospitals in Britain were making patients wait outside accident and emergency units in ambulances, rather than admitting them straight away (Campbell,

2008). This made no sense from the point of view of patient comfort or care, and no sense from the point of view of the ambulance service, since these ambulances were no longer available to respond to new emergencies, but it did make sense to hospital staff trying to meet government targets on waiting times in accident and emergency units. The government target was supposed to improve the performance of these units, or at least to demonstrate that government was 'doing something' about the performance of these units, but the actual result in this case could hardly be said to be in the interests of service users. Arguably some of the targets which social work agencies have to meet are similarly questionable, though of course targets may also serve the useful purpose of keeping staff focused and preventing staff complacency.

A preoccupation with 'targets' is very characteristic of modern public services in Britain. Another kind of activity that is very characteristic of public services is 'restructuring'. Social work agencies are frequently restructured: their hierarchy of teams and managers is rearranged, units are combined or divided up, new names are coined for different parts of the organisation. One social work agency I worked for once restructured twice in a single year, and indeed the university faculty in which I now work was restructured in two successive years, during which time it changed its name twice. There is a good chance that if you are placed in a statutory agency, that agency will have been very recently restructured, or is undergoing a restructuring while you are there. You may want to consider what effect this is having on the way that service operates.

Sometimes these restructurings take place at a national level. The Every Child Matters agenda mentioned earlier was presented by the UK government as a root and branch restructuring of the entire range of services for children and families. This sort of activity certainly gives an impression that something is being done and of course it may serve many useful purposes, but service delivery can suffer while a restructuring is underway, and sometimes the long-term benefit is questionable. A US study (Glisson and Hemmelgarn, 1998) which compared outcomes for users of services for children and families in different local government areas, concluded that 'organizational climate' was more important to service effectiveness than 'service system configuration'. In other words factors like staff confidence and morale were more significant than structure. If this is the case, frequent restructurings, which tend to have a negative effect on staff morale, may sometimes do more harm than good in terms of outcomes for service users. (Interestingly, in view of the huge emphasis now being placed on multi-agency working and interagency co-ordination in the UK, this study also found that 'increased service coordination *decreases* quality' [ibid.: 417: original emphasis].)

Nor are these complications confined to the state sector. Students placed in voluntary agencies may also notice agendas which seem to conflict with the ostensible aims of the service. A student placed in a voluntary agency which is ostensibly led by its own service users commented to me that the staff of the agency seemed in reality to have a great deal of control over the agenda and outcomes of service users' meetings, and made many decisions in unofficial meetings that took place without service users present. I doubt that these staff *intended* to be dishonest, but students (whether in state or voluntary placements) often notice problems and contradictions which staff who work in the agency simply fail to see, rather as a fish may not be aware of the water in which he constantly swims. 'Keep your eyes open!' is perhaps the overall message of this chapter: 'Keep your eyes open and keep asking yourself what is really happening here and why?'

PLACEMENT QUESTIONS 2.4   THE POLITICAL CONTEXT (MACRO AND MICRO)

- What recent government initiatives seem to preoccupy staff or managers in your placement agency? What is it that these initiatives are ostensibly trying to achieve? What actual consequences are they having on the way the agency operates, and to what extent do you think they are making a difference? Are they making a difference in the way intended?
- Are there any activities you notice taking place which seem to you to serve some other purpose than purely the best interests of service users? If so, what seems to be driving these activities? What purpose do they serve? Why do they happen?

CHAPTER SUMMARY

In this chapter I have looked at a few of the ways in which social work agencies differ from one another and, as a result, have different issues to face, different pressures, different priorities and different outlooks. There are many other context-specific factors which I have not covered. (Isabel Williams and Janet Young [2003] for example, draw attention to the transient nature of many social work teams and the difficulty in building a coherent team knowledge base when much of the team is made up of temporary staff recruited from employment agencies.) My overall point has been, though, that the entire context has to be taken into account when trying to understand how a social work agency operates, and that it is often misguided to try to say how things should be done, unless one understands this context.

FURTHER READING

Karen Healy's book on social work theory, referred to above, is a text that places strong emphasis on the context in which social work is practised:

Healy, K. (2005) *Social Work Theories in Context: Creating Frameworks for Practice*. Basingstoke: Palgrave.

For a look at the way social work fits into the broader context of social policy, another text that may be useful is:

Dickens, J. (2010) *Social Work and Social Policy: An Introduction.* London: Routledge.

But I would urge readers to look for books and articles that relate to *their* particular context. If working with elderly people, for instance, seek out books on ageing, on services for older people, on social work with older people. The main point of this chapter has been that guidance that is appropriate in one context is not necessarily appropriate in another.

3 ASSESSMENT

- What and who?
- Assessment over time
- Judgement and discrimination
- Assessment and proportionality
- *Needs-led and service-led assessment*
- Assessment as human interaction
- Values and mandate
- Theories and analysis

'Assessment' is a very important word in social work. Indeed if you spend time in a state-run social work agency (the 'statutory sector' as it tends to be called in the UK) you may well find that 'assessment' is a word you end up using many times every day. And you will also probably find that the agency has an elaborate assessment procedure involving several sets of complex paperwork (or, more likely, inputting data on-line, though I will use the word 'paperwork' for brevity). What you may also notice, though, is that the word 'assessment' is sometimes inaccurately used simply to *mean* the paperwork, as in 'have you completed that assessment yet?' Actually a form, and the information gathered on it, is *not* really an assessment *per se*. It is a tool to be used for the purposes of making an assessment. The assessment itself is the judgement that is reached as a result of the information-gathering exercise.

In contrast to large bureaucratic state agencies, in some small voluntary agencies there may be no formal assessment tools and 'assessment' may not be a defined procedure at all. Students on placement in such agencies sometimes say to me that the agency 'doesn't do assessments'. My response to this is 'Then how does the agency ever know what action to take?' The truth is that, in any context, inside or outside of social work, you need to come to some sort of judgement about what action to take, and that is all an assessment really is: *a judgement made about a situation in order to decide how to act.* Any action is preceded by *some* kind of judgement, so there is *always* an assessment, whether it is a lengthy and formal one, a snap judgement that takes place entirely inside your head, or something in between.

It might be a good assessment or a bad one, a brief one or a long one, an ethically sound one or an ethically questionable one, but some sort of assessment always happens.

Sometimes I feel that we would rather not face up to the fact that our actions are based on our own judgements, and I wonder whether that is why in state agencies we sometimes hide behind the forms, as if pretending to ourselves that it is the forms that make the judgements and not we ourselves. And perhaps, too, it is why in small agencies we may like to persuade ourselves that no assessment is done at all.

Throughout this book we will come back to issues relevant to assessment. This chapter makes a start by raising a range of issues and questions about the assessment process. In inviting you to try to relate these to your placement agency, my suggestion is (as it will be throughout this book) that you ask yourself 'What *really* happens?' (as opposed to what happens in theory, or what is supposed to happen). As well as looking at the mission statements, the guidelines, the legal frameworks, therefore you should also look *behind* them. Students in agencies which claim to do no assessments may find that in fact snap judgements as to whether a client will receive a given service are being made by agency staff on rather dubious grounds. Students in agencies which pride themselves on their exhaustive assessment process may conclude that much of the information that is so laboriously gathered is never actually used.

Before going any further, though, you might like to ask yourself what it would be like to be on the receiving end of an assessment.

PLACEMENT QUESTIONS 3.1   ASSESSMENTS FROM THE POINT OF VIEW OF SERVICE USERS

Consider the service users of your placement agency, and think about what you know about the initial encounters between them and the agency, before the agency has decided what kind of intervention it is going to offer to them (or in some cases, impose on them). In other words think about what happens during the time when the agency is still at the initial stage of finding out about the service user. (This includes the referral stage, which might be followed by a stage that might be called 'an initial assessment' and may sometimes be followed by a more complex and detailed assessment, but which might in some agencies have no specific name at all.)

Try to put yourself in the position of one of those service users, and ask yourself how you would feel in that position. What would your hopes be? What would your fears be? Would you feel encouraged and empowered by the encounter, or discouraged and disempowered? Would you feel supported or undermined? Valued or patronised?

Now notice for a minute what kind of service user you have selected to think about. Is the service user in question representative of the service users of the agency as a whole? For example if you are placed in a children and families agency, you may have chosen to think about a parent, rather than a child. Try now to look at the process from the point of view of other service users that you did not originally think about, and ask yourself the same questions. (If you thought about a parent, think now about a child. If you thought about an elderly person, think now about an elderly person's carer.) Do you come up with the same answers or different ones?

Standing back a bit now from the experience of service users, do you think that the agency conducts the initial contact in a way that is likely to bring the best response? How could it be done differently?

WHAT AND WHO?

Two important questions to ask about any assessment, are 'what is being assessed?' and 'who is responsible for the assessment?' Speaking for myself, I would hate to be on the receiving end of an assessment in which a social worker asked me a lot of questions about my problems and then took the information away and made a decision by herself about what my needs were. I suspect that I would disagree with the worker's decision and would most likely find it clumsy and simplistic. And while, like everyone, I have problems in life, these cannot really be understood if taken in isolation, without also thinking about my strengths, my problem-solving abilities, the relationships I have with other people.

You are unlikely to come up with a reasonably accurate sense of what a person needs without, at minimum, some sort of dialogue with that person. It is true that, as an outsider you may well see useful things that the client does not see, but the converse is definitely also true. There will undoubtedly be things that the client understands about himself that you do not understand. In most circumstances the service user needs to have, at minimum, some input into the conclusions of the assessment process. And there are lots of circumstances in which it makes sense for the service user to decide for himself what he needs in terms of services, as the majority of us do in respect of most aspects of our lives. We do not normally require professional advice to tell us where to live, when to have children, how to spend our money. By the same token, we do not necessarily require professional advice about the social care services we need.

So, as a general rule, assessments will be better, more accurate and more useful if (a) they address strengths as well as problems and (b) they actively involve the subject of the assessment: the client.

But there is another set of reasons too why it is important that assessments are not just problem-orientated and why they should be done *with* rather than just done *to* the client. I would not just be annoyed if a social worker asked me about my problems and then decided for herself what my needs were. I would also feel humiliated and disempowered. I would not feel motivated to work with the social worker, and this could seriously reduce their ability to do productive work with me, since most of the services that are provided by social workers require the active involvement of the client. I would also feel pretty unmotivated if the assessment did not acknowledge strengths.

Imagine you were a social work student receiving one or other of the following two assessments of your learning needs and ask yourself which is more likely to motivate you:

- X has a number of significant problems with his/her academic work. She has difficulties structuring her assignments. She has not learnt the referencing conventions. She does not seem to know how to make effective use of reading.
- X is very enthusiastic. She has great personal warmth and an intuitive understanding of human relationships. She does however need to work on her more academic skills in the area of structuring written work, following academic conventions and making effective use of reading. Improvement in these areas would enhance her analytical skills and enable her to make the best use of her already considerable inter-personal skills.

I think you will probably agree that, while both accounts describe the same problems, the second one feels much more encouraging and optimistic, and is more likely to motivate you, because it balances these problems by acknowledging strengths, and presents the way ahead as building on strengths. This is in essence the underlying idea behind the 'strengths perspective' (Saleebey, 2006). Most of us are prone to some degree of self-doubt, and many users of social work services have received many negative messages to further undermine their self-confidence. Just as a student is more likely to be motivated to learn by a message that acknowledges what she has already achieved, so a service user is more likely to be supported in achieving change by a message that acknowledges that 'people who seek help with problems are more than the problem' (Early and GlenMaye, 2000: 119).

Although assessment can in some ways be seen as a process that precedes intervention, it is also in another sense the first part of the intervention itself. It makes no sense to conduct assessments in a way that will make subsequent interventions less likely to succeed.

ASSESSMENT OVER TIME

Any assessment involves several stages. Milner and O'Byrne (2009: 61–62) divide this into five which I list below with my own commentary added beneath each one.

1   Preparation
    For example, a social worker (Susan) is asked to see a potential client (Mr Brown) who has come into the office. Before talking to Mr Brown, she checks any previous information she has about him and his circumstances, including previous assessments, so as to avoid asking for information that the agency already has, and also to see whether there are particular areas that she will need to explore.
2   Data collection
    To continue the example, Susan interviews Mr Brown and subsequently speaks to other professionals who might have information to contribute, noting down what she has been told. What information she actually obtains will of course depend on her interviewing skills, the quality of her preparation, the amount of time she takes, what questions she chooses to ask (this may be dictated to some degree by her agency's assessment forms, but not entirely), and what Mr Brown and the professionals choose to tell her.
3   Weighing the data
    Susan decides which pieces of information are relevant and important. This 'weighting' process is reflected in her recording: she does not write down the whole conversation verbatim, but extracts from it what she sees as the salient points. There is no reason in principle why it should be just the social worker that carries out this weighting process. She could discuss with Mr Brown what the salient points are, and agree with him how they are to be recorded. Whether this is appropriate or not will depend on the context. What Susan or Mr Brown see as salient, however, will depend in part on their respective life experiences, their values and their views on how the world works.

4   Analysing the data
    Susan uses the information she has gathered (whether or not in collaboration with the client) to come up with some sort of summary of what the main issues are for her agency. What needs does Mr Brown seem to have which the agency might have some responsibility to assist him with? How acute are those needs? The conclusions she reaches will depend on a number of factors including her knowledge, her theoretical orientation and her understanding both of the agency's brief and her own role. Again this stage in the process can in principle be shared with the service user and indeed with others, but this may or may not be appropriate. If Mr Brown is a sex offender, for example, and Susan was assessing the risk he poses to others, then clearly she cannot simply go along with Mr Brown's assessment of his own riskiness.

    A social worker's analysis may also be influenced by how she sees her role – as advocate or gatekeeper? Many social workers will try to do both these jobs as the same time, but there is a basic conflict between the two. As advocate, a social worker should try to make the best possible case for her client, rather as a defence lawyer does in a trial. As a gatekeeper for her agency's resources, the social worker tries to present the client's needs fairly but in a balanced way so as to allow them to be compared with the needs of other service users and let limited resources be distributed as fairly as possible. Vulnerable, marginalised people *need* strong advocates and a social worker may be the only one they have. But, while gatekeeping seems a rather less glamorous function, it can also have a perfectly honourable basis if it is about *equity*. Some social workers may prioritise their advocacy role and deliberately gloss their clients' needs to make them seem as great as possible, though of course this may result in other clients losing out. Others may prioritise their gatekeeping role with the result that their clients may lose out to other clients who have workers advocating strongly on their behalf.

5   Utilising the analysis
    Finally the analysis is used (whether by the social worker herself or by others) to determine what kind of response the agency might make to Mr Brown and to move towards a plan of action.

If you are in an agency where there is no formal assessment process, you may feel that you don't go through all these stages, and I suppose it *is* possible, though not desirable, to miss out the 'preparation' stage. (I say it is not desirable because poorly prepared assessment interviews can result in repetitive questions and time wasted on gathering information that is either irrelevant or already a matter of record.) But, that conceded, and assuming that you do come to *some* conclusion about what you or your agency ought to do for the service user in question, then you *must* have been through the other four stages: you will have gathered some information about that person, you will have made a decision about what is most relevant and important, you will have come to some conclusion about his needs, and you will have reached a decision about what to do on that basis. This will be the case, even if the whole process only took a few seconds and even if it all took place more or less unconsciously inside your own head.

Very brief informal processes have the advantage of minimising the amount of your limited time and your agency's limited resources that is used up on assessment as opposed to actually delivering a service. But they have the disadvantage of not being thorough – needs may be overlooked or not understood – and not being consciously thought through.

If you weigh up information very quickly, without thinking about how you are doing it, then all sorts of prejudices and biases are likely to creep in, and of course you cannot possibly gain as complete a picture as you would from a more thorough process.

PROVISIONALITY

Any given assessment, in social work as in life, can only be provisional, only a part of an ongoing process of assessment and reassessment. Susan's assessment (in the example I have just used to illustrate the stages) should take into account information from previous assessments. And in the event that she recommends that a more detailed assessment of Mr Brown's needs takes place later, then Susan's own preliminary assessment – including her analysis and conclusions – will itself just be one of the pieces of information that the subsequent assessment should gather in, weigh up and incorporate in its own analysis. People and circumstances change and we should not think of assessment as some sort of one-off process that goes through its five stages, comes to a conclusion and then sits on a file as the final and definitive statement about a person's needs. In fact, *as soon as it is placed on the file*, an assessment begins to become out of date. Would you wish for an assessment of your needs or your capabilities to be based on information gathered a year ago?

But nor should we regard each new assessment as taking place in a vacuum, disregarding all the information that has already been gathered. This would mean that the client would be forced to retell stories which she has already told, while we ourselves repeat work that has already been done and deny ourselves the opportunity to learn from previous experience, or to notice the kinds of patterns that only emerge when you look at the present in the light of the past. If you learn, for example, that a young child has been left alone in the house by his parents, this is concerning, but if you were to look back over the child's file and find that this had happened repeatedly over a long period of time, it would be much more so. Sometimes it is only when you compile a chronology of events that have occurred over a period of time that you get a sense of what is happening. The following came from a study undertaken by Bridget McKeigue and myself in which we interviewed social workers involved in care proceedings:

> Case Y concerned a child of eight-and-a-half. This was the second set of proceedings on this child. He was returned home after the first set of proceedings on the recommendation of a psychologist, though against the view of the guardian. 'The nettle should have been grasped then' was the feeling of the social worker who initiated the second set, four years on. The current proceedings were not initiated as a result of a single event but as the result of this social worker compiling a chronology and seeing how bad things looked when events were seen together rather than in isolation. (McKeigue and Beckett, 2010: 159)

Assessments have to take into account the past as well as the present, and in making an assessment we need to bear in mind that things will be different again in the future. Having said this though, an assessment is only useful if *some action flows from it*. Things may change in the future, but it is necessary to reach conclusions about a person's needs at a given point in time, and then act. Otherwise we may be tempted to assess and re-assess forever as an alternative to actually doing anything at all.

JUDGEMENT AND DISCRIMINATION

As I have already said, an assessment involves making judgements. It is *of itself* a judgement, but it also entails a series of judgements that have to be made during the process of completing it. Judgement is involved in deciding what information to collect, how to collect it and how to interpret it.

The fact that assessment involves judgement is what makes it difficult. The decisions that social workers make can have enormous implications for people's lives, in some cases literally lifelong implications. What professionals tend to do when faced with having to make such judgements is to make a mystique out of it, and lay claim to some sort of 'specialized scientific knowledge' (Schön, 1991: 22) which is not accessible to ordinary mortals. But in fact, though specialised knowledge can and does provide quite precise and unambiguous answers to certain types of technical problems, there is no exact science, or even an inexact one, that can guide the majority of social work decisions. To claim some sort of precise quasi-scientific knowledge base for social work would be to mislead both others and yourself.

And yet decisions do have to be made, including some – 'Is the risk of harm to this child so great as to warrant compulsory intervention?' 'Is this elderly person so confused and so much in danger that we must arrange for her to move to residential care?' – on which the course of a whole life may turn. A social worker whose responsibility is to come to judgements about such situations cannot simply throw up her hands and say 'this is too hard', any more than political leaders faced with some new crisis or judges in a court room at the end of a trial can throw up *their* hands and say, 'this is too difficult for us, let someone else decide'. If it is your job to make a decision, you must make a decision, albeit with the support and advice of others. And in fact not making a decision *is itself a decision* which itself has consequences. Drift and delay of various kinds are characteristic of agencies which are finding it hard to come to judgements, and they can have catastrophic consequences for service users. (Indeed I have suggested elsewhere that drift and prevarication in the child care system can be so harmful as to be regarded as a form of child abuse [Beckett, 2007a: 198ff].)

It is important to remember in all this, though, that there is a distinction between coming to a judgement about *what to do*, and coming to a judgement about the *moral worth of a human being*. Making a judgement is not the same thing as *being judgemental*. Admittedly this isn't always an easy distinction for people on the receiving end to see. If I come to a judgement that my agency is not in a position to provide a service to somebody who has requested help, this may well feel to that person that she is being judged and not found sufficiently deserving, but my judgement should not have been based on her worth as a human being or her deservingness, but on her needs and on my agency's capacity to meet those needs, given all the other calls on its resources. To give an example, Mr Roberts cannot get out of bed by himself at all, while Mrs Williams can get out of bed and move around her home, though it is not easy and she could do with some help. If I can only help one of them, I must help Mr Roberts because his needs are more acute. This is not to say that Mrs Williams is not deserving of help, or to say that her problems are not real ones.

PLACEMENT QUESTIONS 3.2   TIMELY DECISION-MAKING

Thinking first about your placement agency:

- How good is your agency at coming to timely judgements about situations?
- Do you see evidence of it coming to judgements too quickly without proper consideration?
- Or do you see evidence of it trying to put off coming to decisions when a decision is needed?
- Have you noticed evidence of delaying tactics to avoid coming to a decision? (For example decisions are deferred to some future date, even when it is unlikely there will be any further evidence to discuss. Or are decisions pushed to and fro up and down the organisation, or between the organisation and other agencies?)

Thinking now about your own practice:

- Have you noticed yourself coming to a judgement too quickly, jumping to a conclusion which later on you felt was not justified?
- Or have you noticed yourself trying to put off decisions which you know need to be made? How have you done this? What have you learnt about yourself?

As well as being about judgement, assessment is also about discrimination. Indeed the whole purpose of an assessment is to enable us to discriminate between one person and another, for if an agency were to deliver the same service to everyone, regardless of their needs or circumstances, there would be no need for an assessment. But people have different needs, face different challenges and threats, and have different strengths and weaknesses. However there is a difference between being *discriminating*, which is necessary – as Neil Thompson says, 'to discriminate' simply means to 'identify a difference' (Thompson, 2006: 12) – and being *discriminatory*, which means basing decisions and judgements on factors which should be irrelevant to the matter in hand.

We need to be clear about these distinctions. If you are delivering a service for disabled people, it is perfectly appropriate to deliver a more comprehensive service to Mr Smith than to Mr Brown on the basis that Mr Smith has a more severe disability and greater needs. That is just being discriminating. But it is obviously *not* appropriate to deliver a more comprehensive service to Mr Smith than Mr Brown on the basis that you like Mr Smith more, or that he reminds you of your brother, or that Mr Smith is white and Mr Brown is black, for all these would be discriminatory.

Likewise it would be discriminatory to initiate child protection procedures on Mr Jones' children purely because he is known to use heroin. But it would *not* be discriminatory to initiate those procedures if you had evidence to suggest that his heroin use was affecting his capacity to parent to the point that his children were being seriously neglected and put at risk. It is important that you are clear about these distinctions. I have encountered social work students who feel anxious about making any judgement at all on the grounds that it might be discriminatory. But that is to misunderstand the meaning of 'discriminatory'.

We will come back to the subject of making judgements in Chapter 5.

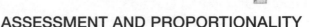

ASSESSMENT AND PROPORTIONALITY

We live in a culture that is very preoccupied by the idea of gathering information and predicting harm. But you can have too much assessment. In my experience students on placement are sometimes concerned that agency assessments seem quite unnecessarily elaborate and time-consuming, and many times out of proportion with the often quite modest services that are provided on the strength of them. They are right to be concerned for several reasons. Firstly, as I pointed out earlier, assessment uses up resources that could otherwise be used for *doing* something. Secondly, assessment represents a substantial intrusion into people's privacy, which can only be justified if it is likely to yield real benefits to the people concerned. Thirdly, an elaborate assessment naturally raises hopes of an equally comprehensive service. Beth Parry-Jones and Judith Soulsby comment that 'practitioners do not wish to discuss needs with users and carers which cannot be met, because they are reluctant to raise false expectations' (2001: 416). This reluctance seems to me to be well-founded. Unless we can be confident that information about unmet need is actually being used to improve the service, and is not simply being filed and forgotten about, then how can we justify wasting service users' time and raising their hopes, by carrying out assessments that will not lead to anything?

Of course it is possible for assessments to be disproportionate in the other direction too. Decisions can be made *too* quickly and/or without an adequate exploration of the situation that they are supposed to address. It is entirely right and proper that a decision that may have long-term implications for a person's life should be based on thorough examination of the problem. But assessment does not take place in a vacuum. It has an impact in itself. While the assessment is going on the situation itself is changing and perhaps deteriorating. (Imagine a doctor taking so long over assessing a patient's heart problem that the patient had heart failure and died before the assessment was complete.) Taking too long over an assessment may even close off options that might otherwise have been available. However, there are a number of political and psychological dynamics in play that can lead to an assessment process getting out of proportion.

THE PURSUIT OF CERTAINTY

You will rarely if ever in social work achieve a conclusion about which you can be absolutely certain. In situations where your conclusion may have very far-reaching consequences, this can be hard to bear. Writing about judges and welfare officials involved in matrimonial custody cases, Jon Elster referred to a 'psychological tension in decision makers that many will be unable to tolerate', resulting from the 'huge significance of the decision but the absence of a non-contentious way of making it' (Elster, 1989: 124). The same kind of tension exists in many areas of social work, and is exacerbated by the very public blaming of social workers who make decisions which, with the benefit of hindsight, turn out to have been wrong. Social workers, alongside other decision-makers, such as judges, often deal with this anxiety by clinging onto what Elster called 'an irrational belief in the possibility of rational preference' (ibid.: 124), the belief that, if only you have enough information and enough expertise, an incontrovertibly 'right' answer will emerge.

AVOIDING AN OBLIGATION

Just as politicians sometimes set up a working party or a public enquiry as a way of avoiding having to act, so in the area of public services, a lengthy assessment can be used as a way of avoiding providing a service at all. For example, an education authority that delays the completion of a Statement of Educational Needs, a form of assessment defined by the 1996 Education Act (s312), may avoid having to commit resources that it otherwise would have to commit if the statement was completed quickly. You may notice this occurring in social work agencies. A further time-consuming assessment may serve the purpose of putting off the moment when resources have to be committed to a costly service.

PUTTING A DECISION OFF

Prolonging the assessment period can also have the attraction, for professionals, of putting off a painful moment of decision to some point in the future, though for the service user this may mean prolonging a period of insecurity and delaying the moment when life can move on again. Suppose you are carrying out an assessment of Mrs George's ability to parent her baby son and it is beginning to look as if Mrs George is really not up to it. Unless you are a very unusual (and not very nice) person you will not be looking forward to telling Mrs George this, and you may be tempted to prolong the assessment in order to put that moment off, but you should be aware that if you delay too long this may have long-term consequences for the baby, who is being denied the opportunity to form long-lasting attachments until the matter is settled one way or the other, and whose actual ability to form such attachments may diminish with the passing of time.

NEEDS-LED AND SERVICE-LED ASSESSMENT

We tend to assume that the assessment is what determines the service that will be provided, but in fact the opposite can often true: the kind of assessment that we carry out is often shaped by the kind of service we think is needed. For example, if you thought someone was likely to need psychotherapy, you would probably ask very different questions and explore very different areas than if you thought what they were looking for was practical care in their home.

Guidance that accompanied the 1990 NHS and Community Care Act introduced a distinction between *needs-led* and *resource-led* assessment. A *resource-led* assessment takes as its starting point the various services an agency has under its control, and determines whether a prospective service user is suitable or eligible for one or other of these services. A *needs-led assessment* does not presuppose what kind of service is going to be provided, and considers what the client's actual needs are before starting to thinking about ways in which they could be met.

> ## Case example 3.1 Does Mr Jones need residential care?
>
> Mr Jones aged 92 is unable to manage at home. He and his extended family have come to the conclusion that he 'needs residential care'. A purely service-led assessment might simply look at whether or not he qualifies for residential care under agency guidelines. What would a needs-led approach be?

COMMENTS

You'd really need to know a lot more about Mr Jones in order to ascertain precisely what it would entail, but instead of assessing Mr Jones' eligibility for residential care, a purely needs-led approach would set aside thoughts about the services that might be provided and look purely and simply at what needs Mr Jones has which might require the provision of services *of some kind*. It might look at his need for company, for assistance with washing, for food to be prepared for him, for assistance in getting out of a chair, etc. Having established the full range of needs that Mr Jones has, the assessor then considers how these needs might be met. Assuming (and it is quite a big assumption) that the necessary resources were available to fund alternatives, residential care *per se* would never, or almost never, be the only possible way to meet his particular set of needs. Perhaps a lodger could be found who would help him with getting up in the morning and provide him with some company in exchange for a rent-free room? Perhaps a local volunteer could take him to the pub along the street for a hot meal?

In theory at least a genuinely needs-led approach avoids pigeonholing service users, pays proper respect to their uniqueness and complexity as human beings and creates an opportunity for more imaginative service-provision tailored to individual need. That said, it can be difficult in practice for busy workers to avoid taking the short-cut of quickly assigning service users to one or other existing service.

ASSESSMENT AS HUMAN INTERACTION

Gathering data for assessment purposes usually involves a series of conversations between human beings. People say different things depending on who is speaking to them, in what context and in what way. You get different answers to the same questions depending on who is being asked and who asks. If you ask an elderly person about what her care needs are you may get a very different picture of her needs from what you would get from her daughter, or her GP. You may also get a very different answer if you yourself were, say, a middle-aged woman, than you would get if, say, you were a young man. We do not reveal all of ourselves to everyone, and what we choose to reveal depends on our perceptions of the person we are talking to.

How the conversation is conducted will depend on a variety of factors, including the purpose of the assessment, the agency requirements and the value base of the social worker and of the agency. Three different basic models for the interaction that are very frequently cited in the literature on social work assessment are the following, suggested by Smale and Tuson (1993):

1 The Procedural Model – here both the worker and service user are obliged to work within a framework laid down by the agency, typically involving the filling in of forms using check-boxes and so on.
2 The Questioning Model – here the worker takes the lead and is assumed to have particular expertise in the area in question. In this approach the social worker takes the lead.
3 The Exchange Model – here the worker doesn't claim special expertise in the problem area in question. The process is shared with the service user. The worker does not impose her own theoretical model or priorities but simply offers her expertise in supporting the service user in thinking through the problem. In this approach the social worker tries not to take the lead but to proceed by negotiation with the client.

A purely *procedural approach* can be cold and alienating. It is not hard to imagine how distressing it could be to have someone ask very personal questions about, for example, your relationships, your bodily functions, your religious beliefs, your sexuality, and then record these in tick-box style on a form, particularly if the relevance of these questions was not obvious to you. If, as a social worker, you have to use forms and checklists then it is important to remember the possible discomfort and even humiliation that such an experience may make a service user feel and to try to make the experience as human as possible. When you yourself have done it many times and it has become ordinary and mundane, it can be harder than it seems to bear in mind that it may not seem ordinary and mundane to a service user at all.

Another disadvantage of the procedural approach is that it restricts the freedom of action both of service user and of social worker to conduct the assessment in the way that seems best to them. Social workers who have been in the field for a while frequently bemoan the reduction in the amount of professional autonomy, as well as the increasing amount of time spent sitting at computer screens, that has accompanied the 'managerialist' ethos that began to emerge in public services during the 1980s. Not surprisingly, since social work academics have often themselves been in the social work field for some time, you will frequently find similar thoughts in social work textbooks (Tony Evans and John Harris [2004] refer collectively to this material as 'curtailment literature'). But we need to recognise that, if social workers' autonomy has indeed been reduced (and Evans and Harris suggest that this may not have occurred as much as is commonly stated) this has advantages as well as disadvantages. Freedom of action for social workers is not *necessarily* a good thing, because social workers can abuse their power as much as anyone else, as well as having their own individual blind spots and biases. (Managerialism causes all kinds of problems, but you only need to look at a few case files from the 1970s and 1980s to realise that the era before managerialism was far from being some sort of 'golden age'.)

'On the plus side' a standard prescribed procedure may at least ensure some consistency and help to prevent social workers from focusing only on the particular aspects of problems that happen to interest them or the ones that happen to occur to them at the time. Given that assessments are often used to determine how resources are divided up between different service users, a standardised assessment format may perhaps help to ensure that the needs of service users are fairly weighed up against one another. A procedural approach also has the advantage that the responsibility for choosing the topics to be covered is taken by the agency as a whole rather than the individual worker. This can mean reduced anxiety for the worker, more consistency for the client.

A *questioning approach* is one that puts the social worker in charge. The social worker asks the questions and the client answers them. This can feel very undermining for the service user or carer – and it can result in something being imposed on the client which is not really helpful. If I had a personal problem and wanted to tell someone about it, I would prefer to tell them what I considered to be important, rather than simply submit to answering questions that they had chosen. But there are many situations in which it is perfectly appropriate for the social worker to insist on her own agenda. For example, when interviewing prospective foster-parents or adoptive parents, the social worker has a decision to make which quite properly cannot be completely handed over to them because it is not only their interests that are at stake. The social worker needs to satisfy herself that they will be able to provide good care to children, and will not pose a risk to children. (The approach actually used for such assessments also includes a substantial *procedural* element.) This is not to say that the process cannot be in large part a collaboration between worker and prospective carer, but the social worker does have a responsibility to establish any possible risk to children placed with this carer, and must be free to obtain information that she judges to be necessary to come to a judgement.

In the *exchange approach* the social worker takes pains not to set herself up as 'the expert', and aims to give at least equal weight to the service user's unique expertise in her own life. I cannot think of any assessment interaction where some element of an exchange approach is not appropriate. However, a pure exchange approach is not appropriate in situations where the client may not be capable of making an informed decision (i.e. a very small child, a person who is suffering from a psychotic illness or dementia), or in situations where you are interviewing someone about the risks they may pose to others, or in situations where you are gathering information that will be used to compare this client's needs with the needs of others. It is worth noting also the deep contradictions involved in using an exchange model in situations where the client is not there by his own choice (a common situation in social work, as discussed in Chapter 2), though this is not to say that you cannot use elements of an exchange approach even in these contexts.

Life is always more complicated than theory and a given interview rarely if ever falls neatly into one or other of these models. An assessment interview is typically a combination of all three. We need to be aware too that a social worker's *perception* of the process may be very different from that of the client. A social worker may feel, for example, that she is using an exchange approach in which there is an equal partnership between herself and the client, but the client may not feel the same thing. He may feel that he is simply responding to what he perceives to be her wishes, and may not really feel like an equal partner at all. (Non-verbal cues may tell the client whether we are interested, whether we think what they are saying is important, whether we approve of what they are saying. You will know this yourself if you have ever been on the receiving end of any kind of counselling or 'talking therapy'.) You may remember the distinction I made in the previous chapter between 'service requesters' and 'nominal service requesters'.

It is important, as far as is practicable, to try to carry out the assessment as a collaboration with the client, a mutual activity done *with* people rather than *to* them, for the reasons discussed earlier on in the chapter. But it is also important to be honest about the limits of this – and not pretend that we don't have our own agendas, or that power differences do not exist. Karen Healy found that service users

> were confused and often disappointed by what they understood to be offers of unconditional support and friendship which appeared to be implicit in service providers' emphasis on mutuality. These clients asked not that social workers entirely abandon ideals such as mutuality but that they be more explicit about the boundaries to these ideals in their work with them. (2005: 58)

VALUES AND MANDATE

Because assessments are not just about collecting information, but also about interpreting information and coming up with a course of action, they cannot be value-free. Indeed, since we do not collect information randomly, but select the topics which seem to us important, even the collection of information is not value-free. Most questions that assessments are intended to address contain a value component.

Case example 3.2   Should Mrs Rani be protected against herself?

Mrs Rani is a somewhat mentally confused elderly person living in her own home, who is known to sometimes forget to turn off electrical appliances, and has recently very nearly caused a serious house fire. Her house stands on its own so a fire is unlikely to be a risk to others, but she is certainly putting herself at some risk. However, she insists she is fine, wants no outside help or support, and wants to remain in her own home.

Since this vulnerable person is placing herself at risk, do social care agencies have a right and/or duty to intervene if Mrs Rani has said she doesn't want this?

COMMENTS

Your conclusions will reflect not only your thoughts about the likelihood of her coming to harm, but also your views (and the views of others) on (a) what level of risk is *acceptable*, and (b) the extent to which this is *anyone's business* other than that of Mrs Rani herself. The facts themselves will not answer these questions for you.

One thing that it is important to be clear about is what the assessment is actually *for*. What *kind* of decision is it that the assessment is supposed to be informing? What is your mandate? Which decisions are yours to make and which are not? Assessments address different kinds of question, and require different kinds of judgement. Clarity about the kind of question that your assessment is supposed to address helps to ensure that it is not unnecessarily intrusive, and not disproportionately elaborate.

Thus, if Ms Schmidt has problems with mobility and you are assessing her for practical help in her own home, then clearly there is no need to go into questions about her sexuality. This would be irrelevant and intrusive. On the other hand, if you are assessing Ms Schmidt as a specialist carer for children who may have been sexually abused and have problems in the area of sexuality, then it might well be appropriate to talk with Ms Schmidt about her own sexuality.

THEORIES AND ANALYSIS

Social work students, in my experience, often struggle with the concept of *social work theory*, and I can't say that I blame them for this. The truth is that there is no such thing as 'social work theory', if what one means by theory is a body of knowledge which serves the same role for social work as, say, medical science does for the practice of medicine. In social work education we tend to offer a very mixed bag of ideas, some of them explanatory models drawn from psychology (for instance 'attachment theory'), some of them working methods developed by therapists of one kind or another (for instance 'cognitive behavioural therapy') or within social work itself (for instance 'task-centred casework'), some of them more akin to belief systems or value positions (for instance 'empowerment'), some of them generalisations about society derived either from academic disciplines such as sociology or from the political stances taken by activists (for instance 'the social model' of disability) and then we lump all these things together as 'theory'. Students struggle to shoehorn the real practice situations they encounter on placement into one or other of these 'theories' and they also notice that most of the qualified practitioners around them don't even attempt to do so. They then wonder what theory is and whether it is really necessary at all.

The fact is, though, that you simply can't do a meaningful assessment without recourse to some kind of theory. Consider the following case example.

Case example 3.3   Theories behind assessment

(a) You work for a mental health agency. A new client of your agency, not known to you personally, has just called. She is 50, widowed (her husband died in the first Gulf War) and has a son aged 30 living in Australia. She has asked for a home visit, but the social worker who normally deals with her is not there and (for whatever reason) you cannot access her

(Continued)

(Continued)

records. She says she is feeling very low lately, and says 'I just don't know any more how to get from one day to the next'.

Think about four questions you might like to ask her, and write these down in a column, as in Table 3.1 below.

(b) You work for a children and families agency. A 24 year old woman self-refers because she feels unable to cope with the destructive, aggressive behaviour of her 5 year old son and thinks he needs to go into care for a while in order to calm him down and to teach him a lesson. You are the duty social worker who sees her.

Again, think about four questions you might like to ask her, and write these down in a column, as in Table 3.1 below.

Now, having written down your questions in both cases, please write down your reason for asking the question in the second column.

Table 3.1   Why ask the question?

Questions	Why ask this?

COMMENTS

My submission to you is that what you have written down in the right-hand column constitutes *theory*. You may not be able to give it a name but it represents the thinking behind your choice of question. Really you would have no business asking a question at all if you could not think of a reason for it (none of us would enjoy being asked a random set of questions by a professional who had no idea what the purpose of these questions was). And if you do have a reason, it ought to be good one, one that you could explain if asked to do so.

This point does not apply just to your choice of questions. In order to explain the decisions you make at *every* stage of the assessment – the decisions you make in weighing the data, the way you analyse the data – you would have to come up with 'theory'. How you carry out an assessment is shaped by your theoretical assumptions, and this is true whether or not you are consciously using named theories of the kind found in books, or are simply applying your own personal theoretical frame. For example:

- If you take a psychodynamic approach – or at least, which is probably more likely, you have a personal approach that is influenced by or akin to psychodynamic theory – you are likely to ask a lot of questions about the early history of the client on the basis that early history is a major factor in problems in the here and now.
- If you take a behavioural approach, whether consciously or unconsciously, there will be less emphasis on the past and more emphasis on the detail of the present circumstances because behaviourist theory suggests that any behaviour which persists must be being reinforced in some way in the here and now.
- If you take a task-centred approach, you will want to identify what are the key problems from the client's point of view and will also want to work with the client on first prioritising them and then developing strategies to address them in order.
- If you take a 'solution-focused' approach, you will try to avoid too much emphasis on problems and will want to explore with the client their *successes* in dealing with problems.
- If you are interested in family systems, you will want to look at the patterns of interactions that take place within the family as much as at what each individual family member *says*.
- If you tend to a more political perspective you may be inclined to look more at people's external circumstances: the neighbourhood they live in, their financial situation, the messages they are given by the rest of society. You will be inclined to see the difficulties faced by service users as the result of oppression, discrimination, poverty and power imbalances, rather than as personal problems.

An assessment is never simply 'the facts'. It is always an interpretation of those facts. Even at its very simplest, an assessment has to move away from the facts of a client's circumstances towards a view about what the client needs. In fact you could say that a completed assessment constitutes, *in itself,* a kind of theory about the circumstances of the service user who is the subject of the assessment. And I suggest that, as a responsible professional, you should be able to be explicit as to what your theory is and spell out the reasons why you think your theory makes sense. 'I believe that Jenny is at significant risk of harm for the following reasons … based on the following evidence …'. Occasionally the facts, properly presented, will almost speak for themselves, in the sense that any reasonable person would agree with them ('I think Jenny is at risk of significant harm because she is only 8 weeks old and has already sustained multiple bruises, some of the them visibly hand-shaped, while with her current carers, as well as a fractured leg for which her carers have offered two different explanations'). Often, though the facts will not speak for themselves, in that some might disagree with the conclusions you draw from them, and you will then need to be able to draw on research evidence, or on the specialist knowledge of others, or on theoretical models soundly based on such evidence and knowledge, in order both to inform and to defend the conclusion you reach.

It is also worth looking at the assessment questions you are required to ask as part of agency procedures, and asking 'Why am I required to ask this question? What is the implicit theory that lies behind this question, if any?' In other words, just as you must in fact have a theory, whether you know it or not, so must your agency, and it is worth thinking about what that theory is, and how well-founded it is.

PLACEMENT QUESTIONS 3.3 THE THEORY BEHIND ASSESSMENT QUESTIONS

How would you summarise the kinds of questions staff in your agency seem to concentrate on when carrying out an assessment? (The agency's formal expectations may well be different from how assessments are carried out in practice.)

For example, would you say that these questions were focused more on the present or on past history? How do they balance an exploration of problems and difficulties as against strengths and opportunities? Do they concentrate more on individuals, or on the social context?

What would seem to be the theories on which your agency's approach is, in practice, based? Are these consistent with the agency's stated objectives? Do they seem to you to be valid and helpful? If not what would seem to you to be their major flaws?

CHAPTER SUMMARY

This chapter has presented an overview of the topic of assessment. I have discussed what exactly it is that we 'assess' in social work (see also Chapters 6 and 7 which will discuss the concepts of *need* and *risk*), drawing attention to the dangers of emphasising problems rather than strengths, and considering the issue of ownership of the process. I have looked at assessment over time, considering the stages that assessment goes through, and noting that in a sense any assessment is necessarily provisional, because it will always be overtaken by events. I have noted that assessment involves judgement, and in fact *is* a judgement (the process of coming to a judgement will be discussed in more detail in Chapter 5). I have looked at questions about the proportionality of assessment, the amount of time and effort that ought to be invested in it as against other activities, and not least the actual provision of a service. I have touched on the distinction between a service-led assessment and a needs-led one that avoids simply 'pigeonholing' service users into existing services. I have looked at the inescapable role of values in assessment and the importance of a mandate (you are not there to assess everything about a person). Finally I have drawn your attention to the equally inescapable role of theory, of *ideas*, and encouraged you to think not only about the ideas on which you base your own assessment practice, but also about the ideas on which the assessment practice of your placement agency seems to be based.

FURTHER READING

This is an excellent general text on social work assessment:

Milner, J. and O'Byrne, P. (2009) *Assessment in Social Work* (3rd edn). Basingstoke: Palgrave.

For more reading on the human aspect of assessment, the communication between social worker and others, I would recommend the following new edition of a classic social work text:

Lishman, J. (2009) *Communication in Social Work* (2nd edn). Basingstoke: Palgrave.

4 INTERVENTION

- Words
- The character of social work intervention
- Roles
- Planning, clarity and coherence
- 'Radical non-intervention'
- Communication and purposefulness
- Theory

Quite often assessment is the easy bit. Recognising the problems that need addressing and even getting a sense of what is causing those problems, though challenging in itself, is very often a relatively straightforward task as compared to deciding what to actually *do*. In fact I think this is one of the reasons why assessments are sometimes dragged out, in the way discussed in the last chapter: social workers putting off the moment when they actually have to *act*. But assessment should be a preparation for action, not a substitute for it. Assessments on their own are no use unless they result in an actual service which in some way improves the quality of life for the recipient of that service.

The subject of this chapter is the service that social workers deliver, the ways in which they act upon the environment of their clients, *the things social workers do to make a difference* (to use a succinct definition of social work intervention that was suggested to me by a student). Every occupation has its own characteristic modes of action, a characteristic service that it provides. Teachers teach, bus drivers drive buses, actors act, surgeons do operations, carpenters make things out of wood. So what is the equivalent for social work? What do we do assessments *for*?

WORDS

Before plunging further into this subject I need to make a brief digression into the question of language, because it so happens that not only is the characteristic action or service of social work hard to define, but we are also not even quite sure what word to use for it.

In the past the word 'treatment' (by analogy with medicine) was the term commonly used for the kinds of services delivered by social work. For example, in the 1980s, programmes of activities for young offenders were described as 'Intermediate Treatment' (it often consisted of things like canoeing courses and motorcycle maintenance) and a book on social work could be given the title *Social Treatment* (Whittaker, 1989). The word 'treatment' seems quite odd to modern ears I think, and even rather distasteful and pretentious, because it equates the problems of social work clients with sickness, suggests that social work is analogous to medicine and implies some kind of precise technology which the social worker expertly applies to social problems. I don't think many of us believe any more that social work is like that. Even medicine itself isn't quite as like that as some people suppose.

The word 'intervention' now seems to have supplanted 'treatment' and is the term most commonly used at the time of writing, but this word also has somewhat uncomfortable connotations. For one thing, as I have pointed out previously, it is one of a number of words used in social work which have a military resonance (Beckett, 2003), given that the phrase 'military intervention' is often used when soldiers are sent in to apply armed force. (I discussed the reasons for our use of this military language in Chapter 2.) Also, like 'treatment', the word 'intervention' is also often used in medicine (we talk about 'surgical intervention', 'medical intervention'). And, as students often observe, 'intervene' also sounds a bit like 'intrude' and 'interfere', both things that social workers are frequently characterised as doing, or like 'invade'. A similar thought is expressed by Jane Dalrymple and Beverley Burke: 'The word "intervention" conveys a notion of intrusion into people's lives and by its very nature indicates where the dominant power relations are situated' (Dalrymple and Burke, 2006: 159).

Certainly it seems quite fitting to describe, for instance, the kind of protective action that is imposed on a family when child abuse is believed to have occurred. Here the social worker insists on getting involved whether the family wants her to or not, and is making it her business to look at some of the family's most intimate and personal aspects. No question about it, she is indeed *intervening*, and we may as well call a spade a spade (something we are not always good at in social work). Dalrymple and Burke agree that in such situations, the word 'intervention' is appropriate and accurate. However they suggest that the word seems to fit rather less well with other kinds of service that are also provided by social workers. For instance, is 'intervention' such a good word to use to describe arranging, at an elderly man's request, for him to have assistance with bathing, or doing life-story work with a child in public care for whom the social worker has had a long-standing case responsibility? These are both quite definitely services which will make a difference to their recipients, but would 'helping' or 'offering a service' be better words to use?

However, I think we are stuck with the word 'intervention' for the present. It at least has the merit of reminding us that our actions (even when they are welcomed) are always an intrusion into people's personal lives. So I use the word 'intervention' both in the title of this chapter and in the title of the book, to describe the whole range of services which social workers offer which are intended to make a difference. It includes an extremely diverse range of services which might include, for instance, providing an elderly person with an opportunity to talk about her past, removing a baby from the care of his mother,

commissioning homecare services for a person with disabilities or representing the interests of a person with mental health problems in his dealings with a housing agency.

THE CHARACTER OF SOCIAL WORK INTERVENTION

What is the common strand, if any, that links all these very different kinds of intervention? Or to put the question another way, what is the nature of the service that social workers provide that distinguishes it from the services that are provided by other professionals? As Martin Davies observed some years ago it has been 'strangely difficult for social work to arrive at a helpful definition of its own role' (Davies, 1991: 39). Davies went on to suggest that there were two 'myths' (I prefer myself to use the more neutral word 'discourses') about the nature of social work which increased this difficulty by confusing us about what social workers in practice actually do. One of these discourses was that social work was necessarily 'directed at client therapy'; the other that social work was necessarily a 'left-wing political activity'. These different discourses persist. There is still a discourse about social work which places quasi-therapeutic interactions at centre stage (look at the number of ideas derived from psychotherapy that appear in books on social work theory and you might indeed imagine that what social workers do is itself a form of psychotherapy). And there is still also a rival discourse (also prominently represented in books on social work theory) that sees tackling structural injustice, discrimination and oppression as the primary focus of social work activity. Lena Dominelli has long been an advocate of this second view of the profession:

> Inegalitarian power relations perpetuated by decision-makers and resource-holders have to be changed at the same time as egalitarian values are enacted. Social workers have an important role to play in promoting these issues. (Dominelli, 2004: 62)

As Davies acknowledged there are 'slivers of truth' in both of these discourses: social work *is* often partly about engaging in conversations with people intended to help them move on in their lives, which is essentially what psychotherapists do; and social work *is* often partly about challenging injustice and speaking up for people who are oppressed, which could at a pinch be described as a left-wing political activity, if one takes the view that the political left is necessarily the part of the political spectrum that aligns itself with the oppressed. (People who have lived in countries with tyrannical but supposedly left-wing regimes – such as the 'eastern bloc' countries in Europe before 1989 – might not necessarily agree with this. Nor might social workers with conservative or liberal political views who could with some justice point out that ideas about personal autonomy and service user choice have as many antecedents on what we would now call the political right as on the political left.)

However, even if one accepts that there is some truth in both accounts, the fact remains that neither of them really describe the service that social workers, in the main, actually deliver most of the time. Organising practical support at home for an elderly person, for example, is not by any stretch of the imagination either therapy or left-wing political activity, but it is nevertheless a useful service of a kind that many social workers spend much of their time delivering. Assessing foster-parents, helping people with learning disabilities manage their finances, investigating allegations of child abuse: these are likewise all useful activities carried out by social workers which really cannot be described, even at a long shot, either as therapy or as political activism.

So what *is* the common theme that links all the services that social workers try to provide? I think that a useful way of describing the job of social workers – and differentiating their work from that of other human service professionals – is to say that they attempt to fill gaps of various kinds in society's informal network of care and support. Most people, whether adults or children, have an informal care network provided by their family, friends and those around them which is adequate to meet their needs for emotional and practical care from other people, and to provide them with a base from which they can grow and live their lives. In some cases, though, and for a variety of reasons, people do not have an adequate network to meet their needs and require additional support. (It could happen to any of us that, at some future point, if not now, we or a member of our families may have care needs which the rest of the family finds it impossible to meet in full.)

What social work and social care services do (I suggest) is attempt to make good these deficits in some combination of the following ways:

1 Substituting for caring networks: Where a person simply does not have an informal network of care to draw upon, social workers attempt to provide services that will substitute for such a network. This might be the case, for example, when working with a young unaccompanied asylum seeker, or with an isolated elderly person.
2 Supplementing caring networks: Where a person's needs are so great that they are beyond the capacity of that person's informal network to cope with, social workers attempt to supplement that informal care either (a) by themselves arranging additional services, for example by providing homecare or respite care for elderly people or people with disabilities, or (b) by supporting the person in requesting and/or demanding additional services, or better services, from elsewhere (the latter being a point where social work can shade into something resembling political activism). For example, a social worker in an agency providing advocacy services for people with disabilities, might assist service users, individually or collectively, with obtaining financial help from the benefit system.
3 Promoting self-care: Where a person's ability to care for themselves or participate in society has been impaired, perhaps by lack of care and support in the past, or by adverse circumstances, social workers sometimes provide services intended to help that person to build or rebuild their own coping capacity. An example would be work with survivors of abuse to try to build up confidence and self-esteem, and to re-empower them after their experience of being profoundly disempowered. (This is an area where social work can shade into something resembling 'therapy'.)
4 Addressing failures in caring networks: Where a person's carers are abusive or neglectful, or for some other reason are not providing appropriate care, social workers attempt either to bring about change in the way that they deliver care or to arrange for alternative care to be provided. This may occur in child protection situations, or in cases of the mistreatment of vulnerable adults, but it might also occur in situations where carers simply lack the necessary skills or understanding.

PLACEMENT QUESTIONS 4.1   THE NATURE OF INTERVENTION

I have just proposed that the unifying theme which links the many kinds of service that social workers provide could be described as filling gaps in society's network of support and care. (I think that this does give social work a distinctive character which sets it apart from other caring professions.) And I have just suggested four broad ways that this occurs.

Does this make sense in relation to your placement agency? If so, what are the predominant kinds of activities that your agency is engaged in:

- Substituting for caring networks
- Supplementing caring networks
- Promoting self-care
- Addressing failures of caring networks

If you look at pieces of work that you yourself are undertaking on behalf of your placement agency, is it possible to describe the focus of your work in these terms?

If not, how would you prefer to describe it?

ROLES

But this has been a description more of the gaps or needs that social workers try to address rather than a description of what they do. The next question, therefore, is *how exactly do they go about addressing these deficiencies and shortcomings in the informal network?* One way of looking at this (as I have suggested previously in Beckett, 2006) is that when they intervene to try to address one or other of the kinds of needs that I have just discussed, social workers take on various different *roles*. These roles can be very broadly divided into three groups which I will here call 'advocacy roles', 'direct work roles' and 'executive roles' (see Table 4.1 for a summary). (I first used this terminology in Beckett [2006] but am modifying it slightly here.) Each of these broad groups of roles have their own characteristic mode of action.

1. ADVOCACY ROLES

A social worker is acting as an advocate when she helps give her clients a voice, either by speaking on their behalf, or by helping them to speak for themselves. This is an important facet of the role of a social worker in most contexts, and in some specialist contexts it may be a social worker's primary task.

There are two distinct sorts of advocacy, *direct* and *indirect*. *Direct* advocacy means speaking on behalf of another person, as a lawyer does in a courtroom. Every time a social worker contacts another agency with a view to resolving a problem that a client has with that agency, she is acting as a direct advocate. There is always a danger inherent in the direct advocacy role

Table 4.1 The three broad groups of social work roles

Type of Role	Characteristics
Advocacy roles	*Speaking on behalf of the service user or helping service users to speak for themselves.*
Direct work roles [*called 'Direct change agent' roles in Beckett, 2006*]	*Engaging in an interaction with a service user, or group of service users, which is intended to be helpful in itself.*
Executive roles	*Using resources external to the social worker (material resources, legal powers or the services of others) in a way intended to be helpful to the service user.*

that, by speaking on someone else's behalf, we may undermine that person's confidence in her ability to speak on her own behalf or even undermine other people's willingness to listen to her. (John has cerebral palsy and has some difficulty speaking clearly. If he uses an advocate to speak to other agencies on his behalf, then those agencies may end up talking exclusively to the advocate, who is easier to understand, and John may end up feeling excluded from a process of negotiation that is supposed to be about him.) Some of the problems inherent in direct advocacy can be avoided by moving to *indirect* advocacy, which means helping people speak on their own behalf. For example a community worker would be doing this if she helped local residents to set up a group to pressure for better services.

As with other kinds of interventions, advocacy (whether direct or indirect) can be focused on an individual or family or on larger groups. We might advocate on behalf of a neighbourhood, for example, or of specific groups within a neighbourhood (Bangladeshi women, parents with mental health problems, young carers, people with learning disabilities, etc.). Indirect advocacy sits particularly well with a collective approach, since assisting people to support one another and to act together is probably one of the most effective ways of helping people to achieve change on their own behalf.

Indirect advocacy shades into *direct* work, the second type of role which I will now discuss, since its aim is usually not only to help people secure particular changes in their lives, but also to help them change themselves, for example by becoming more confident and assertive, or more able to make effective use of their collective power.

2. DIRECT WORK ROLES

I will use the phrase 'direct work' to describe the role played by a social worker in situations where it is the *interaction between social worker and service user itself* that is intended to be the service provided to the service user (or groups of service users), as opposed to the interaction being a means to other ends, as is the case when a social worker is working in an 'advocacy' or 'executive' role. Social workers are acting in a direct work role when they offer some form of counselling or therapy, or act as mediators or educators or facilitators of groups. In my earlier attempt to categorise social work roles, I referred to what I am now calling the 'direct work' role as the 'direct change agent' role. I now feel that the latter term places a little too much emphasis on the social worker as the 'agent', when of course the main player in any direct work interaction is the service user himself, and the social worker may have to settle for making quite a modest contribution. As I will discuss further in Chapter 8, we cannot *make* people change.

In an earlier book (2006) I suggested 'counsellor/therapist', 'mediator', 'educator' and 'catalyst' as different subcategories of the direct work role. But I wonder if these subcategories are a bit limiting, for social workers may perform a direct work role in ways that do not fit neatly under any of them. Therefore, rather than worry too much about the precise subcategories into which 'direct work' can be divided, I suggest that the really important distinction to get hold of is the three-way one between direct work and its alternatives: advocacy and executive work. What I mean by 'direct work' is engaging in an interaction with a service user which is intended, *in itself*, to be of assistance. It is just one distinct form of action that social workers take, and it is quite different from speaking out for someone (direct advocacy), or making material changes in a person's environment (executive work), though both of these will typically also involve a direct interaction with service users, which in itself may be carried out skilfully or badly.

The following are a few characteristic ways in which social workers play a direct work role, but I would not want to suggest that this is by any means an exhaustive list.

- *Problem exploration:* Although I said earlier that assessment is no use unless it results in a service, there are situations where the process of exploring problems with service users is, *of itself*, a useful service, for example: in working with a parent who is finding her child hard to cope with. Such work shades into counselling and therapy, and it certainly benefits from a knowledge of counselling skills (see, for instance, Seden, 2005). We all surely know from personal experience that sometimes what we most need is not that someone *does* something for us, but simply that they listen to us, ask questions, and offer their own perspective on difficult situations which ultimately we will have to deal with ourselves. In fact sometimes what we really need is for people *not* to try to do things for us, or propose answers, something which I'm afraid I sometimes found hard to hold onto when I started out in social work.
- *Preparation for, and support through, transitions:* Social workers often come up with care plans that involve people moving from one place to another, or having other major changes in their life. For example: moving a child from a short-term foster-home to a permanent home. In arranging the placement, a social worker is acting in an *executive* role, but a competent care plan will address not only the actual physical move, but also the equally important work of helping a person prepare for and cope with it at a personal and emotional level (in the case of work with children who must move, see for instance classic work by Vera Fahlberg [1981, 1994]. This will involve talking to the person and listening to them in order to help them make sense of what is happening, manage their anxieties, and preserve some sense of dignity and continuity and control.
- *Historical reconstruction:* In many situations, social workers may be involved in helping service users reconstruct or make sense of past events. For example: Reminiscence work with elderly people (Sim, 2003), or Life Story work with children (Rose and Philpot, 2005). This sort of work also shades into counselling and therapy, with psychodynamic approaches to therapy in particular being concerned to help a client uncover, explore and reinterpret the past.

- *'Support' and encouragement:* As I will discuss presently, the word 'support' can sometimes be misused to describe unfocused visiting with no clear purpose at all. But support is one of the most important things that the majority of us obtain from our friends and families and those around us, and there is no doubt that one of the most useful roles that social workers can perform for people who do not have an informal support network capable of meeting this need is to provide support through difficult times, the challenge being to do so in a way that promotes service users' confidence in their own coping skills, rather than simply making them increasingly reliant on the social worker. In Task-Centred Casework (Reid and Epstein, 1972; Marsh and Doel, 2005) one of the main functions of the social worker, following the initial stage of problem exploration is to support and encourage the client in making incremental stages in her life.
- *Challenging:* Social workers in many contexts need to set boundaries and challenge unacceptable behaviour. For example: a residential social worker may need to challenge a young person who has been bullying other residents. Chris Trotter uses the term 'Pro-social' work (Trotter, 2004, 2007) to describe the way in which social workers use the interaction with a service user to promote positive, socially responsible behaviour and discourage anti-social behaviour (of course this raises questions as to who defines what is 'socially responsible', but I will not go into that further here).

One form of direct work that is necessary for almost any kind of social work interaction is that of *communicator*. Even when direct work is not ostensibly the main kind of intervention being offered, effective communication may be absolutely central. The quality of the communication may make a difference between a service user feeling supported and empowered, and a service user feeling diminished and undermined, even if the actual service being provided is ostensibly the same. This can be seen if you imagine a social worker arranging respite residential care for an elderly person. The ostensible service being delivered here is the care itself (which the social worker arranges in an 'executive' capacity). But the way this is negotiated with the client, and the way that the arrangements are discussed and explained, could make a huge difference to how the old person actually experiences it. Poorly explained, poorly negotiated moves can be very frightening and demeaning indeed.

3. EXECUTIVE ROLES

The executive roles are very characteristic of social work. In many contexts they are the main type of role played by social workers and I myself think that it is the centrality of these executive roles that makes social work such a very different kind of activity either from that of specialist advocates or from that of professionals such as therapists or counsellors who only engage in direct work. Although some might feel that the executive roles are the least glamorous of the roles played by social workers, they are arguably what make social work a separate and distinct activity. They are in a sense its soul.

Acting in an executive role, a social worker aims to bring about change not primarily as a direct result of her personal interaction with the service user (though skilled personal interaction is invariably necessary, with service users and others, if an executive role is to be played well) but by recruiting external resources of one kind or another. These external resources can be material resources (money, accommodation), legal powers (powers conferred by a court order, or powers directly given to a social worker under the law) or the services of others (such as care assistants, foster-parents or specialist workers). In an executive role, then, the action that a social worker takes is directed at the service user's wider environment.

The following are some of the different kinds of 'executive role' characteristically undertaken by social workers (you may perhaps be able to think of others). They are also summarised in Table 4.2 (on page 55).

Gatekeeper

Social workers are frequently a service user's access point to various resources, and are involved in collecting information with a view to distributing those resources to those most in need of them. A duty social worker, for instance, may be involved in gathering preliminary information about potential service users in order to inform decisions on who most needs a service and at what level. This particular kind of executive role is what I am here describing as the gatekeeper role. (In Beckett [2006] I appropriated the obsolete term 'almoner' to describe this role, but I have found this causes confusion.)

When acting as a gatekeeper, the role of a social worker is similar to that of other public service officials such as benefits or housing officers. But other professions also engage in gatekeeping. For example a triage nurse in an Accident and Emergency department is in part a gatekeeper, determining which patients will gain access to priority attention from her colleagues; a medical general practitioner likewise is in large part a gatekeeper for other more specialist parts of the health system.

While the gatekeeper role may seem a rather unglamorous and bureaucratic aspect of social work, it is worth reminding ourselves that in some situations a gatekeeper may be all that is required. For example, a disabled person, or group of disabled people, may be perfectly capable of arranging and managing their own care and would prefer to choose and employ their own carers rather than rely on carers employed or commissioned by a social care agency. Individual Budgets (IBs), promoted in recent years by the UK government, offer service users an alternative to having services provided or commissioned by social care agencies. Instead, their level of need having been assessed, they are provided with a budget of their own to commission services to suit themselves. (Glendenning et al. [2008] compared recipients of IBs with people receiving conventional forms of support from social care agencies. They found that the services commissioned by service users themselves were as cost-effective as the conventionally provided services and that those receiving IBs on average felt more in control of their lives. People needing mental health services and physically disabled people were the most satisfied, older people the least satisfied, perhaps because they did not like the burden of organising their own services.)

Care manager/care co-ordinator

As one of the most commonly practised of all social work roles, and one of the most distinctive to social work, care management is about organising and overseeing the delivery of services by others. For example, a social worker specialising in care services for elderly or physically disabled people may assess the care needs of a service user, identify service providers and commission specific services from them on behalf of the service user, managing and reviewing the resulting 'package' of care as time goes on. A social worker with responsibility for children in public care may likewise find and commission services from foster-parents, perhaps also engaging the services of other providers such as companies providing school transport, independent counsellors and so on.

(In Beckett [2006] I just used the phrase 'care manager' for this role, but since many agencies describe people who carry out this role as 'care co-ordinators', I have added this term to the name for the role.)

Responsibility holder

Social workers are sometimes placed in a position where they take on responsibilities akin to those taken on by family members for people who cannot fully take responsibility for their own lives. In some circumstances, for instance, social workers may take on responsibility for managing the financial affairs of elderly people who are too confused mentally to manage their money for themselves. The social work specialism in which the 'responsibility holder' role is most obvious, though, is that of work with children in public care. In England and Wales, social work agencies are given parental responsibility for children who are under a care order (1989 Children Act s33 (3)). In consultation with natural parents social work agencies are responsible for making the same decisions and meeting the same needs that a parent would normally be expected to make and to meet. This is a rather unique level of responsibility for a professional to be asked to take.

Control agent

Somewhat ironically perhaps, in view of the emancipatory rhetoric and talk of partnership and empowerment that is so very prominent in social work discourse, social workers are frequently in the position of exercising control over people, making requirements of them which they are obliged to meet, or imposing changes on them irrespective of their own wishes. For example, a social worker in a youth offending team may be in the position of insisting that a young person meet him regularly for appointments and may go back to court and ask for legal sanctions to be imposed if the young person fails to do so.

In some cases the control agent role is exercised through specific legal powers which may be backed up if necessary by sanctions or force (for example, in England and Wales, a mentally ill patient can be taken to hospital by the police as the result of a request from a social worker under Section 2 of the 1983 Mental Health Act): in this case service users have a distinct working relationship with their social workers which is different from that of purely voluntary clients. (They will have the relationship either of a 'supervisee' or of a 'protectee', as discussed in Chapter 2.) In other cases the social worker's authority does not have a specific legal power behind it but service users will nevertheless feel they have little choice but to comply (for example a parent reluctantly allowing into her house a social worker who has called to discuss concerns raised about her children at school). As I discussed in Chapter 2 I do not think that social workers always understand the extent to which an apparent partnership with service users may in fact be a relationship based on the social worker's power and the service user's feeling that it would be wiser to go along with the social worker's wishes than to attempt to assert their own views. (I used the term 'nominal service requester' in Chapter 2 to describe people who technically have a choice about receiving service, but do not in fact feel that they have a real choice.)

Multi-agency co-ordinator/keyworker

Perhaps because of the 'jack-of-all-trades' nature of their job, social workers are frequently the ones who, in a multi-professional group, are assigned the role of co-ordinating the activities of the group as a whole. A good example of this would be the role played in England and Wales by the keyworker in a child protection case. The keyworker, who must be a social worker, is responsible for making sure that the outline child protection plan agreed in a child protection conference is developed by the professionals working with the family into a fully-realised plan. She is also the 'lead professional' for the inter-agency work and must run the core group meetings and 'coordinate the contribution of family members and agencies' to working out the details of the plan. She must also make sure that the plan is carried out and that its progress and effectiveness are properly reviewed (DfES, 2006b) This kind of multi-agency co-ordinator role is distinct from the care co-ordinator/care manager role, though the two may often be combined, because the latter involves commissioning and directing the services of others, while the multi-agency co-ordinator role places the social worker in the position of co-ordinating the activities of others over whom she has no direct control.

(I used the word 'co-ordinator' for this role in Beckett [2006] but have changed the name here to distinguish this role from that of 'care manager/care co-ordinator'.)

Service developer

Many social workers have little or no direct involvement with service users at all, but are involved in developing and maintaining the service that is delivered by others. These social workers are actually engaged in a very diverse range of activities which could doubtless be further subdivided into further distinct roles by anyone so inclined. They include managers who are responsible for co-ordinating, supporting and monitoring the work of social workers and other staff, project workers who are involved in developing new services and specialist workers such as those responsible for recruiting, assessing and supporting foster-parents and adoptive parents. Social work educators, like myself, could also be described as service developers in this sense, as could social workers involved in inspection and quality assurance.

When acting in an executive role, a social worker is trying to support change or maintain stability not primarily through the interaction with the service user herself, but through bringing about other changes in the service user's environment. This is what distinguishes executive roles from direct work ones. However, as I have already noted, this does not mean that skills in interpersonal work are not important for executive work. On the contrary, skills in communication and listening, assertiveness, negotiation skills, the ability to use authority are typically needed to act effectively in most of the executive roles. For example to act as a control agent in a child protection or mental health context, while simultaneously

Table 4.2 Different kinds of 'executive' role

Role	Characteristics
Gatekeeper *[Called 'almoner' in Beckett, 2006]*	Acting as an access point to resources, concerned with fairly distributing limited resources.
Care manager/care co-ordinator *[Called 'care manager' in Beckett, 2006]*	Commissioning, and supervising the delivery of, services from others.
Responsibility holder	Taking responsibility, akin to that taken by some family carers, for the well-being of people who lack the capacity to take full responsibility for themselves.
Control agent	Using powers conferred by law to impose constraints on situations or insist upon change.
Multi-agency co-ordinator/keyworker *[Called 'co-ordinator' in Beckett, 2006]*	Co-ordinating the activities of professionals and others over whom the social worker does not have direct control.
Service developer	Developing, enhancing and/or maintaining a service rather than delivering the service directly.

conveying to an angry and distressed service user your willingness to listen, is something that requires interpersonal skills of a high order.

The executive roles, like advocacy, typically require the exercise of these kinds of interpersonal skills not only in relation to the service user, as is the case with direct work, but also in relation to many others too. You may need to negotiate with doctors, policemen, lawyers, concerned neighbours demanding that 'something be done'. You may need to secure the co-operation of five or six other agencies, each with its own different agenda and ethos. You may need to stand up to powerful people in order to drive through an appropriate plan.

At the risk of over-labouring the point I really want to emphasise here that complex interpersonal skills are key to most work in an executive capacity, and are not confined to 'direct work'. In other words, in practice, the interactions that you carry out with service users in an executive capacity do in fact shade into direct work, even if direct work is not the primary aim.

COMBINING DIFFERENT ROLES

Roles do shade into one another and social workers do characteristically combine several roles. This is often a positive. Different roles do indeed often sit very well together. For example, acting in a *care management* role, a social worker arranges a new placement for a child, for whom she is her agency's *responsibility holder*. As part of the process of arranging the placement, acting in an *advocacy* role, she has had to argue for resources to be made available to make a specialist placement possible. Alongside this, acting in a *direct work* capacity, she prepares the child for the transition that this involves.

However, when carrying out multiple roles, it is important to be clear with both yourself and your client what role you are playing at a particular moment in time. For example, if you think direct work is appropriate then there does need to be an understanding between you and the service user that this is what is in fact being offered. It can happen that a social worker believes that he is engaging in some kind of therapeutic work while the service user imagines that the conversation is merely a prelude to the delivery of the practical service or material resource which is what the service user actually wants. 'He was no use at all,' is a not uncommon complaint about social workers, 'all he seemed to want to do was talk.' (This will occur if the social worker has never made clear to the service user that 'talk' is the service that he proposes to deliver, and has never obtained the service user's agreement to this.) Conversely, a social worker may believe that what is being asked of her is to provide material resources or practical help, when in fact what the service user really wants is someone to listen.

Different roles *can* sit very well together in social work as in life generally (teachers, policemen, parents – all play multiple roles). Roles can also shade into one another so that it can be hard to see where one begins and another ends. For example a social worker helps a very unconfident young man to build up his confidence so that he can deal more assertively with other agencies: is this direct work or indirect advocacy?

But there can also be serious conflicts between different roles. For instance, as I pointed out in the previous chapter, you cannot be a whole-hearted advocate for your service user and a committed gatekeeper for your agency at the same time. Social workers do not possess superhuman powers, and cannot split themselves into two. Similarly, if you have a control agent role, then you cannot offer a service user the kind of confidentiality that would be offered by a counsellor or psychotherapist, and you need to be honest with the service user about this, because it can happen that a service user thinks he is being offered a confidential counselling service when in fact the social worker is gathering information that will be discussed with others and used for risk assessment purposes. (If you are a child protection worker, for instance, you need to be clear that what the child or parents tell you will be recorded and may be shared with other agencies or even repeated in a court of law.)

If there is a serious conflict of interest between your roles then you need to relinquish some of them. For instance, if a service user needs an advocate and your other roles prohibit you from being a proper advocate, then you need to have the humility to recognise this and to help the service user to find someone else to advocate for him.

On the other hand, even if your primary role is not that of an advocate, there may be times when you may realise that if you don't advocate for a person than no one else will. A student in his final year was working in a hospital social work team dealing with the discharge of elderly people from hospital. Staff in such teams are under huge pressure to move patients out quickly, either to their own homes, or to relatives, or into residential or nursing care, because of the pressure on hospital beds, and the main role played by social workers in such teams is probably care manager/care co-ordinator. The student – I'll call him Bill – was given the case of an elderly woman ('Mrs Green') who had been diagnosed by a consultant as being seriously demented and in need of residential care in a specialist unit for dementia sufferers. Bill was supposed to organise this, but he became convinced that Mrs Green was not in fact suffering from dementia but was temporarily confused (as can easily happen) as a result of the anxiety and bewilderment caused by the hospital experience. Bill took it on himself to delay Mrs Green's discharge, challenge the consultant to reconsider his view (not an easy thing for a student to do) and ask for time to reassess her needs. As a result, Mrs Green was not discharged to a dementia unit but to a normal residential home, where she would have a chance to socialise with people who were no more mentally confused than herself.

So, although Bill's day-to-day work in this agency was that of a care manager, he recognised that Mrs Green needed an advocate and took on that role himself. As a result he made a huge difference to the quality of Mrs Green's life. (And did so, not as a result of any very complicated theoretical understanding, but simply out of recognising that Mrs Green was a human being, and not simply a logistical problem.)

PLACEMENT QUESTIONS 4.2   SOCIAL WORK ROLES

- Thinking about the work that is done in your placement agency, can you identify which roles are typically played by social workers? (Do they act as advocates, do direct work, carry out executive roles? If they do direct work what kind of direct work is it? If they carry out executive roles, what kind? Do social workers in the agency have a control agent role?)
- How do the various roles played by social workers in the agency sit together? Have you noticed workers playing roles which conflict with one another? Are agency social workers aware of these conflicts and how do they deal with them?
- In your own work for the agency, what kind of role have you been taking on? Do you experience difficulties at times as the result of a conflict – or awareness of a potential conflict – between different roles?

PLANNING, CLARITY AND COHERENCE

Social workers may respond to a situation in many different ways, and may play a number of quite different roles or combinations of roles. Typically they also work alongside other professionals who in turn have a range of different possible contributions to make. So how do you choose what action to take? Lack of analysis, complex and confusing situations and inter-agency politics can often result in poorly chosen actions or combinations of actions. Among the mistakes commonly made are:

- *'Intervention by numbers'.* Offering a particular service not because it necessarily fits well with the needs of the service user, but because it happens to be available, or because it is always offered in cases of this kind (a service-led, as opposed to a needs-led, approach).
- *'Going through the motions'.* Minimal, tokenistic responses which demonstrate that an agency is 'doing something' but in fact do not contribute in any meaningful way to changing things for the better. Sometimes agency and inter-agency politics can make it very difficult to avoid such actions.

- *'Unilateral casework'*. Services are provided without a mutual understanding being reached with the service user about what is to be provided, and/or services are provided which simply are not appropriate within the working relationship that exists. William Reid and Laura Epstein spoke about social workers engaging in

  > fruitless efforts, sometimes extending over months, to engage semi-captive clients in helping relationships that they have not asked for, do not want, and probably cannot use. (1972: 49)

- *'Social work on paper'*. Lots of meetings are held and lots of paperwork is generated but the service user is not offered anything which he or she experiences as actually being helpful.
- *The 'scattergun' approach*. A large number of different services are simultaneously provided to an extent which is simply overwhelming and is therefore likely to achieve nothing at all. This is particularly prone to happen in cases where the professional system feels vulnerable to accusations of not having done enough, but the scattergun approach is also often a consequence of 'social work by numbers': an assessment identifies a variety of needs and the social worker (alone or as part of a multi-professional team) tries to address those needs in tick box fashion by trying to match each one with its own separate service.

Case example 4.1 Planning care for Tina

Tina, aged 7, has been removed from her own family where she has suffered serious neglect and also some abuse. A plan is being drawn up for her care. It has been identified that (a) she needs a secure permanent substitute family where she can form attachments in a secure environment; (b) her relationship with her mother, though difficult, is very important to her, and she is very close to her maternal grandmother and aunt, who want to have regular contact with her, though they are unable to provide her with a home; (c) she is very confused about what has happened in her own past and could benefit from some form of therapy; (d) she plays football, and this is a very positive part of her life and needs to be encouraged; (e) her present school is also a positive part of her life and very important to her.

(For the purpose of this exercise we will ignore the question of her legal status and make the assumption that the social work agency is in a position to decide on a plan for her.)

Her social worker proposes the following:

- Placement with a permanent foster-home
- Tina to continue to attend the same school, and if necessary taxi transport to the foster-home will be provided
- Tina will attend child psychotherapy once a week after school
- She will see her mother once a week after school for one hour's supervised contact in the social work office. The social worker will collect Tina from school or arrange for a taxi to collect her, and then take her back to her foster-home
- She will visit her aunt and grandmother together once a week after school
- She will stay after school on Wednesdays and play football and have a taxi to take her home.

What are your thoughts about this plan?

COMMENT

Every element in the social worker's plan addresses something that she has identified as a need, or something important to Tina. However, as you will have noticed, the upshot of this plan is that for four out of five school days, Tina, who is only 7, will be doing something else after school. This will be a long day for her, especially if the foster-parents are at some distance. At least two of these four activities are likely to be emotionally quite demanding: the psychotherapy and the contacts with her mother. She will have little opportunity to go home and unwind after school like most children do. In fact, while ostensibly the plan addresses all of Tina's needs, it actually pulls in different directions. The first aim, of a secure permanent family environment where she can form attachments, is in fact under-mined by the sheer busyness of the rest of the plan. It may well also be undermined by the heavy emphasis being given to her existing family relationships.

Social work interventions can be frankly bewildering to service users. 'I didn't know what he was after, he wouldn't say,' is the comment of one client quoted by Joyce Lishman (2009: 15). They can be unhelpful or undermining. They can make matters worse. In order to provide a service that is actually in some way helpful, we need to pay careful attention to the following:

- *Boundaries and mandate.* What are our responsibilities in a given situation and where do our responsibilities end?
- *Ethical complexity.* In many situations there is more than one important ethical issue at stake, and good practice requires that we try to balance these as best we can. For example, in a child protection situation, we should be aware of a responsibility to protect vulnerable children, but we should balance this with an awareness of our responsibility not to undermine family rela-tionships. It is often dangerous to privilege one ethical principle at the expense of others.
- *Communication.* It's important to ensure that there is an understanding between ourselves and service users about what is going on in any given interaction and what can be expected from us, and not just to assume that such an understanding exists. Joyce Lishman illustrates the gap in understanding that can occur with the following example:

    'I was frightened [says a mother attending a child and family psychiatry clinic]. I thought they would say I was a bad mother and take him away from me. When they took him away (to see a psychiatrist while she saw a social worker) I wondered where he was going. I did not ask.'

- With characteristic humility, Lishman adds:

    I was the social worker and was unaware at the time of this intense anxiety. For me the initial encounter was a regular everyday experience. For my client it was unique and I should have been more aware of her anxiety and conveyed my recognition of it. (Lishman, 2009: 11)

- *Purpose.* You yourself ought to be clear about what it is you are trying to achieve – both over-all and in any given interaction – and how you propose to go about achieving it. If you your-self do not know what it is you have come to see the service user about, then it is inevitable that the service user will not know either.
- *Coherence.* The different parts of a plan need to fit together. They need to pull in the same direction. All the elements of the plan should, taken together, be a realistic proposition.

But while it is important to be very clear about the purpose of your work with a client, it is also possible to be *too* rigid. As is so often the case there is a balance to be struck. You have to be careful, in your efforts to avoid vagueness, not to end up being so rigid and impatient for results – and so frightened of wasting time – that no space is left for negotiation to occur or for anything constructive to emerge. The culture of managerialism and the current preoccupation in the public services with time-scales, measurable outcomes and so on can often result in the loss of this important element of flexibility, though these managerialist tools do possibly offer some degree of protection against the kind of unfocused intrusion into personal life that Reid and Epstein's quote above exemplifies.

You might like to ask yourself whether, if you had a social worker come round to your house, you would prefer for that social worker to have a clearly prescribed role and to have to account in detail for her practice to her agency or for her to be free to do whatever she wanted and to try out whatever approach struck her as useful at the time? (Perhaps it would depend on who the social worker was?)

'RADICAL NON-INTERVENTION'

I have suggested that social work is about filling gaps in informal networks of support, but this does not mean that a social worker should attempt to be her client's best friend, parent and fairy godmother rolled into one. A good social worker does not try to do everything. When a social worker fails to recognise or accept the limits of her role, this is confusing to service users, and in my view often reflects a lack of ability on the part of the social worker to unravel her own emotional needs from those of her client. A good social worker is clear about what her responsibilities are in a given situation and what kind of working relationship should flow from those responsibilities. She is clear that she is a paid worker with a defined job description whose involvement in the life of a service user is likely to be temporary and whose relationship with that service user exists within certain parameters.

As well as being clear about boundaries with service users, social workers often need to assert their own boundaries in dealing with other professionals and the general public. Social work is not a magical cure to every worrying situation. Social workers should only become involved in work with people where either:

a   this is requested or at least welcomed by the people themselves, or
b   in specific circumstances where the law permits compulsory action to protect vulnerable people – and then only where there are reasonable grounds for thinking that compulsory action will make things better.

Social workers are often put under a lot of pressure to 'do something' – to intervene – in respect of people who are worrying other professionals or the general public, but who fall into neither of the above two categories. It can happen that an individual or family ends up with a bewildering array of different services 'going in' with very little overall rationale (other than '*something must be done*') and no clear mandate at all. The clients have not asked for the service, yet it has not been made clear to them that they actually have a choice in the matter. Such involvement can be both oppressive and wasteful of resources, and it may well not only be unhelpful but actually counter-productive. But when under pressure to 'do something', *any* action, however useless it will be, may seem tempting, simply to demonstrate that one is indeed doing something. Politicians are often under a similar kind of pressure. The false reasoning that can result was pinpointed many years ago by the British satirical TV programme *Yes, Minister*, which once offered the following pseudo-logical account of a politician's reasoning:

'Politician's Logic'

1 Something must be done.
2 This is something.
3 Therefore, we must do it.

An important element of good ethical practice is therefore the willingness to refuse to act if it seems to you that action will not help or will make things worse, or if it is simply not your business to act. Sometimes this might entail refusing to get involved at all. Sometimes it might entail resisting the 'scatter gun' approach in which certain service users are subjected to a barrage of different services which they cannot possibly constructively use, and insisting on services being provided at the service user's pace.

When I first became a social worker, my more experienced colleagues would sometimes jokingly use the term 'radical non-intervention' as a fancy way of saying 'doing nothing' or 'leaving well alone'. I did not know it at the time but I have since found out that the expression actually came from the title of a book by Edwin Schur (1973) who argued that services intended to address the problem of youth offending often made things worse rather than better, because of the way that young people are labelled once they enter the formal professional system. (Some evidence that such interventions can indeed make things worse will be discussed in Chapter 9.) Schur argued that the formal system should '*leave kids alone wherever possible*' (Schur, 1973: 155, his emphasis). In the UK, the state is constantly introducing new initiatives to address all kinds of problems that occur in communities and families, but I suggest that non-intervention should always, and in all seriousness, be considered. Just as in medicine, overuse of medication may weaken the body's own capacity to heal itself, perhaps excessive social work intervention can weaken the ability of individuals, families and communities to solve their own problems?

For this reason (as I discussed in Chapter 1) I feel uneasy when social workers and social work academics set overly broad and ambitious goals for themselves and their profession. I also feel uneasy when such goals are set *for* social workers by politicians. We are only a small part of the picture and we should have the humility to leave room for other forces to come into play.

> **PLACEMENT QUESTIONS 4.3   CLARITY OF PURPOSE IN RESPECT OF INTERVENTIONS**
>
> (These relate to both previous sections: 'Planning, clarity and coherence' and 'Radical non-intervention'.)
>
> - Do you ever wonder about the value of the interventions carried out by your placement agency? Do they sometimes strike you as pointless, counter-productive or tokenistic?
> - If so, why do you think they are carried out at all? Do you think the agency sometimes feels under pressure to 'do something', no matter what?
> - How good is your placement agency at agreeing with its partners a coherent basis for intervention? Do its plans hang together, or do you think its service users may sometimes experience interventions as unco-ordinated, piecemeal or incoherent?
> - Have you ever found yourself in a position, in your work on placement, where you feel obliged to act, though you are not convinced that to act will really be better than leaving things alone?
> - Does it ever strike you that it seems more pressing to do *something*, than to think about what would be a genuinely helpful thing to do? If so where does the pressure come from, and how might one resist it?

COMMUNICATION AND PURPOSEFULNESS

I have already made the point that the mandate of the social worker, her limitations and her boundaries, should be clear not only to the social worker herself, but to the service user too. For a variety of reasons social workers are not always good at being clear with service users about what is going on. Sometimes it may simply be the result of thought-lessness. It is easy to forget that what is obvious to us about the job we do every day may not be obvious to a member of the public who only encounters social workers infrequently or may never have encountered one before (see the example from Lishman given above). But there are other reasons too why social workers may avoid communicating clearly. A desire to be liked, or to be seen as helpful, or to avoid conflict, can result in social workers not being clear about the limits to what they can offer, or being evasive about the aspects of their job that they suspect clients will find less appealing. Helen McClaren (2007) explored Australian social workers' attitudes to 'forewarning' service users that they would have to report child abuse concerns, even if this meant breaching confidentiality. She found that many workers avoided forewarning, either because they thought it would 'scare' clients, or because it made the social workers themselves feel uncomfortable.

Social workers in the statutory sector, like other public service workers, are also often under political pressure to conceal resource limitations and to offer other explanations for limitations on the service they are offering, as Michael Lipsky observed many years ago:

> Street-level bureaucracies devote a relatively high proportion of energies to concealing lack of service and generating appearances of responsiveness. (Lipsky, 1980: 76)

If you have worked in a public service for any length of time, or if you have had to negotiate with a public service as a service user, you will know just how reluctant such services are to admit to their limitations and how prone they are to find rationalisations for not providing a service where one is asked for.

Use of jargon, whether deliberate or not, is one way in which professionals, including social workers, confuse service users about what they are saying. I suspect that very often we are not clear what we mean ourselves and use jargon to free ourselves both from having to think and from making ourselves vulnerable to challenge. Obviously it is impossible to be clear with service users if you yourself are not clear about what you mean.

The truth is that not all social work activity *is* purposeful. The word 'support' is often used to describe contact with service users which has no clear purpose. This is not to say that offering support is not a valid purpose in its own right, as discussed earlier, but, if you think that support is the service that you are providing, you might want to ask:

- Does my client understand that I am giving 'support' and does she find it 'supportive'? If the service user finds it intrusive, annoying or patronising, then it really *can't* be described as support.
- Is the support I am offering helping her to deal with her own problems, or am I inadvertently undermining her belief in her capacity to solve her own problems? Even if the service user experiences you as helpful, you may not actually be helping her if you are preventing her from learning from her own mistakes.
- What am I supporting the service user *with* exactly?

The word 'monitor' (as in 'we are going in every week to monitor the situation') is also commonly used to describe unfocused visiting taking place in respect of cases where there are some anxieties about the safety of vulnerable people. Again, one could ask the questions:

- What information am I actually obtaining through these visits?
- Is this information useful and am I gathering it in the best possible way?
- What is the effect of my contact on the service user? (If the effect is to make the service user feel thoroughly disempowered, you may be preventing the service user from making the very changes that your actions are supposed to promote.)

Clarity of purpose requires that you must be clear about what your overall aim is, as well as being clear about what you are trying to achieve in every contact with the service user. It means being able to unpack vague general statements about what you are doing and be specific. It also means being able to distinguish purely formal steps from substantive actions that will actually make a difference. 'Holding a planning meeting' for example, is not an action in itself. The planning meeting is only as useful as the actions – or positive decisions not to act – that flow from it.

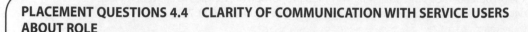

PLACEMENT QUESTIONS 4.4   CLARITY OF COMMUNICATION WITH SERVICE USERS ABOUT ROLE

- How clear have you found staff in your placement agency when communicating with their service users? If you were a service user of this agency how do you think you would feel about the kinds of communication that occurred? Would you feel that you were being kept in the picture? Would you feel that you understood what it was that the agency was trying to do?
- What feedback have you had, if any, from actual service users about this?
- Have you found it easy to be clear with service users themselves about what your role is? Have you noticed anything that makes this difficult in any way, and if so what is it? Is it perhaps that you yourself are not clear? Or is it a reluctance to say things to service users that they may not like to hear? How might you work on these difficulties?

THEORY

Depending on the role being performed by the social worker, the action she takes could be anything from providing financial assistance, to arranging personal care, to arranging for a person to be removed to a place of safety, to carrying out a piece of life-story work.

The purpose of some social work actions is, of course, so straightforward and obvious that it is hardly necessary to spell out the theory on which they are based. You don't need much of a theory to know that, if a person is having difficulty using the bath, it may be useful to provide bathing aids. Or even in my earlier example of the social work student Bill standing up for Mrs Green, there was not much need of a theory, even though in my opinion this was an excellent piece of social work.

However, when it comes to more complex action – and this applies whether the social worker is operating in a direct work capacity, or as a care manager, or as a control agent – there is a need for the social worker to have a thought-through basis for acting, a reason for believing that a given course of action is likely to have positive outcomes. Why do I think this action will help the service user, and what evidence if any am I drawing on? What are the likely and possible outcomes for the service user of my taking this action?

Case example 4.2   Does Mrs Robinson need a parenting skills class?

Mrs Robinson, a lone carer, has two children who seem to have no behavioural boundaries. They will not settle in class. They take things from other children whenever they feel like it. They refuse to accept the authority of teachers. They scream and fly into a rage if challenged in any way. One of the services that your agency is able to offer is parenting skills classes, and your manager proposes that Mrs Robinson is referred for classes. How would you decide whether this was a suitable intervention?

COMMENTS

Superficially this may seem a similar case to that of the elderly person who is having difficulty getting in and out of the bath. The elderly person has difficulty getting in and out of the bath, therefore bathing aids are needed. By the same token, you might be tempted to argue, the children do not seem to have been properly parented, therefore their parent needs training. But of course it is not that simple. You would need to know more about the situation to know if parenting skills classes were really appropriate. A range of other questions need to be considered. Is Mrs Robinson really lacking in the necessary skills, or is she just not able or willing to apply them at the moment? (She might be depressed for example.) Is it possible that classes will further undermine her confidence? Is it possible that the children's behaviour is connected to something other than the parenting provided by Mrs Robinson? What is the role played by the children's father? Would respite care, counselling, family therapy be more appropriate? Is there any possibility that the children are being abused? If you simply apply 'solutions' mechanically to 'problems' which they superficially seem to fit, you may make the situation worse.

(Incidentally, even the bathing issue may not be as straightforward as I have suggested. Perhaps the real problem is obesity? Perhaps the old person has a drink problem and it is this that causes problems with bathing?)

Good social work actions are characterised by clear thinking and are based on a genuine attempt to respond, within the limits of possibility, to the specific needs of the individual service user, as opposed to the 'by-numbers' approach which assigns a standard 'action' to a standard 'problem'. Bad actions are reactive and respond to specific aspects of problems in a superficial way without any overall plan and without any depth of understanding. Good actions are not necessarily based on a formal 'theory' in the sense of being based on one specific theory from a book, but they *are* characterised by an ability to theorise – or at any rate to think analytically – and to draw as necessary on ideas other than the social workers' own. If you can't clearly explain why your plan of action is a good idea, it probably isn't. If you have no reasonable basis for believing that your action will have a positive outcome, you need to ask yourself why you are doing it.

The emphasis on 'theory' in social work education sometimes has the unfortunate consequence that students feel they have to find a theory in a book and, so to speak, staple it onto their descriptions of their work, so that we find phrases in student essays like:

… I discussed Mrs Brown's relationship with her father (attachment theory) …
… I set Mr Jones three tasks to do before we next met (task-centred work) …
… I used empowerment to help Michael fill in his benefit form …

But an ability to theorise is not really about stapling a name onto an action after the event, it is about thinking clearly about the basis on which you act.

PLACEMENT QUESTIONS 4.5   TAILORING INTERVENTIONS TO SPECIFIC SITUATIONS

- Does your placement agency tailor its interventions to individual situations, or does it sometimes adopt more of a 'by-numbers' approach, applying a standard response regardless of specific circumstances?
- How careful do you think the agency is to think through the possible interventions that it might offer and their possible positive and negative consequences?
- Would you be able to explain the ideas behind your own interventions? (As just discussed, this is not the same thing as finding a 'theory' in a book.)

CHAPTER SUMMARY

In this chapter I have explored the nature of 'intervention' in the social work field, taking intervention to mean the services that social workers offer that are intended to make a difference of some kind in the lives of service users. After discussing the word itself and its connotations, I looked at what characterises social work intervention and makes it distinctive from the kinds of interventions that are offered by other professionals. I moved on to look at the 'roles' undertaken by social workers. I then looked at a range of issues which all had to do with the need for clarity of purpose in deciding first whether to intervene at all and secondly, what kind of intervention to make. This chapter does not represent everything this book has to say about intervention. If you want to carry on reading more about intervention I'd refer you in particular to Chapter 8, which is about 'Change'.

FURTHER READING

Interestingly, in view of my comments at the beginning of this chapter about 'assessment being the easy bit', there are fewer books about social work intervention than about social work assessment (though there are several books, like this one, on 'assessment and intervention'). Books on 'social work theory' however are also relevant because they describe methods and approaches to intervention. The following are some general texts, but I do wish to stress (as I did at the end of the introductory chapter) the importance of also seeking out books and articles relating to the particular context in which you are working, and also books about particular methods of intervention (for example, if you are interested in a task-centred approach, seek out books about task-centred work).

Beckett, C. (2006) *Essential Theory for Social Work Practice*. London: Sage.

Lindsay, T. (ed.) (2009) *Social Work Intervention*. Exeter: Learning Matters.

Payne, M. (2005) *Modern Social Work Theory* (3rd edn). Basingstoke: Palgrave.

5 JUDGEMENT

- The necessity of judgement
- Reaching a conclusion
- Unwarranted assumptions
- Judgement and emotion
- Dangers of group decision-making
- Making the best possible judgement

In the introductory chapter I observed that one of the things that make social work particularly challenging is that it is an activity that combines an exceptional potential for transforming lives, for worse as well as better, with an absence of a precise science to guide it. But social work is hardly unique in this respect. Across a whole range of professions, as Donald Schön observes,

> there is a high, hard ground where practitioners can make effective use of research-based theory and technique, and there is a swampy lowland where situations are confusing 'messes' incapable of technical solution. The difficulty is that the problems of the high ground, however great their technical interest, are often relatively unimportant to clients or to the larger society, while in the swamp are the problems of greatest human concern. (Schön, 1991: 42)

Indeed, not only in professional practice but in life generally, the most important decisions we make are typically ones which we have to make in the 'swamp', in conditions of uncertainty. Choosing a partner, deciding when to have children, deciding whether to end a relationship or keep working at it, choosing a career: these are all decisions whose outcomes we cannot be certain about but which we have to make anyway if we are to progress through our lives at all.

Even avoiding a decision *is* a decision. If, for instance, for fear of making the wrong choice, you never choose a partner, then you are effectively deciding to remain single. And in social work and other professions the same applies. You may have several different courses of action to consider, or you may decide not to act at all, but non-action in itself can have consequences, sometimes catastrophic ones, just as action can. (Think of a medical decision whether or not to carry out a risky surgical procedure). You may not know for certain what the right action is to take, but, having considered the information available, you, if not on your own, then as part of a team, may still need to make a 'judgement call'.

THE NECESSITY OF JUDGEMENT

In Chapter 3, I discussed the five stages of assessment proposed by Milner and O'Byrne (2009: 61–62):

1 Preparation
2 Data collection
3 Weighing the data
4 Analysing the data
5 Utilising the analysis.

Social workers sometimes mistakenly refer to the second step in this process as if it was, in itself, the assessment. To some extent government guidance (such as, in the UK, the *Framework for the Assessment of Needs* in childcare social work [Department of Health, 2000]) may help to perpetuate this confusion by placing a great deal of emphasis on stage 2, and rather less emphasis on the later stages, even though these are in many ways the most difficult. Let us be clear that data, simply as data, cannot tell you how to act. You have only really completed an assessment when you have drawn some conclusions from those data, and drawing conclusions is what is going on in Milner and O'Byrne's stages 3–5. In other words, you have only completed the assessment when you have come to some sort of judgement. But how do you arrive at a decision about which course of action to take, when you do not have access to an entirely objective basis on which to make it?

The chapter will explore this. The following is a case example which may help to illustrate some of the issues.

> ### Case example 5.1   Jackie's contact with her children
>
> Jackie, aged 22, has two small children who have been taken into public care because of a number of concerns about neglect (there are numerous instances of the children being left in the care of different people who they don't know and Jackie then disappearing and not collecting them for sometimes as much as three days). They have been placed with Sue, Jackie's mother, pending investigations. The social work agency responsible has arranged daily contact sessions for her with the children at her mother's home. Jackie herself had insisted that she wanted these, that she loved her children and that she was committed to working for their return.

However Jackie is not turning up for the contact sessions and is out when the social worker calls by appointment to discuss this with her. Her failure to show up causes distress to the children. According to Sue, Jackie has a new boyfriend in a neighbouring town, is obsessed with this relationship and is spending as much time as she can with the boyfriend, going out to clubs and pubs, buying clothes, talking about the boyfriend to the exclusion of just about everything else.

The social worker has, among other things, the task of assessing Jackie's willingness to commit herself to her children, something that has considerable bearing on whether or not the children will be returned to her. What do you think the above information tells you about this?

COMMENTS

The first thing to notice in the case example is that when presented with information like this you will, almost unavoidably, make some sort of judgement almost straightaway. If you reflect about your thought processes as you read the case material above you will notice that some sort of picture will have already formed in your mind as to what is going on here, and what the information signifies. You may even find that you have formed a mental image of the people themselves.

Many people would come to the conclusion on the basis of the above information that Jackie simply does not care about her children much. Certainly, Jackie does not seem to be showing much commitment to her children at the moment and it sounds as if she didn't show that much in the past either. It would be easy to conclude that she is simply unable to prioritise her children's needs over her own, and this could indeed be the case. But here are a few thoughts which might make you want to modify such a judgement, or at least suspend it pending further enquiries.

- To what extent is your judgement influenced by Sue's reports? If so, why are you giving so much weight to information provided by someone about whom you know nothing at all? Do you know what her agenda is, or what kind of relationship she has with Jackie? (The answer of course is that you don't know anything about any of these things because I haven't told you!)
- Suppose that you discovered that Sue had been dismissive and punitive towards Jackie throughout her childhood, had consistently told Jackie as a child that she was useless and incapable. Suppose she has been telling Jackie since the birth of her children that she is unfit to be a parent and that she should hand the children over to her. Would this shed a different light on what Sue has told you? Would it shed a different light on Jackie's reluctance to visit the children at her mother's house?
- Is it possible that Jackie really loves her children very much and that her biggest problem is that she feels unworthy of them? Is it possible that far from showing a lack of interest in her children's needs, what we are really seeing is a reflection of her fear that she is unable to meet their needs, or to be loved by them? Perhaps the new boyfriend is her way of seeking some comfort and reassurance in this situation, rather than a sign of indifference?

Of course the latter is simply speculation – I am not saying that it would necessarily turn out to be true – but the notion that Jackie does not care about her children is also speculation. In truth these are simply two possible interpretations out of many that could be based on the information given.

You might like to ask yourself how your judgement might be affected in any way if we added one of the following to the case scenario above:

- You were aware of the negative aspects of Sue's relationship with Jackie, and this reminded you very much of your own relationship with one of your parents so that you found it very easy to empathise with Jackie's position.
- You found either Sue or Jackie very intimidating and/or very attractive.
- You were white and Sue and Jackie were black (or you were black and they were white…).
- There had very recently been a high-profile case in the press where a social worker was lambasted for returning a child from a relative to a young mother with a history of neglectful parenting, and the child had had a fatal accident as a result (or, alternatively, there had recently been a high-profile case in the press where a grandmother was accused of abusing two children placed in her care).

I think that you will be able to see, in at least some of these situations, that your judgement would probably be affected by factors which are not really directly relevant to the matter in hand. In order to come to the best possible judgement about this situation you would want to try to avoid being overly influenced by such factors.

You would also want to feel that your judgement was based on a solid foundation, but (as I observed in Chapter 3) you would not be able to go on assessing the situation forever just to make sure. A time would have to come when you (you personally and those you were working with) would need to decide what situation you seemed to be dealing with, and would then have to act accordingly. In this case that action might include making recommendations to the court as to the future care of the children. The rest of those children's lives could be shaped by the decision that the court made as a result.

REACHING A CONCLUSION

As I hope was illustrated by my discussion of the case example above, new information, properly considered, can alter or even completely overturn our original impressions. New information about Sue and her relationship with Jackie, for instance, might well change the way you interpreted Sue's reports of Jackie's behaviour. If you are to come to the best possible decision, you need to avoid coming to a conclusion too hastily, but you do need to come to a conclusion *at some point*. This means that one of the many judgements you have to make about assessments is how long to go on assessing: when is the benefit of gaining more information offset by disadvantages?

There is a difficult balance to be struck between the need for a thorough assessment and the need for a speedy resolution. One area in which this is particularly difficult is in the case of care proceedings (legal proceedings which determine among other things whether children should be in the care of their parents). As was the case in the example above, the outcome of these proceedings can have literally life-long consequences for the children involved and their parents, and the process therefore needs to be as fair and as thorough as possible. But it *also* needs to be as quick as possible, because while a court is deliberating a childhood is ticking by and a child is being left in a situation of uncertainty and anxiety at a time of life when she needs the security of carers to whom she can form a long-term attachment. It can be difficult to know when the point is reached where further assessments will do more harm than good, but there must *be* such a point. My impression is that the process often goes well past such a point. The following, for example, are some comments made by myself and my colleague Bridget McKeigue on a real case which we looked at as part of a study on lengthy care proceedings. The four 'James' children (not their real name) were the subjects of care proceedings that had lasted 2 years and 11 months. At the outset of proceedings the youngest was 3 months and the oldest 5 years:

> In the case of the James children, concerns about neglect, hygiene, safety and possible physical abuse went back five years before the case was brought to court. Immediately after the making of the first interim care order an assessment was embarked upon by the social worker and a family centre, with some respite being provided by foster carers. Twenty two months later the children were placed full-time with foster parents and two months later (two years into the proceedings) a care plan in the file included the comment that 'further assessment' was needed as to whether the parents could 'realistically work in partnership with the department'.

> The local authority had worked with this family for seven years and had just spent 22 months assessing and supporting the family under interim care orders. Under these circumstances we wondered what new information one could reasonably hope to obtain by yet another 'assessment'? (Beckett and McKeigue, 2003: 38)

UNWARRANTED ASSUMPTIONS

Sometimes painful decisions are put off longer than they should be, and this can have very harmful consequences. But, that said, human beings also have a strong tendency to come to judgements much too quickly on the basis of limited information. Indeed, as I pointed out above, it is virtually impossible not to start drawing conclusions almost straightaway, however limited our data.

Our brains are not computers. They are biological entities which have evolved to make 'best guesses' on the basis of limited information. Imagine one of our hominid ancestors on the plains of Africa confronted by a hungry lion. She would not have the luxury of being able to carefully weigh up every aspect of the situation. She would have been extremely foolish to have undertaken a detailed risk assessment. Her best bet would be to make a snap judgement and then act. In fact, the ones who made detailed risk assessments were probably also the ones who did not go on to have a lot of descendants. So we have a strong predisposition to make judgements quickly, and although this may have served us in good stead when confronted with lions, it may in other situations result in us jumping too quickly to reach conclusions.

Additionally, the human mind also possesses a formidable battery of defence mechanisms which allow it to protect itself against anxiety by excluding things from consciousness. As a result there are certain characteristic ways in which our judgement tends to be distorted and our thinking tends to go astray if we are not aware of the dangers. For a whole variety of reasons, we can easily give excessive weight to some evidence, and not enough weight to the rest. Some of these reasons may be personal – our own life experiences may predispose us to notice some things and ignore others – while some will be more general. Some of them will be cognitive (that is: to do with the way we analyse information), while others will be more emotional (to do with the way we manage feelings).

SELECTIVE ATTENTION

As a general rule, as Milner and O'Byrne (2009: 10) note 'vivid, distinctive or unexpected data are perceptually more salient' (a single odd, unexpected and interesting fact about a person, for instance, may make more of an impression on us than other facts which are less unusual, even if these are actually more to the point) and a 'primacy effect' (ibid.: 12) also tends to operate which means that first impressions usually stick. These effects may have a profoundly negative impact on social work assessments.

> The subjects of social work assessments are most likely to encourage these effects, the reason for their referral being usually one which is distinctive. As they will initially be seen when they are at their 'worst' …, they will then present the assessor with a first impression that is difficult to dislodge. (Milner and O'Byrne, 2009: 10)

An overly positive first impression can, however, be as dangerous as an overly negative one. A 'halo' effect occurs when an initial positive impression of a person becomes so set in our minds that we are unable to see less positive aspects later.

Often, too, social workers rely a great deal on other people to provide first hand information, and this can easily magnify the effects of selective attention because a selection process will have already taken place before the information even reaches us. Rather like the way that messages are gradually transformed into something completely new in the children's game 'Chinese whispers', information at second and third hand is gradually distorted as each hearer selects what seems to him or her to be the really important detail (which may in fact be the most vivid, or sensational, or exciting detail) and passes that on.

Representatives from a parents' advocacy agency who come to talk to students at the university where I teach, regularly complain that social workers tend to build up an overly negative picture of parents based on isolated incidents, or incidents taken out of context. If it is not too painful an exercise, consider what kind of opinion people might form of you, if they did so on the basis of a list of the things in your life that you feel most ashamed about.

PAST/PRESENT AND SELF/OTHER

Although 'first impressions' do stick, there can also be a tendency for information from the past not to be fully taken into account, and this can result in unnecessarily repetitive assessments.

This may be particularly the case when the information comes from someone else and perhaps particularly when it is in written form. In the following exchange a social worker is commenting on how she carries out assessments of families in cases which are subject to care proceedings:

> Researcher: 'How do you deal with information that comes from a source that is just on paper, with no personal experience of it. How do you weight that?'
>
> [Social worker]: 'It's very hard for me. I tend to go out and do my own assessments.'
>
> (Beckett et al., 2007: 58)

This attitude is very understandable but if each new person involved in a case were always to choose to disregard the assessments that had already been done it would mean that the same things may be reassessed and the same questions asked over and over again. (There is a saying 'those who do not learn from the past are condemned to repeat it'.) Taken to the extreme, in a situation where there are frequent changes of workers, this could result in an effective paralysis of decision-making. (One situation where this can happen is where a family or individual is moving frequently from one area to another, so that each agency *can* only begin to build up a picture of the circumstances if it takes the trouble to obtain and take on board assessments conducted by other agencies. Families who move about like this have been a feature of a number of child abuse tragedies in the UK.)

However, just as we are sometimes prone to discount information that we haven't 'seen with our own eyes', we can also sometimes place an exaggerated faith in the judgement of others, particularly those who are presented as 'experts'. In the following real-life example (again names have been changed) a professional consensus, based on a great deal of experience, including an actual previous unsuccessful attempt to rehabilitate a child with his mother, is overturned on the basis of the opinion of a single expert whose direct contact with the child and adults in question was limited to a single meeting:

> In the case of Michael Thomas … the professional consensus, a year-and-a-half into care proceedings, was that he should be adopted. This was based on a family centre assessment and a failed attempt to settle Michael into his father's new family. Michael had, by this time, spent over half of his life 'in limbo'. However, the court ordered a new psychiatric expert to be instructed. This expert, on the basis of a single interview with Michael, his parents and his foster carers, took the view that his father's family could meet his needs, so the plan then became a new family centre assessment and a further attempt at rehabilitation. This arrangement was to break down as the first one had done, another 18 months later, suggesting that the earlier consensus of those who knew the case had been right and the view of the 'expert' had been wrong. By this time Michael was … at an age where it proved difficult to find him a suitable adoptive home. (Beckett and McKeigue, 2003: 37).

The human reluctance to place credence in the findings of others, and the equally human willingness to place a quite unrealistic amount of faith in the opinions of people we choose to view as expert, are in a way opposite to one another, but they are both tendencies which we need to try to avoid.

It seems to me that, in our efforts to reduce the anxiety that is inevitably caused by making a decision on an important matter, we very readily resort to various psychological defensive strategies. One of these is to suppress our own doubts and persuade ourselves that our own judgement is necessarily right. The other is to place an irrational degree of faith in the judgement of others (as was the case, I think, when a judge and a whole multi-professional group were persuaded to change their mind in the case of 'Michael' discussed above), absolving us of the need to decide ourselves. Both of these are dangerous. Both involve a kind of childish 'magical thinking', in one case involving an unrealistic faith in our own infallibility, in the other case involving an unrealistic faith in the infallibility of someone else.

STEREOTYPES

We all have stereotypes in our heads: stereotypes about men and women, for instance or stereotypes about people from different parts of the country in which we live (conjure up in your mind a 'typical' Yorkshireman, New Yorker, Glaswegian, Liverpudlian, and you will see that it is so). Stereotypes, whether positive or negative, can distort judgements and decisions, but we are not necessarily conscious of our own stereotypes and can discriminate against people without any conscious intention of doing so.

For example, it seems that white people are more prone to judge black people as being violent than they are likely to judge white people as being violent in the same situation. Argyle (1994: 86) cites a study by Duncan (1976) in which white people were shown film of an argument which ended with people pushing one another. Otherwise identical versions of the film were made, some with white actors, some with black ones. Black people who pushed were judged to be violent in over 70 per cent of cases. White people who behaved in exactly the same way were judged as violent only in 13 per cent of cases. A much more recent US study (Plant and Peruche, 2005) resulted in similar findings. In a computer simulation, police officers were more likely to shoot unarmed suspects when they were black than when they were white. Black people were perceived as more of a threat than white people. Here surely is one of the reasons that, in predominantly white societies, black people are over-represented in prisons and mental hospitals. One census conducted by the Mental Health Act Commission in 2005 and 2006, for instance, found that 'African-Caribbean people are three times more likely to be admitted to hospital [and] up to 44% more likely to be sectioned under mental health legislation' (Brooker and Repper, 2009: 57).

In social situations we are constantly 'decoding' the signals that other people give through their actions and body language. What these studies illustrate is that the same signal may be decoded in a different way depending on whether it is delivered by a black person or a white one, and depending on who is doing the decoding. The process is not necessarily conscious. My guess is that if the white people in Duncan's study were asked the question 'Do you consider black people more prone to violence than white people?' many of them might well quite truthfully have said that they did not. In fact, the US study mentioned above found that police officers are influenced by cultural stereotypes of black people 'even when the officers making the decisions do not personally espouse those beliefs' (Blaine, 2007: 92, discussing Plant and Peruche, 2005). There is a difference between our rational views and our hunches and gut reactions. Many of us may have many prejudices which we ourselves are not fully aware of. Consider the following scenario. You are walking home alone late at night on a deserted city street. There is no traffic and there is no one else in sight other than three people in a group who are walking towards you. Many people would find this a little bit intimidating. Ask yourself how different your response would be if:

- They were three young black men
- They were three young white men
- They were three elderly men
- They were three young women
- They were three young male Orthodox Jews.

I suspect that you will notice some differences in your responses. I suspect too that your responses will to some extent be determined by your own identity and context. If you are black then you may have different feelings about the first two scenarios than you would if you were white. If you were a Palestinian in the occupied West Bank you might have a very different response to the last one than you would if you were a Londoner.

The point here is that these kinds of initial gut reaction will be factors in the judgements you form when carrying out assessments. This is not to say that there is not an element of reality in these judgements. Stereotypes often have some factual basis (for instance, I think there are objective reasons for a Palestinian in the West Bank to be wary of a group of young Orthodox men, for instance), but, even if they do have some factual basis, they are crude rules of thumb which should not be treated as if they were always true. You need to notice them and make corrective adjustments to allow for them.

LABELLING

The sociologist Howard Becker (1997 [1963]) described how deviant groups are created by the application of labels, and the word 'labelling theory' is commonly used to describe his idea (though Becker himself did not describe it as a 'theory'). The sociological literature on labelling 'stresses the importance of the process through which society defines acts as deviant and the role of negative social sanctions in influencing individuals to engage in subsequent deviant acts' (Clinnard and Meier, 2008: 86). To give an example: Helen, aged 15, is arrested and charged with criminal damage. She becomes a 'young offender' as a result of her behaviour being treated as an offence (rather than, say, as 'youthful high spirits', 'a cry for help' or in some other way). The label 'young offender' results in her being treated differently in some ways. For example, she may be required to have meetings with a youth justice worker, or to attend groups with other offenders. While ostensibly intended to deflect her from offending behaviour, this may have an unintended opposite effect. If people start to treat her as 'a youth offender' she may start to feel less at home with those who do not have such a label and more at home with others who do. (With a little reflection it is not difficult to see how other labels too – 'mental health problem', 'confused', 'unco-operative' – might also have the effect of increasing the behaviours which led to the label being applied.)

This is an idea from sociology, but all sociological models are in a sense also psychological ones, since sociological phenomena are made up of decisions made by human beings. And psychological evidence does indeed abundantly confirm that the application of a label to something has, as Pohl (2004a: 327) says, 'a distorting influence in subsequent judgement or recall'. Pohl goes on to cite a number of examples. For example, he cites an experiment by Loftus and Palmer (1974) in which people were shown a car accident on video and were asked to guess the speed of the cars involved. They estimated a higher speed if asked the question 'About how fast were the cars going when they *smashed* into each other?' than they did when asked the question 'How fast were the cars going when they *hit* each other?' (Pohl, 2004a: 327).

Labels do not only affect perception but also memory. Loftus (1977, cited by Pohl, 2004a: 334) used slides of another car accident, in which a green car was seen passing the scene. Participants were asked a series of questions about the scene, including a question about this car. For half of the participants the question took the form 'Did the blue car that drove past have a ski rack on the roof?' The other half were simply asked 'Did the car that drove past have a ski rack on the roof?' Twenty minutes later, after performing another task, both groups were asked to use a colour chart to identify the colour of (among other things) the passing car. Those in the group where the car had been described as 'blue' selected bluer colours than those in the other group (the 'control' group), and their percentage of correct colour choices was only 8 per cent, as compared to 28 per cent in the control group. The misuse of the word 'blue' to describe the car had affected the way that the colour of the car was recalled, even though both groups had seen with their own eyes the colour of the car itself.

What has this to do with judgement in social work? I suggest that it has two implications. First of all, it suggests that our judgement is likely to be affected by labels that have already been applied by other people. If an elderly person is described to you as 'very confused', you may be more likely to see him as very confused than you would otherwise. If a young man is described to you as 'aggressive' you may be more likely to interpret his behaviour as aggressive, and subsequently remember it as such, than you would otherwise have done. Secondly it suggests that we ourselves, by applying descriptions to people, are likely to impact on the way that people are subsequently seen by others. (What impact do you think the notes that you write in service users' files might have, for instance, after your placement is over and your cases have to be reallocated?)

Incidentally, to make things more complicated, it is worth noting that 'labels' are sometimes welcomed or even demanded by those they are applied to. A label of 'dyslexic', for instance, may well be welcomed by someone who has great difficulty with writing and spelling. The label makes the problem more comprehensible, and it may well be a passport to services. Many labels are double-edged in this respect, though. A 'mental illness' label may help you to access services and may allow you to take a much-needed break from work, but it comes with a stigma attached and may have other long-term negative consequences, such as an effect on your employability. We should be careful about the labels that we dispense, even if they are welcomed at the time.

QUESTIONABLE HEURISTICS

Akin to stereotypes are rough heuristics ('rules of thumb') that agencies use to come to judgements quickly. I mentioned these in Chapter 2, referring to the work of Karen Broadhurst and her colleagues. The following is a further quotation in which they describe some of these strategies. They note that these strategies are in a sense forced on busy workers because the pressure of work requires (a) that quick decisions are made, and (b) that some demands on the service are deflected away. But of course this does not alter the fact that these judgements are questionable and in some cases could well be proved by hindsight to have been dangerously mistaken:

> In order to manage the volume of referrals, we consistently observed that the teams had well established 'general deflection strategies' that included: strategic deferment, namely sending the referral back to the referrer to ask for more information; and signposting, deflecting the case to a more 'appropriate' agency … Where insufficient time precluded the pursuit of more detailed information from a referrer, other decision-making heuristics came into play. These included the routine categorization of anonymous referrals as malicious (indeed, referrals from neighbours and family members were also often treated as suspect). We were told that children aged thirteen, fourteen and fifteen were routinely 'NFA-ed' (i.e. 'No Further Action' was recorded) on the basis that these children and young people 'must have lived with these concerns for a long time and be quite resilient' … We found that well intentioned, but very busy, workers became habituated to these methods of rationing, with little time to reflect on, or question, such rationales and the risks they entailed. (Broadhurst et al., 2010: 360)

PLACEMENT QUESTIONS 5.1   LABELS, STEREOTYPES AND 'RULES OF THUMB'

- Consider the terminology your placement agency uses in order to describe and categorise the users of its services. In what way could it be said to be labelling service users, and what consequences, negative or positive, do you think this has for them?
- To what extent are the agency's judgements influenced by labels applied by others, for example by medical professionals?
- What stereotypes or 'rules of thumb' do you notice being applied in your placement agency when it comes to making quick judgements about what to do? How, for example, does the agency go about determining how to prioritise new referrals?

ATTRIBUTIONAL BIAS

This refers to biases in the way we look for causes and make inferences about the meaning of events. For example a 'self-serving attributional bias' is occurring when people 'attribute positive events to themselves and dismiss negative events as attributable to other causes or people' (Walshe et al., 2008: 270). I remember a meeting I once had with a head teacher and a boy who was under threat of exclusion from the school. When the boy tried to shift responsibility for his poor behaviour onto others, the head teacher quite rightly insisted that he take responsibility himself. However, when the discussion moved on to areas in which the boy had made some progress, the head was not prepared to give him any credit, insisting that progress was entirely the result of efforts by her staff. I pointed out to the head teacher that she couldn't have it both ways. Either the boy was to be held responsible for how he performed or he was not. (Of course it would equally be an error to give him credit for his achievements but to allow him to blame others for his shortcomings, an error which I think social workers do sometimes make.)

A self-serving attributional bias may be occurring in situations where service users seem to be being judged by harsher standards from those which we apply to ourselves. For example, a service user is late for, or fails to attend, an appointment or a meeting, and this is interpreted as a lack of commitment, but when the social worker is late for an appointment or meeting, this is explained as being due to being very busy or to having other more urgent priorities. Here the social worker is excusing her own conduct by reference to external factors (pressure of work), but she is insisting that the service user's conduct is explained by factors internal to that person (lack of commitment).

A self-serving attributional bias is also often evident in the ways in which professional agencies view one another. The other lot are bureaucratic, elitist, uncaring, idle or inefficient when they fail to respond to requests for a service. We, on the other hand, are having unreasonable demands made upon us which we cannot realistically meet within the resources available. A study of how various different professionals working in the palliative care field viewed one another found the following:

> People tailor their judgements of others to affirm their own self-worth and that of their group, and ensure their evaluations of others place themselves and their own attributes in a positive light.
>
> In addition to these self- and group-serving behaviours, there is strong evidence that people perceive their own actions in a different way to those of others. People consider their own behaviour to be influenced by the situation and the pressures exerted by circumstances, whereas they are more likely to believe the actions of others are influenced by stable traits such as character or temperament … . For example, those not in a person's own professional grouping are referred to … as lacking in expertise, elitist, or uncooperative – all more stable trait dispositions rather than being influenced by a particular situation. (Walshe et al., 2008: 270)

It is possible to be biased in the other direction, and to attribute our own actions to our personal failings while excusing similar actions by others as the result of external factors. In a review of research in this area, Mezulis et al. (2004) conclude that (unsurprisingly) attributional bias operates most of the time in a self-serving way to allow people to place themselves in a favourable light, rather than in the opposite direction (which they term 'negativity bias'). They note that some researchers have suggested that 'the bias may be absent or even reversed in some psychopathological samples, such as individuals with depression' (Mezulis et al., 2004: 712). However (perhaps surprisingly, given the very negative evaluations of themselves that depressed people are prone to) they do not find much evidence that attributional bias actually operates in a negative way even here, but only that it acts in a less positive and self-serving way than it does in other populations. I wonder, though, if social workers do sometimes fall into the negative version when, in trying to avoid a self-serving attributional bias, they overcompensate by 'beating themselves up' about things for which they really cannot be held responsible and/or by failing to hold others responsible when perhaps this would be reasonable.

CONFIRMATORY BIAS

It is important to keep in mind that making a proper judgement involves *holding back from coming to a conclusion* until the end of the assessment process. This sounds obvious but requires a considerable amount of honesty and self-awareness. It is actually quite easy to pretend to yourself that you are still weighing up the evidence when in fact you have already made up your mind. Having formed a provisional judgement the human tendency is to look for evidence that confirms this judgement and overlook the evidence against it: this is what is meant by a 'confirmatory bias'. It is good discipline, therefore, to actively seek out evidence that contradicts your working hypothesis and to actively consider other alternative hypotheses to test against the evidence. One way to do this in a group setting is for someone in the group to consciously play the role of 'devil's advocate' and present arguments against the prevailing view in order to test it out. Unless we make a conscious effort of this kind, we will tend not to look for evidence that contradicts what we think we already know. The British magician and illusionist Derren Brown, who surely knows more than most people about the ways in which people can be deceived, puts it like this:

> We are not dispassionate judges where we have a belief, however tenuous, already in place. To look at things objectively and step outside our beliefs is almost impossible. (Brown, 2007: 276–277)

An illusionist like Brown can exploit this tendency by establishing a firm belief in our minds about what he is doing, which then allows him to do something quite different without us noticing it. As a result he can perform tricks whose only possible explanation seems to be that he has some kind of 'psychic' ability, even though he himself has repeatedly stated that he does not have such powers and does not believe that such phenomena exist. In a social work context, we can easily be deceived in a similar way (whether deliberately or not) if we enter a situation feeling that we already have some sort of understanding of what is going on. Brown notes that, presented with a statement such as 'Dave is an extrovert' and asked to find out whether this is true, people tend to ask questions which will tend to confirm the statement, rather than finding questions which might open up a different way of looking at Dave.

COGNITIVE DISSONANCE

Leon Festinger (1962) developed the idea of cognitive dissonance to describe the way in which people adjust their view of reality in order to avoid an uncomfortable tension between incompatible 'cognitions'. He originally came up with the idea after studying an apocalyptic cult whose leader claimed to have been told by aliens that the world would end on a given day. When the world did not end on that day, there was clearly a tension between the cult's beliefs and their actual experience, but rather than come to the uncomfortable conclusion that the prophesy was mistaken and that they had been fooled, some cult members came up with the idea that the world *had* been about to be destroyed on that day, but that the aliens had decided to spare it thanks to their intervention. In social work I have seen people similarly reluctant to let go of beliefs in which they have invested heavily. Even when the original basis for the belief has proved unfounded, we may be tempted to find other rationalisations for it rather than admit that we were simply wrong.

I remember a real-life situation in which a small child was placed on a child protection register ('made subject to a child protection plan' would be the modern terminology), and removed from his mother's care, because the professionals involved believed that his mother may have broken his arm. This was actually a reasonable conclusion to draw from the evidence available at the time, but subsequently other evidence emerged that revealed another innocent explanation. A case conference was accordingly held and the child returned to the mother, but rather than apologise to the mother for a distressing, though not maliciously intended, mistake, some of the professionals present tried to find other reasons for being concerned about the mother's parenting, reasons which had not in any way been part of the initial reasons for the child being registered. I think this was an instance of cognitive dissonance. Rather than have to feel uncomfortable about the distress caused to mother and child by an intervention which turned out not to have been necessary, these professionals found it easier to persuade themselves that there were still good reasons for their original concern.

(I am tempted to draw a political parallel here with the new justifications that were given for the 2003 invasion of Iraq by the US and the UK after the initial reason, the country's possession of weapons of mass destruction, proved to be unfounded. However I am not entirely sure that Iraq's weapons *ever* were the real reason.)

PLACEMENT QUESTIONS 5.2   ATTRIBUTION BIAS AND COGNITIVE DISSONANCE

- What comments do staff in your placement agency make about the responsiveness or otherwise of other agencies? (You could try making a list of the main agencies with which your placement agency works, and noting how each one seems to be characterised by your agency staff.) In contrast, how do staff in your agency respond to the demands made upon them by other agencies? Do you notice a double standard at all?
- What negative attributions, if any, is your agency prone to make about service users or carers?
- How do your agency staff talk about interventions that don't work out? How do they explain what happened and where (if anywhere) do they locate the cause of the failure?

JUDGEMENT AND EMOTION

Decision-making in social work often occurs in contexts which trigger powerful emotions such as pity, fear and anger. We may feel a strong attraction or affinity for some service users, we may feel distaste and repugnance for others. If we like someone and feel a connection with them, we may find it harder to come to a judgement that they will not like, and may be prone to overlook important information which might lead us to come to such a judgement. We may avoid raising issues that we think they will dislike talking about. We may even avoid *seeing* things that might make us feel obliged to confront them, or we may see these things but then somehow manage to minimise them or put them out of our minds.

Interestingly the same is also true if we find people frightening. In the presence of people whose anger we find intimidating, our efforts may end up going into placating them and looking after them. This may be one reason that social workers working with violent and disturbed adults sometimes fail to see evidence that, with the benefit of hindsight, looks to have been 'staring them in the face'. Stanley and Goddard, two Australian authors who have looked at the distorting effect of fear on the judgement of child protection workers, carried out a study in which they asked a number of child protection workers to discuss whether one of nine different categories of family violence was present in families they were working with. They found that workers consistently underestimated the level of violence that was actually on record in the current case files. 'On average, violence was recorded in the case file twice as often as that reported by the workers' (Stanley and Goddard, 2002: 130). It would be interesting to know, incidentally, how the violence recorded in the case files compared with the violence that actually *happened*.

DISTRESS

A former colleague of mine used to say that many jobs cause just as much *stress* as social work, but not many jobs involve so much *distress*. Social work often deals with very difficult subjects which touch on deep feelings in all of us, perhaps going back to our early childhood. It also often involves working in difficult places where society's deepest values come into collision. Sometimes *whatever* you decide to do can feel terribly wrong. People who have been doing the job for some time may feel that they have to some extent 'got used to' all this but both the powerful feelings that the subject can evoke *and* the psychological defences that we all put in place to protect ourselves against painful feelings (defences which may give us the impression that we have 'got used to it') can distort our judgement, leading us to misinterpret, over-react to, or under-react to the information in front of us.

COUNTER-TRANSFERENCE

'Transference' is a term originating in psychoanalytic psychology which describes a process which happens 'when someone treats another person as if they were a significant figure from the past and behaves towards them as if they were that person' (Seden, 2005: 63).

'Transference' effects can occur in both directions in a working relationship with a client but transference effects experienced by the professional are usually referred to as 'counter-transference'. The term 'counter-transference' is also used to refer to the emotional reaction of the professional to the client's transference.

If you find yourself having very strong, or even overwhelming, feelings in a situation, protective or punitive, which seem to others to be rather extreme and out of kilter, then it is worth asking yourself whether the feelings do arise entirely from the situation at hand, or whether the situation is triggering something from the past.

It would be too simple to say that counter-transference is a factor that distorts your judgement (as, say, cognitive dissonance does), because counter-transference is double-edged in respect of judgement. Your emotional reaction is likely to have been triggered by something real in the case, and to that extent may actually be a *source of additional information*, but since the strength of your reaction is a product of events that happened in a different context, you need to be careful not to assume that your reaction is a reliable guide to what you see in front of you.

In fact the point of all the discussion so far about emotion is not to suggest that you set emotion aside when making a judgement, but rather to suggest that you need to pay close attention to your emotional responses, and evaluate carefully what they are really telling you.

Case example 5.2 Is Mr Rogers really happy with his daughter's care?

A social worker has been asked to carry out an assessment of the care needs of Mr Rogers, a very frail, though apparently mentally alert, elderly man of 94 whose main carer is his daughter, Mrs Hicks, who lives about a mile away. Mr Rogers' GP is concerned that Mr Rogers is not coping at home and feels that he might be happier in some form of residential care where there would be other people around him.

Mrs Hicks is present when the social worker visits Mr Rogers and she does almost all of the talking. Her position is that Mr Rogers is fine and does not need any help other than that which she provides or arranges for him. She says they are really very grateful that the social worker has taken the trouble to visit, but they really do not need anything. When the social worker requests that Mr Rogers reply for himself, Mr Rogers does so in a very tentative way and keeps looking at his daughter while speaking. He confirms what Mrs Rogers herself has just been saying, that they do not need any help.

Mrs Hicks is a forceful woman, and though she is perfectly polite, she does seem annoyed about the fact that the GP referred Mr Rogers for this assessment, and seems keen that the interview should come to an end so that she can press on with other things. The social worker is actually not averse to ending it either, as he finds Mrs Hicks a little intimidating and her unspoken irritation makes him uncomfortable. He feels relieved when he gets out into the street again and relieved too about the fact that, since neither Mr Rogers or Mrs Hicks are asking for a service, there looks to be no need to continue to be involved.

What are your thoughts about what is going on in this situation?

COMMENTS

The social worker's sense of relief at getting out of the house, and at the possibility of not having to visit again, is very human and natural, but it may have the effect of deflecting his attention. Perhaps instead he should think about his reaction in a different way? If he finds Mrs Hicks intimidating, then how much more intimidating might she be for Mr Rogers, who is physically frail and is in a position of dependency on her? Mr Rogers' body language does suggest that he felt intimidated by his daughter. Can the social worker really be confident that he has given Mr Rogers a chance to express his own views about what he needs? Although I am not suggesting that physical abuse is necessarily involved here, it is worth noting that a lot of elder abuse by carers will go undetected if social workers are willing to close cases on the basis of interviews such as the one above. Would the social worker do better to get back to the GP to discuss this further? It is possible that the GP would have more to say about the reasons for making the referral and perhaps about the relationship between Mr Rogers and his daughter, and possibly that by talking to the GP and other professionals the social worker may be able to find a better way of establishing Mr Rogers' own real feelings.

Incidentally, while finding Mrs Hicks intimidating is certainly one reason why the social worker likes the idea of closing the case quickly, another reason is likely to be pressure of work. Anxiety about being overwhelmed by work is another way in which fear can affect our judgement. I have touched on this previously in the chapter under the subheading 'questionable heuristics'. I suggest that this particular anxiety is in fact a very powerful influence indeed on the way we see things. (For more on this, see McKeigue and Beckett [2010] and Taylor et al. [2008].) Reluctance to get in touch with Mr Rogers' distress may be yet another factor here. The fear of being overwhelmed by other people's distress is another powerful and pervasive anxiety in social work and other caring professions, which is surely aggravated when pressure of work sometimes gives us little or no time to really respond to the distress we do allow ourselves to notice. (See, for instance, Elizabeth Lyth Menzies' classic study of the defences that nurses put in place [Lyth Menzies, 1988].)

DANGERS OF GROUP DECISION-MAKING

One safeguard against personal bias and cognitive distortion is to come to a judgement as a group rather than individually. In most of the areas in which social workers operate – child and families, mental health, learning disability, work with older people – current practice and organisational frameworks place a great deal of emphasis on working as part of multi-disciplinary and multi-agency teams within which workers with different kinds of training and different areas of expertise come to decisions together, along with service users. But, whatever the other advantages and disadvantages of collaborative working, group decision-making may not be as much of a safeguard as it might appear because, just as there are certain predicable ways in which individual judgements can be biased, as I have discussed above, so there are also certain characteristic dynamics that occur in groups which can result in group decisions being distorted and sometimes dangerous.

As I have already noted, we are biological entities, not machines. We have a nature and part of our nature is that we are social beings: we have a need to be accepted and liked by members of the groups to which we belong. Groupthink (Janis, 1982; Munro, 2002) occurs when group members' desire to achieve a consensus and avoid conflict has the effect of inhibiting their ability to weigh up the situation under discussion. When everyone seems to be agreeing on something, it can feel very uncomfortable to challenge the consensus. It can make you feel like a 'party-pooper'. It can result in your knowledge and competence being called into question (particularly if you are a student or relatively junior). On the other hand if you yourself produce arguments in support of the apparent consensus, your contribution is likely to be greeted warmly and make you feel good about yourself. So there is often a strong incentive to go along with what everyone seems to think. (I say 'seems to think,' because sometimes the effect of groupthink can be that a group votes for a course of action which the majority of the group privately has reservations about. If no one expresses their reservations, no one gets to find out that others think as they do!) We feel safer when we are part of a group, even if that group is in fact making a dangerous decision, and we are prone to start thinking of 'our' group as necessarily being 'the good guys'.

A well-run group is one in which people are encouraged to talk freely and to disagree with one another. To avoid groupthink taking over, it may be helpful sometimes to ask a group member to be a 'devil's advocate', in the way discussed earlier, and set out the arguments for the opposite point of view to what seems to be the group consensus.

POLARISATION

Incidentally, although the human tendency to try to avoid conflict is a well-known dynamic in groups, it can also happen that groups split into two or more factions, each taking a different point of view. This too creates dangers. Firstly, it can and does paralyse effective decision-making. Secondly, it can result in the subgroups taking increasingly extreme positions (polarising) in their desire to differentiate themselves from one another. Different agencies, which inevitably have different priorities, can sometimes fall into this trap if they refuse to try to understand each others' different perspectives. Jon Glasby describes how this can occur in relation to hospital discharges, where 'partners seeking to work in a multi-disciplinary fashion quickly polarise, retreating into their "healthcare" or "social care" identities' (2003: 1).

This sort of polarisation can happen between two individuals also. One example from my own experience is the following. Myself and another social worker were both involved in discussions about whether some children should stay long-term with their current foster-parents, who wanted to keep them. The other social worker was extremely negative about the foster-parents and spoke about them in very derogatory terms. I felt this was unfair, and in my desire to defend the foster-parents, I ended up finding it difficult to hear anything negative about them at all. We were very angry with each other. With the benefit of hindsight I now feel that the other social worker, whose view did eventually prevail, was right and that I was wrong. I still think that the other social worker was unnecessarily derogatory in the way she spoke about them and I think this was unhelpful, but I can also see that my own position was unreasonable and that in a sense we were both pushing each other into extreme positions, each feeling the need to overcompensate for the one-sided position of the other.

PLACEMENT QUESTIONS 5.3   GROUP DECISION-MAKING

To examine group phenomena of the kind we have been discussing, you could look at the team or unit in which you are placed, or you could look at the multi-agency networks in which the agency participates and the various forums that this involves (for example planning meetings, ward rounds, or case conferences).

- Do you notice instances of professionals saying different things in a group context to those they say privately, going along in a group situation with views that you know they do not really agree with?
- Have you found it difficult yourself to express your genuine views in a group context, and if so what is it about the behaviour of the rest of the group that makes it hard?
- If you do manage to speak your mind, even when your view does not completely conform to the apparent consensus, what kind of reaction do you get and what effect does it have on you?
- Have you encountered conflict, perhaps between staff in your own agency and those in another agency? What caused the conflict and what got in the way of resolving it?

MAKING THE BEST POSSIBLE JUDGEMENTS

If we come to a judgement in conditions of uncertainty where a decision may have to be made in a limited amount of time, with a limited amount of information, we can never guarantee that the judgement will prove to have been correct in the light of subsequent events. (The hindsight fallacy, to be discussed further in Chapter 7, is itself a 'cognitive illusion' [Pohl, 2004c].) This is true whatever sort of judgement we are talking about. (It might be a judgement about the level of risk that is present in a situation, a judgement about what action to take, or a judgement about how best to support a client in making decisions on her own behalf.) There is no way of guaranteeing that all our judgements will prove, after the event, to have been right. Infallibility is not an option, nor even something close to infallibility. Nevertheless there is a difference between good judgement and poor judgement.

Good judgement is informed by appropriate knowledge and a theoretical understanding of the situation at hand. If you are assessing the needs of a person who is autistic, for instance, you are unlikely to make the best possible judgement if you know nothing about autism. These sorts of context-specific appropriate knowledge have not been discussed in this chapter, and are only referred to in passing throughout this book. You need to refer to literature related to the particular specialist area in question: the literature on disabilities, the literature on services for old people, the literature on working with families, etc.

But a good judgement also requires self-knowledge and an understanding of the social and institutional context in which a judgement occurs. By highlighting in this chapter some of the ways in which our judgement can be shaped, and sometimes distorted, I hope to have drawn your attention to things to attend to, watch out for and, if necessary, correct, if you are to achieve not necessarily the right judgement every time (for that is impossible) but the best possible judgement that can be made in a given set of circumstances.

CHAPTER SUMMARY

In this chapter I began by pointing out the difficulty of making judgements in a field such as social work where you may have no choice but to make a far-reaching decision in a context where you have no means of being certain that any given choice is the right one. I discussed the process of coming to a conclusion and the anxieties associated with it, and noted that putting off the decision again and again is sometimes a consequence of such anxiety. I looked at a range of ways in which our judgement could be affected by errors in thinking or interpreting information, and at the ways in which our emotional responses could colour our judgement but could also provide information that might be useful in coming to the best decision. I briefly looked at the way in which group dynamics could impact on decision-making, sometimes negatively. Finally I suggested that the best possible judgements required not only specific knowledge, but also self-awareness.

FURTHER READING

I would strongly recommend Schön's study of the way that professionals make judgements in practice:

Schön, D. (1991) *The Reflective Practitioner: How Professionals Think in Action*. Aldershot: Arena.

Milner and O'Byrne's book has a good deal to say on this subject and has been an influence on this chapter:

Milner, J. and O'Byrne, P. (2009) *Assessment in Social Work* (3rd edn). Basingstoke: Palgrave.

For those interested in the psychology and sociology of 'cognitive illusions', stereotypes and labelling the following provide overviews:

Blaine, B. (2007) *Understanding the Psychology of Diversity*. London: Sage.

Clinnard, M. and Meier, R. (2008) *Sociology of Deviant Behaviour*. Belmont, CA: Wadsworth.

Pohl, R. (ed.) (2004) *Cognitive Illusions*. Hove: Psychology Press.

It is not often that books by magicians are recommended in social work texts, but the book by Derren Brown, mentioned above, is very interesting on the ways that the human mind can be, predictably, fooled. And it is a somewhat more entertaining read than Pohl's book:

Brown, D. (2007) *Tricks of the Mind*. London: Channel 4 Books.

6 NEED

- Varieties of need
- 'Need' in the social work context
- Expressed need, felt need, inferred need
- Heard need, recognised need, legitimated need
- The politics of need

From talking about judgement, I will now move on to one of the things that social workers have to make judgements *about*: 'Need' is a word that is very frequently used in social work, and a word that I used many times in Chapter 3 when discussing assessment. We speak of *needs-led* assessments, unmet *needs*, children in *need*. We talk about social and medical *needs*. We ask whether parents are capable of meeting their children's *needs*, or putting their own children's *needs* before their own. The purpose of assessment is typically to establish needs; the purpose of intervention is to try to meet them, and the concept of need is embedded in the legislation under which social workers operate. The following are extracts from the two pieces of legislation which, at the time of writing, remain the legal foundations under which social care services for children and adults respectively are delivered in England and Wales. (You may notice that the adult legislation seems to grant more discretion as to whether or not needs, once identified, should actually be *met*.)

From Section 17, 1989 Children Act:

17. — (1) It shall be the general duty of every local authority (in addition to the other duties imposed on them by this Part) —

   (a) to safeguard and promote the welfare of children within their area who are in need; and
   (b) so far as is consistent with that duty, to promote the upbringing of such children by their families,
   by providing a range and level of services appropriate to those children's needs ...

From Section 47, 1990 NHS and Community Care Act:

(1)   Subject to subsections (5) and (6) below, where it appears to a local authority that any person for whom they may provide or arrange for the provision of community care services may be in need of any such services, the authority —

   (a)   shall carry out an assessment of his needs for those services; and
   (b)   having regard to the results of that assessment, shall then decide whether his needs call for the provision by them of any such services …

Although assessments do not only look at need, closer examination reveals that the other things they look at are closely related to need. For example *capacity* relates to need in the sense that what you are looking at is either a person's capacity to *meet their own needs*, or – as is the case in a parenting assessment, for instance – their capacity to *meet the needs of others*. *Risk* is something that assessments look at as well. 'Risk', as I will discuss in the next chapter, means the likelihood of harm, and 'harm' too is linked to need. It could be defined as the flip-side of need, the thing that happens, or at any rate becomes more likely to happen, when needs are not met. Indeed the guidance accompanying the 1989 Children Act does relate 'need' and 'harm' in just such a way, as we will see presently. (And because of this close relationship between unmet need and risk, the subject matter of this chapter inevitably overlaps with that of the next one.)

VARIETIES OF NEED

Given the frequency with which the word is used it is interesting how difficult 'need' is to actually define. The word itself is difficult to pin down, as I think you will find if you try to write a definition of it without resorting to other words, such as 'necessity', which more or less mean the same thing anyway. And it does not get any easier if you try to define the word as it is used in a particular social work context, such as your placement. A study of workers attempting to carry out needs-led assessments under the NHS and Community Act found that 'no consensus about the meaning of need seems to exist' (Parry-Jones and Soulsby, 2001: 415). Other difficulties identified by this same study, to do with carrying out needs-led assessment and rationing simultaneously, and to do with the power that is placed in the hands of the professional who assesses need, are topics we will touch on later in this chapter, but for the present, let us consider the difficulty of definition.

What do we mean by 'need'? Do we mean something that is essential for survival, or something that is essential for happiness or health (assuming that we can define happiness or health), or do we mean something that is essential in order to participate in society? Can we really define need at all except in relation to a purpose? If someone were to ask you out of the blue 'What do you need?' you would probably reply 'What do I need for *what*?' If the purpose in question is to stay alive, you need food, air, water and warmth. But what if the purpose in question is to participate fully in society? Here things start to get more complicated and there is more scope for disagreement.

ABSOLUTE NEEDS

Air, food, water, warmth … No one would dispute these are human needs in whatever context, because humans cannot exist without them. They are absolute needs. They apply in any society and at any point in time.

I would also define as absolute needs a range of things which may not be necessary for us to stay alive, but are necessary, in any social context, for us to operate as fully functioning human beings: things whose absence will result in extreme distress and psychological damage. One of these, I'd suggest, is human company. If you have seen the film *Castaway* in which the character played by Tom Hanks is marooned on a desert island, you will remember how his loneliness became so desperate that he painted a crude image of a face on a football, gave it the name Wilson, and talked to it, apologised to it and grieved when it was lost. The image of 'Wilson' (you can find it on the internet by searching 'wilson castaway') has always struck me as a powerful representation of the sheer intensity of our need for others.

And more than just human company, we need attachment (or perhaps we could simply call it 'love'?). There is abundant evidence that children deprived of reasonably secure attachment figures in childhood can suffer long-term psychological harm into adult life. For example Rutter et al. (1998) found that gross early privation was a major cause of cognitive deficits in Romanian orphans who were adopted in the UK after living as small children in institutions where there was little or no opportunity to form attachments to adult carers. The cruel animal experiments on attachment carried out by Harlow (1963) provide another iconic image which graphically illustrates the sheer power of this need which humans share with other mammals: a baby rhesus monkey clinging to a monkey doll covered in terrycloth (it can also be readily found on the internet: search 'harlow monkey'). The baby's need for the reassurance of a cuddle is so strong that, in the absence of a mother, it tries to meet it with an inanimate substitute rather than leave it completely unmet (just as the Tom Hanks character used the football to meet his need for someone to talk to, rather than give up altogether on talking to anyone).

These two images raise questions for me about the extent to which many of the things that we subjectively experience ourselves as needing ('I need a cigarette') are in fact substitutes of a similar kind. How many of the things that we feel ourselves to 'need' are in fact stand-ins for other more basic needs? Is a heroin addict putting a needle in his arm a bit like the baby monkey clinging to a stuffed doll? I have heard that the immediate result of injecting heroin is a feeling of peace and security and calm, which is surely what a baby also seeks in the comfort of a carer's arms.

We are still talking here about *absolute* needs, things that all human beings need, regardless of social context, but even here it is difficult to put our finger on what needs we should include. I think we can agree that human beings need some degree of security, some degree of control over their environment, a need to know that our needs can be met. Many people with whom you come into contact as social workers will have issues and problems to do with control: some will find it difficult to control their own behaviour (people with addictions, eating disorders, self-harming behaviours or obsessive disorders), perhaps because these behaviours themselves provide, in the short-run, a desperately-needed sense of *having* some control. ('My eating disorder was not a girlish fad or a diet gone wrong,' writes an anorexic, 'but a private, violent strategy for exerting control on the body when life felt beyond my control' [Penny, 2009: 11]). Other people you encounter will try to control those around them in violent and abusive ways. (In one study, women victims of domestic violence report that their abusive partners sometimes control them to the extent of not allowing them to visit the toilet on their own, trying to 'eradicate the woman's sense of self and create instead a "puppet woman" subject to their authority' [Humphreys and Thiara, 2003: 215]).

Long-term harm is associated with a sustained exposure to extreme situations in which people feel under threat in situations over which they have no control. This is apparent in adults who have suffered neglect or abuse in childhood, for instance (Stovall-McClough and Cloitre, 2006), or victims of domestic violence (Harne and Radford, 2008), or (a group that social workers now regularly encounter in work with asylum seekers) adults who have experienced torture (Johnson and Thompson, 2008).

What other absolute needs are there? I would suggest that sexual expression of some kind is for most people a need, even though a minority of people seem happy to go through life without being sexually active at all (and even though it is possible to argue that, in a highly sexualised society, sex is often used as a substitute or stand-in for other unmet needs). Disabled people in particular have suffered from society's unwillingness to recognise that they too have this need. The following comes from a study conducted in Belgium on barriers to intimacy and sexuality experienced by people with learning disabilities:

> Regardless of setting, people with developmental disabilities often are limited in the development of a full (sexual) life because of prevalent attitudes and structural and organizational obstacles … [M]any people with developmental disabilities are … obliged to live with people not of their choosing – only rarely do they get the opportunity to make this choice themselves. Organizational and structural factors cause people to be parted from friends and loved ones, so relationships often end because of excessive distance. Many couples barely get to see each other, maybe once a month, and then only at organized events or fixed dates, and only infrequently in settings designed for intimacy. Some community facilities still have a policy advocating that kissing and petting should be reprimanded. Sexual expression is often limited to what can be supervised; therefore, to what must occur in public. (Lesseliers and Van Hove, 2002: 78–79)

Other absolute needs surely include a need for stimulation (something to do and think about), a need for identity, a need to be a part of society, to have a purpose, and to have some way of making sense of life. These are all needs which social workers are in the business of trying to meet. Social workers in the foster-care field, for instance, often have to juggle 'identity needs' and 'attachment needs' when making placement decisions. Social workers who are working with the elderly are often trying to balance people's needs for autonomy with their need for physical safety, or even their need for a moderately hygienic environment as the following case example illustrates.

Case example 6.1   Patience Toller and her cats

Patience Toller is an elderly woman living by herself in a house in the rural fens of East Anglia. She is 82 years old. Her mobility is very limited as a result of severe arthritis, and she only uses the downstairs of the house, spending her time in the kitchen, which is where she also sleeps. There are no other dwellings within half a mile. She shares the house with more than 30 cats. She has never married and has always lived in this house, which she shared, until their deaths some years ago, with her father and brother, her mother having died when Miss Toller was a child.

Workmen clearing drainage ditches near her house called on Miss Toller to let her know what they were doing. They were so shocked to discover the conditions she was living in that they contacted the local adult social care services. 'It's a scandal that she's just been left there,' they say, 'it shouldn't be allowed. Something has got to be done.'

A social work visit confirms that Miss Toller's clothes and bedding smell overpoweringly of urine. The house is littered with cat faeces and food scraps. Miss Toller is suffering from a skin condition likely to be connected to the poor hygiene. She has a black eye and cuts to her face which Mrs Toller dismisses as the result of a small accident, but are clearly the result of numerous incidents and not just one. Her eyesight is extremely poor and it would appear that she is developing cataracts. She appears to have overlooked altogether the remains of a dead kitten in the corner of the living room.

However Miss Toller, while she comes over as rather eccentric and very out of touch with the outside world (a local farmer who is a distant relative apparently collects her pension and buys groceries on her behalf), does not seem to be seriously mentally confused. And she insists (a) that she has no intention of leaving the home until she dies, and (b) that she does not want any help of any kind in the home. What should the social worker do?

COMMENTS

In social work you will often encounter people who, like the workmen in the above story, demand that 'something is done' about situations like this. It is a very understandable reaction. But there is no legal or moral basis for *forcing* Miss Toller to accept services or to move elsewhere. The only appropriate approach is one of gentle negotiation, working closely with other people who have some knowledge of her (including her GP, and perhaps the farmer who brings her groceries) and ensuring that Miss Toller has the information she needs to make a genuinely informed decision. Only Miss Toller herself knows how important her independence is to her, as compared to her physical safety. And she would not be unusual for a person of her age if she did not place as high a priority as younger people do on simply maximising the length of her life. (Indeed a heavy handed intervention that frightened and unsettled her might well have negative consequences for her health anyway.)

But her resistance to outside help – and even to a possible move elsewhere – might well be a result of fear, distrust and a lack of understanding about the options. It is quite possible that given time and a patient explanation, she might actually welcome help that would improve the quality of her life. She surely cannot, for instance, relish the prospect of going blind which will happen eventually if her cataracts are not dealt with. It may still be that she will chose to take some risks for the sake of her autonomy and independence (as indeed we all do) but that is not to say that she will necessarily want to stick to her original position of rejecting any help at all.

A HIERARCHY OF ABSOLUTE NEEDS?

Abraham Maslow's famous 'hierarchy of needs' (1970) is often referred to in discussions of this kind (and can readily be found on the internet). It continues to be cited long after the original theoretical model of which it formed a part has been largely forgotten. I have some doubts about the value of that. The basic point it illustrates, though, is an important one: we tend to want to meet our more basic needs before we worry too much about our more complex ones. If the room you are sitting in were suddenly drained of oxygen, for instance, the only need you would be worrying about would be the need to breathe. All the other needs that might otherwise be on your mind – your relationship needs, your sexual needs, your need for a purpose in life, etc. – would be of no concern to you at all until you had got some oxygen back in your lungs again.

Social workers, like myself, who come from a relatively comfortable middle-class background, do sometimes need to remind themselves of this. Service users who have very basic practical needs – they need money to buy food, or a roof over their heads, or a reassurance that they won't be deported back to a country where they may be tortured – will usually not be very interested in receiving help with other 'higher-order' problems, such as relationship problems, unless some attention is first given to addressing their more basic needs, whether or not the social worker finds those higher-order needs more interesting and rewarding to work on. A failure to understand this can result in clients 'receiving treatment when they were asking for representation' (Brandon and Brandon, 2001: 63).

Having made this point about the hierarchy of needs, though, it is important to recognise that it is not by any means always the case that people prioritise basic or physiological needs over higher-order needs. We can all think of examples of people who have risked their lives, or indeed knowingly sacrificed their lives, in the service of what they saw as higher goals. Even situations such as that of Patience Toller in case example 6.1 above, where people place themselves in some physical danger rather than give up their independence or sense of dignity, could be said to demonstrate that there is not a straightforward hierarchy. And such situations are not at all uncommon.

RELATIVE NEED

But as well as needs that apply to human beings in any social context, there are also needs that are specific to particular contexts:

… minimum needs are not simply satisfied by providing the physical necessities of life, for example adequate food, clothing and shelter, but require also for their satisfaction a level of provision for persons that is suitable for social agents, interacting with others in a specific society. (Weale, 1983, cited by Ware and Goodin, 1990: 2)

To give an example, literacy is clearly not an absolute need because for many tens of thousands of years human beings lived with no form of writing system. Schooling is not an absolute need for the same reason. Nor are television, telephones and the internet. Yet it is surely the case that in a modern Western society, an inability to read and write, a lack of education, and a lack of access to electronic media would prevent a person from participating fully in the society in which they live.

'Relative need' relates to 'absolute need' in the same way that 'relative poverty' relates to 'absolute poverty'. As a social worker you are likely to meet many people who are very obviously poor, in the sense that they experience social exclusion as a result of their material circumstances, even though in terms of income or material possessions they might be regarded as quite comfortably off in other parts of the world. Such people are experiencing 'relative poverty'. And just as relative poverty is still 'real' poverty, so relative needs are still 'real' needs. In fact relative needs are not so different from absolute needs as would appear at first sight. 'Ability to participate in the community' could be argued to be an *absolute* need, and relative needs such as literacy can be seen merely as different means whereby that particular absolute need is met in particular contexts. A psychiatrist who had once worked in the highlands of Papua New Guinea told me that, in that part of the world, ownership of pigs is an important marker of status. He had worked with patients who felt depressed and had low self-esteem because they did not own any pigs. In that context, ownership of pigs may be a relative need, a particular, local expression of the absolute need to have some standing in the community of which you are part.

One of the challenges of a multi-cultural society is being able to recognise that something that does not seem like a need at all to one person, may for another be a very pressing need indeed. This applies for example to religious rules and observances. For Jewish or Muslim people (or indeed vegetarians) not eating pork may be very important, certainly to the extent that they would rather go hungry. Yet to a non-believing meat eater, this need to follow dietary rules simply does not exist at all. Again the point is that, although the expression of the need may seem entirely culture-specific, it does relate to needs which we all share: needs to do with identity, purpose, standing in the community and in the greater scheme of things.

It seems that the higher up the hierarchy of needs one goes, the more varied are the particular ways in which needs are met in different social contexts. There is no variety in the way that the need for oxygen is acted out in different societies, or the need for water. Food varies from culture to culture but is nevertheless almost invariably still recognisable as food to everyone. But when it comes to needs for love and belonging, or the need for esteem, then there are huge differences between the ways in which people understand and meet these needs in different social contexts, to a point where the way in which one culture addresses these needs may be almost unrecognisable to a person from another culture.

'NEED' IN THE SOCIAL WORK CONTEXT

Certainly, social workers are not in the business of assessing absolute needs alone. They are looking at people in their social context and therefore must look at relative need. In England and Wales, the 1989 Children Act defines 'need' as follows in Section 17 (10):

> (10)   For the purposes of this Part a child shall be taken to be in need if –
>
> > (a)   he is unlikely to achieve or maintain, or to have the opportunity of achieving or maintaining, a reasonable standard of health or development without the provision for him of services by a local authority under this Part;
> >
> > (b)   his health or development is likely to be significantly impaired, or further impaired, without the provision for him of such services; or he is disabled …

It is obvious that a child's health and development could be impaired by a failure to meet relative needs (such as schooling) as well as a failure to meet absolute needs (food, warmth, attachment).

But how are social workers supposed to go about the business of determining what it is that people really need and what services to provide to meet them? Assessing needs is one of the necessary but inevitably inexact judgements discussed in the last chapter. We cannot 'read off' the needs of a human being (not even our own needs) as we can read off say the fuel gauge of a car. We can often only infer needs, or guess at them. This makes needs assessment challenging. And needs assessment is made still more challenging by the fact that resources are always finite, so that social work agencies are not simply assessing the needs of service users, but trying to *weigh up the needs of service users against one another*, so as to try to ensure that services go to those who are most in need.

In some areas of welfare provision, such as the benefit system, legislation and regulations set benchmarks which are used to determine whether or not someone is entitled to provision ('need' as measured against a standardised benchmark is sometimes described as 'normative need' [Bradshaw, 1972]). In such a system you are entitled to provision as of right if your circumstances come within the benchmark. But, by and large, the kind of provision that is offered by social work agencies does not work like that. There may be eligibility criteria, as is the case in adult care services, which in England and Wales are required to categorise needs as 'critical', 'substantial', 'moderate' or 'low' on the basis of the 'seriousness of the risk to independence or other consequences if needs are not addressed' (Department of Health, 2003: 4), but this certainly does not eliminate the substantial element of judgement involved on the part of the individual worker. In practice the business of determining what counts as needs is a complex negotiation. To think about how this works we need to go beyond the attempt made in the previous section at an objective definition of needs, and look at need in a more subjective way.

EXPRESSED NEED, FELT NEED, INFERRED NEED

How do you go about finding out what someone needs? The obvious answer is 'ask them!' We are each of us uniquely expert in our own needs and circumstances and, however much they may know about us, no one else can ever feel the direct pull of our own needs or have direct access to our memories and feelings. It would be very poor practice to carry out an assessment of needs that did not place at centre stage the perspective of the person being assessed. But then again, simply to ask service users what they think they need and then write down the answers would not really be an assessment. There are a number of reasons why the service user's perspective is not the *only* relevant one and why a judgement on the part of the social worker and others is usually also required.

There are, for one thing, some service users who cannot articulate or explain their needs. Small babies, for instance, and some people with severe learning disabilities, have no language. They are able to draw attention to unmet needs by showing their distress, and express satisfaction by showing pleasure, but they cannot explain their needs or look ahead and identify needs that they might have in the future. Even small children who do have language cannot be expected to understand their own long-term needs, though they are able to express their feelings about their current circumstances. Adults have responsibilities to think about the needs of children on their behalf, and to simply ask children what they need would be an abrogation of that responsibility.

But even when people *are* quite able to articulate their own experience and discuss their own needs, there are complications. Expressed need is not the same thing as felt need, and neither the needs we express or the needs we feel are necessarily the same as what we *actually do need.* For one thing, we do not necessarily fully understand our own needs, even as mature adults, and it is sometimes the case that we need help from others identifying what our needs really are. (I can certainly think of times during my own adult life when others have helped me understand needs that I did not fully understand myself.) And sometimes people are embarrassed to speak about their needs, or worried about seeming to complain, or afraid of being a nuisance (as is sometimes the case with old people), or afraid of the way other people will react. For instance Peter, aged 16, is disturbed and distressed by finding himself strongly sexually attracted to other boys and does not feel able to talk about it with his family or friends. Gay and lesbian adolescents are a vulnerable group which has, among other things, a higher incidence of suicide than adolescents in general (see Eisenberg and Resnick, 2006), so Peter may badly need some help to make some sense of what is happening to him. But he may not look for or ask for help for fear of the reaction he might get. He may fear ridicule or censure. He may simply be reluctant to speak out loud about something that he would rather not face up to himself.

There are many other circumstances in which people might be afraid of the consequences of being honest. It is suggested, for instance (and indeed I have heard women confirm it from their own personal experience), that mothers may be reluctant to admit to post-natal depression and obtain help because they are afraid that they may be seen as unfit to care for a baby and have their child taken from them (Association for Improvements in Mental Health Services, 2004). Some women are afraid to disclose domestic violence for similar reasons (Farmer and Owen, 1995). Other people might feel reluctant to admit to needs that are not being met out of loyalty to their carers, or alternatively out of fear of their carers (Mr Rogers, discussed in Case example 5.2 in the previous chapter, was perhaps a case in point).

Sometimes, people are also reluctant to admit even to themselves to having needs which others might infer from their behaviour (this might be the case for instance when someone has a drink problem). Sometimes people will confuse desires that feel like needs with need itself. Heroin addicts may feel such a strong craving for heroin that they are willing to prioritise is over their basic needs, and sometimes over the needs of their loved ones too. It feels to them like an urgent need. But it may be harder for them to face the underlying needs which led to the heroin use in the first place.

Often we express our needs by speaking about something that we think would solve the problem, rather than speaking of the need itself. For example when someone says 'I need a holiday' they are, strictly speaking, talking about something that they think will help meet a need, rather than a need itself. People often try to express their needs to social workers in this way (a service-led way, to use a term discussed in Chapter 3), talking in terms of services that they imagine the agency could provide, rather than in terms of the need itself. And social workers sometimes have to work with service users who present their needs as a demand for a specific service which the social worker does not feel is likely to solve their problems at all.

Case example 6.2   Will 'care' teach Michael a lesson?

Mr and Mrs Gavaghan telephone a children's social care office and speak to a duty social worker about their son Michael, who is 15. He is abusive and foul-mouthed when challenged about anything whatsoever, and if pushed will fly into a rage, slam doors and smash whatever is to hand. He hangs out with older boys and stays out into the early hours of the morning, refusing to accept any sort of coming-in time. 'He is wrecking our family,' they say. They also say he is setting a bad example to his younger brothers who are starting to imitate him. 'We're not prepared to put up with it anymore,' they say. 'What he needs is a sharp shock. We want you to take him into care immediately to teach him a lesson'. How should the duty social worker respond?

COMMENTS

In my experience it is not uncommon for parents to seek to use 'putting into care' as a punishment in this way. But of course Mr and Mrs Gavaghan's idea of what being 'in care' might entail, or what consequences it might have, are unrealistic. 'Care' is not intended as a punishment and is not run that way. It is not likely to have the deterrent effect that the Gavaghans imagine. In any case it would not be appropriate for a children and families agency to accept the parents' view of the problem without seeking the perspective of Michael and his brothers, or considering the way the family works as a whole, or finding out the perspective of others who know Michael and his family, such as his school.

Although it does not sound very similar, the situation has something in common with that of Patience Toller in the previous case example. In both cases the social worker is presented with a rather rigid position which may be based on lack of understanding about how things work. In both cases the social worker will need to try somehow to negotiate some space to explore options and consider different perspectives.

HEARD NEED, RECOGNISED NEED, LEGITIMATED NEED

There are many reasons for assessment needing to be an exploration, rather than simply asking questions and recording answers, and many reasons why the judgement of the social worker is involved, as well as the stated wishes of service users. But this does raise a number of potential problems. Delivering services based on a social work agency's assessment, rather than on the basis of a fixed right or entitlement does concentrate a great deal of power in the hands of the social work agency. It therefore has the potential to be profoundly disempowering to service users, giving out the negative and demeaning message that a 'client's own definitions of their personal problems' cannot be relied upon and that 'the more profound and relevant reasons for their difficult situations and relationships lay outside the direct knowledge of the distressed individual and within the competence of the professional' (Brandon and Brandon, 2001: 63).

And just as there are a variety of factors that might mean that clients may not *express* their needs, so there are also an equally wide variety of reasons why social workers and their agencies may not always be able to *hear* or *recognise* their needs. Social workers, after all, are human beings, just like service users, and have their own needs, their own unique but limited knowledge and experience, and they work within specific institutional contexts which very much shape the way they see things. (As a student coming to an agency from outside, you will notice the way that staff in the agency have attitudes that have been shaped by the particular context in which they work. It is harder to retain a sense of this, the longer you work in the same place!)

We are more likely to hear or recognise needs with which we are personally familiar, than to hear and recognise needs of which we have no personal experience at all. If you have been a single mother living on state benefits for instance, you are likely to be sensitive to the needs of other women in the same position. If you are a black person you are likely to be more attuned to the particular challenges facing black people in a predominantly white society where racism is still endemic. (I am white, and if I did not have black friends to tell me about it, I would, for instance, have little real sense of the extent to which being stopped and questioned by the police is a normal part of the experience of being black in the UK.)

But personal experience has quite a complex relationship with our ability to accurately assess other people's needs. There is a distinct danger that, when we see some resemblance between our client's situation and our own experience, we will over-identify the client with ourselves, and make a false assumption that the client's position is exactly the same as our own, as is sometimes expressed by the telling phrase 'I know exactly how you feel'. This is never true, of course. One person's experience is never exactly like another's.

There are also ways in which our own needs may make us not more but *less* likely to hear or be responsive to similar needs in others. A worker who has yet to come to terms with his homosexuality, for example, may find it hard to hear a service user (such as 'Peter' discussed above) who is struggling with his or her own sexuality. A worker who has not faced up to a childhood history of abuse may find it easier not to notice signs of abuse in others, for in confronting the abuse of another, she might be forced to confront her own abuse. If we are in denial about aspects of our own unmet needs, we may similarly go into denial about the needs of others. We may avoid looking at needs that we ourselves don't know how to deal with.

We may also find it hard to recognise needs which we lack the skills or resources to address. This is one reason why professionals tend to pick up on needs in their own particular area of expertise (or alternatively pick up on needs which are very clearly the responsibility of someone else entirely!). If to recognise a need is going to make us feel impotent or incompetent, or is going to put us in a difficult position, it may be psychologically easier not to recognise it at all. Our capacity not to see things is a defence against anxiety that should not be underestimated, and can be very dangerous. I remember once visiting a house where the children's names were (in the term used at the times) on the child protection register (in modern terminology 'subject to a child protection plan'). Leaving after a long and difficult interview with the parents (I confess I found them very intimidating), I noticed on the way out that one of the children had a bruise on his face that I had not seen before. I no longer remember all the details of the case, but I still quite vividly remember a strong impulse to pretend to myself that I had not seen this, so as to avoid having to ask more questions which would mean having to spend more time in a place where I really did not want to be. Because this took place (just) at a conscious level I was able to fight the impulse, but if it had happened at an unconscious level, I would not have been able to do so.

People can and do suppress from consciousness things that their own eyes have actually seen. It is even easier to suppress powerful intuitions and hunches, particularly in situations when we feel overwhelmed. Our brains protect us against things that we cannot cope with.

PLACEMENT QUESTIONS 6.1   THINGS WE SEE AND THINGS WE AVOID SEEING

Within the frame of the kinds of assessment that take place within your placement agency, what are the things that you might be reluctant to see or notice? And what are the things that you might be most inclined to home in on in an assessment of need?

In other words, which part of the territory that the agency is supposed to assess do you feel least comfortable dealing with, and which parts do you feel most comfortable with? Do you understand yourself well enough to know why this is so?

What things might this agency's service users find it hard to tell the agency about? (If it is a child protection agency, for instance, parents might be scared to admit to angry feelings they had about their children.)

Watching the way that people work in this agency, what do you notice them homing in on and what do you see them finding it harder to hear? What do you think are the reasons?

To make things more complicated, in most assessments there are more than one person's needs to take into account. In family social work, we are likely to be considering the needs of both children and parents. In adult social work, we are often looking at the needs of a client and a carer. The needs of the different parties are not necessarily the same and may pull in different directions. And the needs of one person may be 'louder', because they are more likeable, or more like ourselves, or more intimidating, or less distressing to be with, or easier to understand, and may drown out entirely the needs of the other.

Just as sometimes our *own* needs become so 'loud' that they prevent us from hearing other people's needs, so sometimes the needs of one person we are working with become so loud that they drown out the others. And sometimes, too, the needs of the agency come so much to the fore, that it is these needs rather than the needs of a service user *or* carer that become the loudest voice. Completing the assessment on time or in the correct format, for instance, may become the priority rather than getting a real understanding of the service user's needs. Broadhurst et al. (2010) describe exactly this dynamic in relation to 'Initial Assessments' in children's social care, as they apply in England and Wales. A similar dynamic exists in adult social care as a result of the Community Care (delayed discharges etc.) Act, 2003, which makes responsible local authorities liable to pay a financial penalty if a patient's discharge from hospital is delayed as a result of that authority not having completed an assessment and identified appropriate services. This creates a pressure which is in danger of over-riding the needs of individual service users and resulting in a premature and poorly planned discharge home, which may result in patients feeling 'unsupported, overwhelmed and unable to cope', with the risk of a deterioration in their medical condition which could result in further readmissions to hospital that could have been avoided (Glasby, 2003: 2).

Sometimes too there are strong pressures *not* to identify needs which the agency would then be required to meet, or could be criticised for not meeting, so that as well as heard needs and recognised needs, we may speak of needs which are seen as acknowledged or legitimated as against needs which are not. Social workers sometimes find themselves under pressure not to place on record needs which an agency cannot meet for resource reasons. It is something which is not infrequently encountered by students on placement.

And there may be other reasons, apart from resources, why an agency might find it hard to acknowledge what a service user sees as a need. A multiple sclerosis sufferer finds smoking cannabis is helpful for her condition, but is no longer able to roll up cannabis cigarettes for herself. She could argue that this is a real need, since the drug does indeed relieve symptoms which are distressing and disabling (Iskedjian et al., 2007), but a social care agency is unlikely to accept this as a need because cannabis is illegal and it cannot be seen to condone an illegal practice.

A young man with a physical disability once suggested to me that the local social care agency should provide him with assistance in obtaining the services of a prostitute in order to meet his sexual needs. These, to him, seemed more distressing and urgent than other needs which the agency was prepared to help with. Was this a demand that the agency was likely to meet? In the UK, the answer would be no, and of course (apart from any other consideration) the request does raise wider issues about the sex trade and the exploitation of women. Some might argue that many people, whether disabled or not, find it difficult to find sexual partners, and this is not a matter that social care agencies ought to be involved with. Others might argue that social care agencies *do* have a responsibility to help people like this young man meet their sexual needs but that the needs ought to be addressed in other ways, such as helping him meet women of his own age (like the Gavaghans in case example 6.2, he is actually asking for a specific service rather than identifying a need). But he is not alone in arguing that such services should indeed be provided (Croydon, 2009), and indeed they are, or have been, provided in other countries.

PLACEMENT QUESTIONS 6.2   WHAT COUNTS AS A NEED?

- When carrying out needs assessment, do workers at your placement agency feel free to record any need, regardless of whether or not the agency is likely to meet it, or is there an expectation that needs will not be identified unless the agency has a service to meet them? (If you are not sure about the answer to this question you could try asking those who work there.)
- Are there other pressures within the agency – to complete assessments quickly, or to come to particular conclusions – which might prevent a balanced picture of a service user's needs emerging? (In other words, to what extent do the agency's needs take priority over the needs of individual service users?)
- Whose voices seem the loudest in the process of negotiation that results in an assessment of need, and whose voices are least likely to be heard? Whose voices do you yourself find yourself hearing most, and whose do you have to work hard to hear at all?

THE POLITICS OF NEED

I have several times used the word 'negotiation' to describe needs assessment. What this highlights is the fact that needs assessment is a political process, involving a number of different participants with different amounts of power at their disposal. These participants include the primary service user, secondary service users such as parents and carers, you yourself as a social worker, other professionals, and the management hierarchy of your own agency. But they also include many forces that are not physically present, for questions about what needs should be met by the public provision of services and whether or not those needs are in fact being met, are intensely political matters. Their ramifications stretch away from your interview with a client in her living room out into the realms of local and national government, the media and society at large. The kinds of dynamics that I have described at an individual level – the fact that we tend to notice needs with which we can personally identify, for instance, or avoid noticing needs which make us uncomfortable or which place us in a difficult situation – apply at all these other levels too.

MET AND UNMET NEEDS

Many of the pressures I have described earlier in this chapter, the pressure not to recognise need or record need that cannot be met, the pressure to complete needs assessments quickly rather than thoroughly, can be traced back to the needs of the government of the day, which wishes to be seen to be meeting the needs of its citizens, because it knows that is what its citizens want from it. Arguably the very fact that so much discretion is given to agencies and individual workers to assess and prioritise needs, is part of this dynamic, since it distances government from the decisions being made on the ground, and from problems and shortcomings that occur. It has the result, even if we would rather it wasn't so, of making social workers seem very powerful to service users, since social workers are the gateway to services. But social workers do not necessarily feel powerful themselves, and the political process will often make them feel like they are being pulled in two directions at once. On the one hand they may be given the message that their task is to identify and meet need, and they may be sent on training courses (as I remember being sent myself) in which they are exhorted to be creative and imaginative and think outside the box. On the other hand they may receive messages that tell them they should not actually identify too much need at all. The contradiction itself is a consequence of the fact that, in politics, to be seen to be doing something is as important, and often more important, than actually doing it. Politics involves a kind of ritual in which 'a simplified model or semblance of reality is created, and facts that do not fit are screened out of it' (Edelman, 1985: 17). In the simplified model presented on the political stage, social workers identify people in need and meet those needs. Unmet needs are the facts that have to be screened out. And where they nevertheless come to the fore, the problem is likely to be presented as a local failure rather than a failure of the system as a whole.

DEPENDENCY AND THE MANUFACTURE OF NEED

Having discussed the ways in a political process can serve to conceal unmet need, I would like to balance this by offering some very tentative thoughts on an opposite process. It is possible to argue that a capitalist society, which seeks always to increase consumption, is in the business of manufacturing needs. Through marketing and advertising, a capitalist society is able to take things that we did not even know existed and turn them, first into things that we want and desire, then into things which we feel we need, and finally into things which we arguably really do need in the sense of 'relative need' as discussed above (personal computers and mobile phones would be good examples) because everyone else has them and not to have them would place us at a disadvantage. (Since this process is one of the things that is leading us towards environmental catastrophe, it may be that we need to learn to have less needs.) The idea of needs being artificially created in this way has been part of the Marxist critique of capitalism since Marx himself (see Dean, 2010: 33ff).

But this process of manufacturing needs surely extends beyond the marketing of desirable new consumer items like phones. I have already discussed eating disorders earlier in the chapter when I placed them among problems related to our needs and anxieties in relation to control. But it is possible to see eating disorders as being in part a result of manufactured 'needs': needs to consume, needs for women to have bodies like models and film stars. (For more on eating disorders as a product of cultural context, see Bordo [2003].) Is it possible that, in the same way, the high incidence of divorce and relationship breakdowns in industrialised countries could be part of a manufactured 'need' created by idealised depictions of couple love with which we are constantly bombarded?

A final question to consider about what I am calling 'manufactured needs' is whether any sort of equivalent process exists in the field of social work and social care, given that social care services now reach into areas of life which they would not have touched in the past? Are new needs being manufactured here also? Is it possible that some of the people who now contact social work offices feeling themselves to be badly in need of the help of social care services would in the past have solved their problems for themselves without feeling such a need, just as in the past they would have managed without a mobile phone?

CHAPTER SUMMARY

In this chapter, after noting the prevalence of the word 'need' in social work discourse generally, I looked first at need as a concept, introducing the ideas of 'absolute' and 'relative' needs. I then moved on to consider the meaning of 'need' in a specific social work context, and the considerable challenges involved in the process of identifying need. I looked at the ways in which people's expressed needs might be different from the needs which they felt, and the ways in which the latter might be different again from what they actually need, and I considered factors that might make people reluctant to speak of their needs. I then looked at the opposite side of the business of communicating needs: the factors which might shape what social workers recognised as needs, or acknowledged as being within the agency's brief to meet. I concluded with a few thoughts about the ways in which the political process and the dynamics of a capitalist society might on the one hand result in unmet need not being recognised, and on the other hand result in new needs being generated.

FURTHER READING

It is important when thinking about needs to think about the specific needs that might apply within the particular field in which you are working. (If writing about assessing the needs of adopted children, then you need to look at texts on adopted children. If writing about assessing the needs of parents with learning disability, then look at texts on this subject.) I will not attempt to offer reading suggestions for the many specialist areas. The following however is helpful on the concept of 'need' in the context of social work and social policy:

Dickens, J. (2010) 'Needs and rights', in J. Dickens, *Social Work and Social Policy: An Introduction.* London: Routledge, pp. 63–80.

The following book by a social policy academic provides a interesting and very comprehensive exploration of the whole concept of 'need', including the relationship of needs to rights. It also provides a glossary of terms used for different kinds of need:

Dean, H. (2010) *Understanding Human Need.* Bristol: Policy Press.

7 RISK

- Social work and the politics of risk
- Risk equals probability of harm
- Common confusions about probability
- Probability and thresholds: a model
- The necessity of risk
- Risk assessment and risk management

The words 'needs' and 'needs assessment' may be used a great deal in social work, but the words 'risk' and 'risk assessment' are surely at least as commonly used. In fact, the concepts of 'need' and 'risk' are closely intertwined, and are often defined in relation to one another, as is the case in guidance for adult social care which I referred to in the previous chapter: *Fair Access to Care Services* requires local authorities to determine priorities on a basis of the 'seriousness of the risk to independence or other consequences if needs are not addressed' (Department of Health, 2003: 4).

In the child and family field, social workers in England and Wales must decide whether to respond to new referrals under Section 17 of the 1989 Children Act (which deals with 'children in need') or under Section 47, which deals with a local authority's 'duty to investigate' when it has 'reasonable cause to suspect that a child who lives, or is found, in their area is suffering, or is likely to suffer, significant harm' (Children Act 1989, S47 (1b)). In other words, this section of the Act deals with the duty to investigate when a child is thought to be at risk. But since, as we saw in the last chapter, 'need' is also defined in terms of the likelihood of harm, the distinction between 'in need' and 'likely to suffer significant harm' is not a particularly precise one. And as I will discuss further shortly, 'likelihood of harm' is really what is meant by the word 'risk'. (In practice the distinction between cases dealt with under s17 and s47 relates to the acuteness and immediacy of risks, and to the kind of intervention that is indicated, with interventions under s47 being more coercive and adversarial.)

SOCIAL WORK AND THE POLITICS OF RISK

Many commentators on child and family social work argue that 'defensive practice' – or 'risk averse' practice – has resulted in practice becoming too narrowly focused on 'risk' (this was a theme for instance of *Messages from Research* [Department of Health, 2001]). What is really meant by this is that practice has become too preoccupied with *immediate acute risks*, such as the risk of physical abuse, which are more likely to be associated with calamitous consequences for the reputation of agencies, as against less spectacular long-term risks, such as those associated with poverty and social exclusion, which are rather less dramatic and newsworthy, and tend to provoke less public concern.

But there are other commentators (see, for example, Davies, 2008) who argue, on the contrary, that too much emphasis on supporting families has led to an insufficient focus, in policy guidelines, on the acute risks that some adults pose to the children in their care. Davies reports a private conversation between herself and Lisa Arthurworrey, one of the social workers involved in the case of Victoria Climbié, in which Arthurworrey said 'she was following the family support model of social work … Child protection was only for emergencies' (Davies, 2008: 24). Davies's concern is that too much emphasis on 'support' may get in the way of spotting serious abuse.

Debate about the correct balance to be struck between 'family support' and 'child protection' is not really a debate about whether we should focus on risk *per se*, though, but rather a debate about which *kinds* of risk we should focus on: the risks posed to children by their carers, or on the risks posed to families by their social circumstances. It is a debate that has been going on for more than a century (see Guterman [2001] for instance, on similar arguments in nineteenth-century America) and it reminds us of the intensely political and contested field in which social work is practised. A similar tension is present in the mental health field, where public concern often seems to focus on the risk posed to the general public by a minority of people with mental health problems, as opposed to the risks faced *by* people with mental health problems. (See Morris [2006] for more on the tendency of the news media to present people with mental illness as dangerous.)

But there are many other ways in which questions about risk impinge on social work. Social workers in the learning disability field are often involved in debates about the extent to which people with learning disabilities should be supported in taking the kinds of risks that other people are free to take. 'The right to take risks' is a phrase that is commonly used in this field (see for example Alaszewski and Alaszewski, 2002) and others. (Herring and Thom [1997] for instance, discuss the right of elderly people to engage in risky drinking behaviour if they want to.) All parents have to make decisions as to the extent they allow their children to engage in behaviour that carries significant risks (from playing football, to staying out late, to riding bicycles on busy roads) and social workers too have to engage with these questions, both in relation to their work with parents, and in situations where they themselves are involved in parental decision-making in relation to children in care for whom their agencies have parental responsibility.

PLACEMENT QUESTIONS 7.1   AGENCY'S ATTITUDE TO RISK

- What kinds of decisions about risk are typically made by your placement agency?
- What is your impression of the agency's approach to the management of risk?
- Does it strike you as risk averse (that is: prone to be wary of taking risks which perhaps it *should* take in the interests of service users), or does it seem to you to take *unnecessary* risks?
- What *kinds* of risks seem to be of most concern in your agency? Are there some risks that it seems to be preoccupied with at the expense of others?
- Inevitably agencies and their staff are concerned about risk to themselves as well as risk to service users: for example risks to their reputation or their careers, or the risk of litigation. What risks to itself does the agency seem to worry about?
- What issues arise about 'the right to take risks' of service users, and how are they dealt with by your placement agency?

RISK EQUALS PROBABILITY OF HARM

We will come back to these difficult questions about risk and risk-taking, but for the moment let us return to the notion of risk itself, for it is a concept which it is very easy to get confused about.

The idea of risk really includes two elements:

a   some form of harm,
b   the probability (which can also be called 'likelihood') of that harm occurring.

Judgements about risk are judgements about the *likelihood of harmful outcomes.* When we carry out a risk assessment of a situation we are looking at factors in that situation that could have harmful consequences, and we are making judgements about the severity of the harm that could be caused and the likelihood of it. (We should also be weighing up these risks against positive outcomes that might flow from the same set of circumstances, and often we should also be comparing this with the risks and benefits of alternative scenarios, but I will come back to this later.)

The fact that risk includes these two elements is the first cause of confusion. When we speak about something being a 'high-risk' activity or a 'low-risk' activity, do the words 'high' and 'low' refer to a high likelihood or to a high degree of harm? Usually they refer to both. We speak of something as high risk only when the harm that might occur is severe *and* the likelihood of it is relatively high. Travelling by rail can result in very serious harm, since train crashes are nasty and often involve fatalities, but train crashes are also very rare, so that we still describe train travel as low risk, in spite of the severity of the possible harm.

However we are not consistent about this. We may persist in seeing an activity as high-risk, if the harm that could result looms large in our mind for some reason, even if it is very unlikely, and we may persist in dismissing the risks of other activities which are actually more likely to cause harm. Many people are more afraid of air travel, for example, than of travel by car, even though the chance of a fatal accident is much lower in a plane. Some people who refuse to travel on aeroplanes nevertheless continue to smoke cigarettes, even though the latter activity is much more likely to have a fatal outcome, and the death involved is more likely to be a slow and unpleasant one.

This brings us to the second reason why we get confused about risk, which is that most of us find it difficult to grasp the idea of probability.

COMMON CONFUSIONS ABOUT PROBABILITY

If you have studied developmental psychology, you may remember the work of Jean Piaget, who proposed that, before they learned to reason as adults do, children went through the 'preoperational stage', in which their judgements were based on perception and hunches rather than logic (see Beckett and Taylor [2010], for a brief summary of the idea). A child at the preoperational stage, for instance, seeing water poured from a short fat container into a long tall container, may happily state that there is now more water, simply because it looks that way.

It seems to me that, even as adults, many of us are still in the preoperational stage when it comes to probability. We rely on hunches and perception rather than on logic. For example, if I am playing a dice game where it is desirable to throw a six and I get several sixes in a row, my rational head knows that the chances of my getting another six on my next throw remain the same as always (one in six, assuming that the dice is not loaded). But often there is a powerful irrational part of me that cannot help thinking 'I'm on a roll, I'm having a lucky streak, I bet the next throw will be a six as well,' while at other times I might think 'I've already had a row of sixes, no way will my next throw be a six'. Either way I am making the mistake of thinking that the rolls that have already occurred will, in some magical way, have an influence on a roll which has not yet happened. For more examples of this, consider all the various ways in which people persuade themselves they will somehow better their tiny odds of winning the national lottery.

In Chapter 5, I discussed the tendency of the human mind to look for certainty and jump to conclusions on insufficient evidence, and I discussed the factors which might cause this, some of which are cognitive (to do with the way we organise information) and some of which are emotional (to do with the way we manage feelings). Factors of both these kinds are in play when we think about risk. Risk of harm to children or vulnerable adults is a painful and anxiety-making subject. There is a lot of distress associated with it, and this may be aggravated by a climate in which social workers are sometimes publicly pilloried in very frightening and humiliating ways over cases where it is thought that mistakes have been made.

But there are also a number of 'cognitive illusions' associated with risk, ways in which we are predictably misled, regardless of any emotional factors, in just the same way as we are predictably misled by optical illusions because of the way in which 'our perceptual system automatically transforms uncertainty into certainty' (Gigerenzer, 2002: 9). The following are a few common errors that we make in our thinking about risk, all of which can result in dangerously misguided decisions being made.

THE HINDSIGHT FALLACY

I am about to throw five dice. How likely is it that every one of them will come up six?

You will probably agree with me that it is pretty unlikely. If you are mathematically inclined you may have worked out that the chance of this occurring is actually 1 in 7,776. (This is because there are five dice, each of which can come up in six different ways, which means that the total number of combinations is $6 \times 6 \times 6 \times 6 \times 6$.)

Now suppose that I go ahead and throw the dice and they *do* all come up as six. Does that mean that I was wrong in thinking that it was unlikely? No, of course not. I never said that it would not happen, I just said that it was very unlikely to happen. It is unlikely, *but it will sometimes happen*. In fact it will happen, on average, once out of every 7,776 throws.

In the same way, if you carry out a risk assessment as a social worker and you conclude that the likelihood of a particular negative outcome occurring is very low, but the negative outcome does subsequently occur, then it does not necessarily follow that you made a mistake or that your assessment was wrong. Unlikely events do still happen, and the fact that they happen does not prove we were wrong in thinking them unlikely. This is not always understood. If something bad happens, it is commonly assumed that someone *must* have made a mistake and that the judgements they made must have been wrong. This is called the hindsight fallacy because it results from the misconception that what can be seen after the event must have been possible to see before the event. When a child abuse tragedy is reported in the newspapers, this mistake is often made. It is now obvious to us, for instance, that if more time had been spent on the case of Victoria Climbié, she might quite easily have been saved from the dreadful fate that she in fact suffered. What is harder for us to see, looking back at this tragic story with our full knowledge of the outcome, is, that things would have looked very different before the outcome was known. Her case would only have been one of many cases with worrying elements, all of which would have been competing for the limited time of the various professionals. As I have put it elsewhere:

> It is difficult to hold in mind that if more time had been given to her – more time doing the things like making the phone calls and checking the records that we now know led to the failure of the system to recognise the severity of her situation – less time would have been available to other children whose names we don't even know. Without the benefit of hindsight these other children might well have appeared, even to a highly skilled observer, as every bit in need of attention as she was, given that there was limited information about all of them and given that gathering more information about any of them would in itself have required diversion of resources from elsewhere. (Beckett, 2008: 41)

In fact we really cannot tell whether or not a mistake was made if we look only at the particular case which, with the benefit of hindsight, we know to have had a tragic outcome. In order to determine whether a mistake was made we would need to look at all the other situations which the social workers concerned were also dealing with.

So the hindsight fallacy can result in social workers and managers being blamed and punished for decisions which turned out to have negative consequences, even if the decision was at the time a reasonable one. The trouble with this (apart, of course, from being unfair to those concerned) is that it allows us to deal with harmful events by attributing blame, rather than by trying to understand. Finding scapegoats to punish may serve the ritual purpose of assuaging the guilt of the rest of the community, but it does not necessarily result in a better service. A culture in which scapegoating is a prominent feature becomes fearful and defensive and may in the long run be less helpful for service users.

But the hindsight fallacy does not only result in social workers being unfairly judged. It can also sometimes have a negative impact on service users. Service users too are sometimes blamed by professionals for behaviour that had negative consequences, even if in fact those negative consequences were most unlikely. For example: a parent is criticised by professionals for leaving a child alone in a room for a short while, during which time the child incurred an injury, even though no one would have criticised the parent for exactly the same behaviour if the injury had not occurred.

BASE RATE FALLACY

Confusion about base rates (I will explain the term presently) can result in very serious misunderstandings. In order to explain this I will use an imaginary example. It is unrealistic in a number of ways, as will become apparent, but please ignore this for the purposes of the argument.

Suppose that you were a manager in a social work agency and you were debating whether or not to buy a new assessment instrument for use by your social workers. Let us call it the X Instrument. It has been developed as a tool for identifying families where there is a risk of fatal child abuse. How it works (let us imagine) is that social workers enter data about the family into a computer, using a standard questionnaire, and the X Instrument then informs them whether or not the family should be assigned to a 'Dangerous' group or a 'Safe' group.

Let us imagine that the X Instrument has been tested by reputable independent researchers. Details of several million families (this is one of the unrealistic parts!) were entered on the questionnaire, and each was duly assigned by the X Instrument to the 'Dangerous' or 'Safe' groups. For the purposes of this discussion, (and this is the other unrealistic part) please assume that no preventative action was taken in respect of families rated as Dangerous: events were allowed to take their course in all of the families, without outside interference. Researchers then checked out the families' subsequent histories from medical records and other sources. They compared these histories with the ratings given to each family by the X Instrument. The following, let us imagine, were the results:

- Of the families in the trial, some were subsequently involved in fatal child abuse. The independent researchers confirm that *100 per cent* of these families had been rated as 'Dangerous' by the X Instrument. No family which was subsequently involved in fatal child abuse was rated as 'Safe'.
- Of the families who were *not* subsequently involved in fatal child abuse, 99 per cent had been rated as 'Safe' by the X Instrument. Just 1 per cent of these families (families where fatal child abuse did not occur) had been rated by the Instrument as 'Dangerous'.

Assume for the sake of this discussion that these claims are true. The implications are that, if you used the X Instrument to place new families above or below a fatal abuse threshold, it would accurately place above the threshold *every single one* of the five families per million or so where children would die without protective intervention. If you were the manager deciding whether to buy the X instrument, what would you do?

Many managers, I suspect, would be persuaded to buy the X Instrument for a considerable sum, believing that it would allow them to pinpoint all the families where fatal child abuse would otherwise occur. Possibly you also came to this conclusion? But if this were so, you would be wrong. The Instrument would *not* allow you to pinpoint those families in any meaningful sense. It is true that in every million families, the Instrument would correctly identify as 'Dangerous' the five or so where fatal child abuse would take place without intervention. But it is also true that these families would be hidden, like a needle in a haystack, among some *ten thousand* others. This is because, with something as rare as fatal child abuse, the apparently low 1 per cent of families who were assigned to the 'Dangerous' group, but did not go on to be involved in fatal abuse, is sufficiently numerous to completely swamp the accurate predictions, because it is 1 per cent *of a million*.

The 'base rate' (also known as 'prevalence') is the incidence in the general population of the problem in question (in this particular case fatal child abuse, for which I have offered a rough base rate of five per million). The base rate fallacy is to fail to take the base rate into account when interpreting the kind of percentages I cited earlier. One hundred per cent *sounds* more than 1 per cent, but in this case it was 100 per cent of five families and 1 per cent of a million families, and the latter is in fact a much larger number.

One problem caused by the base rate fallacy is that, just like the hindsight fallacy, it can make decisions about risk look like incompetent blunders when in fact they are not. If you pick any well-publicised case where a child has died at the hands of his or her carers and compare the circumstances of the family in question with an average family, the differences do indeed seem obvious, but it is a mistake to think that an ability to distinguish these families from average families is where the problem lies. Yes, it is often not very difficult to distinguish families where there are many problems and risk factors from families where there are not, and generally speaking social workers are not failing in that regard. But that is only a preliminary stage in the judgements that child protection professionals have to make. They then have to do something much more difficult, which is the very thing that Instrument X completely failed to do, in spite of its superficial attractions. The difficult part is to decide which families to focus on *within* the large number of families in which there are obvious risk factors (that is: within a group of families all of which, with the benefit of hindsight, would look like ones that ought to have been picked!). The general public, politicians, the media, and social workers themselves, often completely fail to understand this, not only in respect to child protection but also in respect of other risks (such as those posed to the general public by a small minority of people with mental health problems). The result is that social workers and their professional colleagues operate in a climate of completely unrealistic expectations.

So the base rate fallacy can result in a fundamental misunderstanding about the nature of decisions being made by social workers and others assessing risks. But the base rate fallacy can also cause errors of judgement about risk on the part of individual social workers, who fail to understand the nature of 'risk factors'. Suppose you were informed that one of your clients had a profile that placed him in a high-risk category for suicide. Or suppose that you were working with a lone single mother aged 17 who grew up in care and you discovered that being a lone mother, being a young parent and growing up in care were all risk factors in fatal child abuse (Greenland, 1987). It is important to understand that being in a high-risk group for suicide or fatal child abuse does not mean that the individual concerned is necessarily at all likely to commit suicide, or kill her children, only that she belongs to a group that has a higher incidence of these behaviours than is the case in the population at large. To give a non-social work example, young men have to pay high car insurance premiums because they are in a high-risk group with respect to car accidents, but this does not mean that any given young man is very likely to have a car accident. It just means that he belongs to a group of drivers which is more likely to have accidents than drivers taken as a whole.

THE PROSECUTOR'S FALLACY

Joe is a street cleaner with no educational qualifications. He comes from a poor family, as does his wife, and they support their family on wages that are only a little above the national minimum. Every week, without fail, Joe buys a single national lottery ticket. How likely is he to win the jackpot? The answer of course is that it is extremely unlikely. I believe that in the case of the UK national lottery the chance of picking the winning numbers in any given week is something like 1 in 14,000,000.

One Thursday morning, only two days after seeing Joe in the street, and hearing from him about his financial worries, you are surprised to see him driving by in a gold-plated Rolls-Royce with his wife beside him in a diamond tiara. What are the chances that he has won the lottery this week? If you were to say 'still 1 in 14,000,000' then you have fallen for the 'prosecutor's fallacy'. It is quite true that if he were to buy a lottery ticket now his chances of winning would indeed be the same as ever, but that is not the question here. Joe and his wife suddenly becoming fabulously rich overnight was an extremely unlikely thing to happen, but it *has now* happened. What possible explanations are there? Winning the lottery may well be one of the most likely.

A real-life example of the prosecutor's fallacy comes from the tragic case of Sally Clark, who lost two children and maintained that they had been victims of sudden infant death syndrome ('SIDS', also known as 'cot death'). She was however convicted of murdering them, partly on the basis of expert evidence from an eminent paediatrician that the chances of two children dying in the same family were so minute that this possibility could effectively be discounted. (After serving three years in prison, she successfully appealed against her conviction and was released, but died a few years later, still in her forties.) Ben Goldacre explains the fallacy of the argument used to convict her as follows:

> Two babies in one family have died. This in itself is very rare. Once this rare event has occurred, the jury needs to weigh up two competing explanations: double Sids or double murder. Under normal circumstances – before any babies have died – double Sids is very unlikely, and so is double murder. But now that the rare event of two babies dying in one family has occurred, the two explanations are suddenly both very likely. (Goldacre, 2006)

In other words, when a very rare event has occurred, whether it is a street cleaner suddenly acquiring a Rolls-Royce, or a tragic event such as the death of two babies, then whatever caused that event is *also* going to be something that happens very rarely. Those who prosecuted Sally Clark needed to prove, not that double SIDS is in general very unlikely, but that it was far less likely to have occurred *in this particular case* than child murder. As the case illustrates, failing to understand this has the potential to lead to very serious mistakes being made in the child protection field.

PROBABILITY AND THRESHOLDS: A MODEL

The errors I have been discussing are all connected by a basic confusion about the nature of an assessment of risk. When we assess the risks in a given situation we are coming to an informed judgement about the *likelihood* of an event happening. That is *not* the same thing as determining for certain whether or not it *will* happen. The fact that young men are regarded by insurance companies as a high risk for car accidents is the result of calculations carried out by professionals called actuaries using data about accidents that have actually occurred. Young men really *are* a high-risk group for car accidents. But this does not mean that all young men will have car accidents, or even that most of them will, and it does not mean that people in low-risk groups will have no car accidents. It just means that young men, taken overall, are more likely to have car accidents than people in other groups.

By the same token, some groups can be shown to have a higher risk of suicide, or a higher risk of offending, or a higher risk of causing the deaths of their children, but that does not mean that they will do these things, or even necessarily that they are likely to do these things, only that they are more likely to commit suicide, or offend, or harm children (or whatever else is being looked at), than other members of the population.

Your placement agency will come to judgements that some individuals or families should be seen as being at high risk (in relation to some form of harm that you are trying to avoid), or posing a high risk to others. Other individuals or families you will assign to low-risk groups. The kind of intervention that will be delivered, and often whether a service is delivered at all, will depend in part on these judgements. Typically agencies will have risk thresholds at which a service is initiated, and then thresholds for different levels of service. See *Fair Access to Care Services*, cited earlier, which sets out just such a framework for adult care services. (Other thresholds) will include the threshold at which a person is detained under mental health legislation, the threshold at which a child is made subject to a child protection plan or the threshold at which children are taken into public care.

If you assign an individual to a low-risk category when in fact the evidence available to you should be sufficient for you to assign them to a high-risk category, then this is a mistake on your part for which you could, quite justly, be criticised. But, as we have discussed, even if you do *not* make a mistake of this kind and quite correctly assign an individual to a high-risk or low-risk group, things may still come out the wrong way, because you were making a judgement about the likelihood of harmful events and not about what would actually happen.

I have developed a simplified way of representing the situation diagrammatically (see Beckett [2008] for a more detailed account). Figure 7.1 represents a group of individuals or families who have been rated for risk in relation to some undesirable outcome (suicide, falling and hurting themselves … for the purposes of this discussion it does not matter, so choose whatever

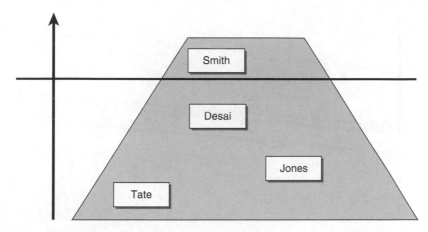

Figure 7.1   A risk threshold

you like). The vertical arrow represents the dimension of risk, with high risk at the top and low risk at the bottom. The horizontal line represents the threshold at which the agency involved assigns people to a high-risk group (it might be the threshold at which a certain service is provided, or the threshold at which certain steps are taken, such as compulsory detention under mental health legislation). Smith is above the threshold, the others are below.

In Figure 7.2 below, I imagine, for the sake of argument, that we can look forward into the future and see whether or not the undesirable outcome will actually occur. The band marked 'event happens' is narrow at the bottom of the pyramid because that is the low-risk end, where the likelihood of the event happening has been judged small compared to the likelihood of the event not happening. It is broad at the top of the pyramid because here, at the high-risk end, the likelihood of it happening has been deemed to be higher. The proportion of the pyramid's width that is taken up by the 'event happens' band gets greater as we go up the pyramid because that is what we mean by higher risk: we mean increasing the likelihood of an undesirable event happening.

Finally, in Figure 7.3 I have put the threshold back into the diagram. What we see now is that above the line, in the high-risk category, there are two groups: one where the event will happen, the other where it will not, even if there is no intervention. The first group are known as 'true positives', the second are known as 'false positives'. If we were talking about a high risk for, say, falling at home and sustaining a serious injury requiring hospitalisation, the true positives would be those identified as being at high risk of such an accident who did in fact have one, while the false positives would be those who were also identified as at high risk but did not in fact have an accident, and would not have had one even if there was no intervention. Below the line, in the low-risk group, we have 'true negatives', where the event deemed unlikely for this group will indeed not occur (they were not judged likely to fall and injure themselves, and they do not do so) and another smaller group marked 'false negatives', where the event, though deemed unlikely, does nevertheless occur (they were not deemed likely to injure themselves, yet in fact they do).

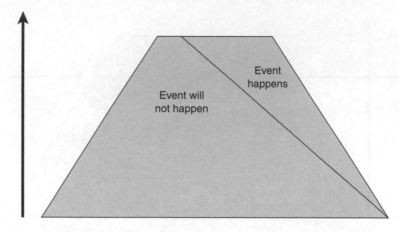

Figure 7.2   Looking into the future

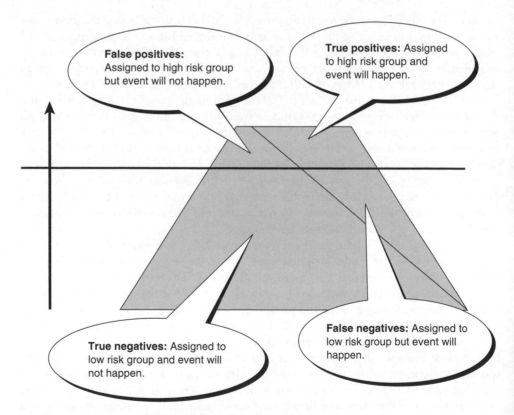

Figure 7.3   True and false positives and negatives

One thing you may notice is that if the threshold were to be moved upwards you would get more false negatives and less false positives. If it were to be moved down, you would get more false positives and less false negatives. In the various fields within which social work operates, and notably in the field of child and family work, thresholds are prone to move up and down in response to society's current concerns. For example, following publicity about a child abuse tragedy in which a child dies at the hands of his or her family, there is typically concern about social workers and other professionals being too naïve and trusting and failing to notice signs of abuse. As a result the threshold at which children are removed into public care tends to move down: more children are taken into care. At other times concerns about excessive interference into family life come to the fore. (This occurred, for instance, following the Cleveland crisis in 1987.) These concerns may result in thresholds being moved upwards. Thresholds tend to be moved, whether up or down, in the name of avoiding errors. The point I wish to make here is that, in conditions of uncertainty where we are dealing with probabilities rather than exact predictions, we cannot eliminate error. We can decrease one kind of error, but only at the cost of increasing another kind of error.

Another point I would like to make about false positives and false negatives is this. True and false negatives are typically easier to spot than true and false positives, because if you choose to place someone in a high-risk category and act to prevent the harmful event occurring, you will never know whether or not that event would have occurred if you had not acted. If you detain someone in a mental hospital, for instance, in the belief that they are likely to harm themselves or others if left in the community, you cannot know whether in fact they would have harmed someone if you did not act. As a result it is often harder to get accurate feedback as to the reliability of our decisions to assign people to a category which triggers intrusive action, then it is to gain feedback about our decisions *not* to assign people to such a category. Does this lack of symmetry between the visibility of false negatives and the lack of visibility of false positives carry a danger of making us more concerned about false negatives than false positives? Given that intrusive interventions such as detaining people under mental health legislation, or removing children into care, can have very serious consequences indeed, this would be worrying.

Before moving on from this model, I will briefly return to the fictional example of the 'X instrument' discussed above. You will remember that it correctly assigned all families where fatal abuse would occur to the 'Dangerous' category, so it generated no false negatives at all, but that unfortunately, the false positives it generated had the effect of completely swamping the true positives. This situation is very roughly represented in Figure 7.4, though in fact the size of the true positive group vis-à-vis the false positives is still represented in the diagram as being larger than it really would be on the basis of the figures in the example, and the size of the true negative group is *far* too small vis-à-vis the positives.

THE NECESSITY OF RISK

But now I want to look at risk in a different and more positive way. Many of the activities which people find the most fulfilling in life include a significant element of risk. All sports, for

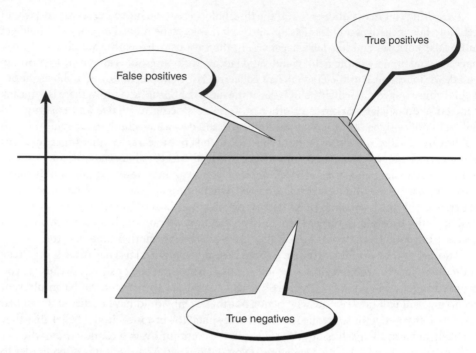

Figure 7.4 True positives swamped by false negatives

instance, contain risks. (Gordon Brown, the former Prime Minister of the UK, provides an example here: he is blind in one eye as the result of a rugby incident.) Many people find facing a degree of danger to be exhilarating and life enhancing (think of mountaineers and people who sail solo round the world), and are willing to set these benefits against the possibility of a harmful or even fatal outcome. Life would be dull and flavourless if no one was willing to take risks. And of course even ordinary everyday life involves risk-taking. We run risks when we go up and down stairs, use knives or electrical appliances, cross the street, or travel by car or public transport.

What is more, we may actually create new risks, if we try too much to avoid taking risks. Being 'risk averse' itself carries dangers. Tim Gill (2007) persuasively argues, for instance, that in our desire to protect children from the kinds of risks that are found in the outside world (accidents, 'stranger danger', and so on) we may actually be putting them at more risk in other ways. Children perhaps need to be exposed to *some* degree of risk in order to learn how to manage risk at all, rather in the way that we need to be exposed to germs in order to be able to develop resistance to them. Most parents recognise this. They do not try to protect their children against any risk, but rather try to pace their children's exposure to risk.

It can be argued too that 'children have an appetite for risk-taking that, if not fed somehow, will lead them to seek out situations in which they may be exposed to greater risks' (Gill, 2007: 16). Perhaps over-protected children, who have not been given any opportunities for adventure (and it is hard to imagine an adventure with no risks!) will end up engaging in activities that are more dangerous than those that they have been protected from?

Even if they do not go out and seek other kinds of adventure, over-protected children may perhaps become vulnerable to other forms of harm. Is obesity not likely to become more of a problem, for instance, if parents are reluctant to let their children play outside or engage in vigorous sports? Could boredom, and a sense of not ever having successfully dealt with a challenge, lead to lower self-esteem, apathy, depression? Is it possible that children 'build their character and personality through facing up to adverse circumstances where they know there is the possibility of injury or loss' (Gill, 2007: 16)?

Although Gill is talking specifically about children, exactly these same kinds of issue arise in work with vulnerable adults. If risk-taking has benefits, then surely these benefits should not be denied to people with learning disabilities, or frail elderly people, simply on the grounds that risk-taking does sometimes have harmful outcomes (for that is what risk-taking *means*!). As I will now discuss, risk management must entail looking at the benefits of acting in certain way, as well as the potential harm.

RISK ASSESSMENT AND RISK MANAGEMENT

We need to be aware that there are really two quite distinct kinds of risk assessment that are carried out in social work with the aim of managing risks in the best way possible. For the purpose of this discussion, I will call them 'Single-context risk assessments' and 'Multi-context risk assessments'. As I will explain, I think the distinction is not always understood and sometimes people believe they are making a single-context risk assessment when in fact they should be doing a multi-context one.

SINGLE-CONTEXT RISK ASSESSMENTS

Suppose that you are going to make a long car journey on your own to the far side of the country. You are aware that there are some risks involved and you spend a bit of time thinking about those risks and trying to minimise them. You might make up your mind to get a good night's sleep before the journey. You might check the route and memorise the various turnings you would have to take, in order to avoid having to try to consult the map while driving. You might check the tyre pressure. This is a single-context assessment in the sense that you have already made up your mind what you are going to do. You are simply thinking about the risks that are present within this single context and trying to minimise them.

There are many examples of single-context assessments that you might undertake in a social work capacity:

- You are arranging an annual visit to a seaside resort for a group of people with severe learning disabilities. You think about the needs and vulnerabilities of the individuals concerned. You identify ways in which they might be at risk in the context of the trip (John has no traffic sense and may step out into the road; Gill is prone to be inappropriate and over-friendly with strangers and could face a hurtful hostile response; Peter is prone to wander off and could get lost; Suzie cannot swim but loves going out into the sea ...). You find means of minimising those risks (John will have a member of staff assigned to him on a one-to-basis while in the streets of the town; some work will be done with Gill about how to talk to people ... and so on).

- You are carrying out a home visit with an elderly woman, who is to be discharged from a hospital where she was admitted following a bad fall. You look with her at the times during the day when she might be most in danger of a similar injury. You also look at possible hazards in the layout of the house. You consider possible ways of changing her daily routine and the layout of the house so as to minimise the risk of further falls. In addition you consider aids and adaptations that might help.
- You are looking over the house of a couple who want to become foster-parents. Is there anything that needs to change in order to make it safe for small children? You might identify a need for a stair gate, or a fireguard, or childproof locks, or perhaps a cover over the garden pond.

These assessments could be represented by a table with two columns. In the first column you list possible sources of risk, in the second column you list ways in which you are going to reduce or eliminate those risks. Often your agency will have checklists that you can use to avoid you having to 'reinvent the wheel'.

MULTI-CONTEXT RISK ASSESSMENTS

If you were planning to travel to the far side of the country but you had not yet decided how to get there, you might, if you were worried about the risks of travel, make a multi-context risk assessment. You might consider the risks entailed in travelling by car, and compare these with the risks involved in making the journey by train, bus or plane. But of course the risks would not be your only consideration. You would be looking at the benefits of each alternative too, and balancing these against the drawbacks. A multi-context risk assessment is one in which you are not just looking at the risks of a given course of action and trying to minimise them, but are (a) weighing those risks against the benefits of that course of action, and then (b) weighing both the risks and benefits of that course of action against the risks and benefits of one or more other courses of action, as represented by Table 7.1.

Table 7.1   Multi-context risk assessment

	No Intervention	Intervention A	Intervention B
Possible harm			
Likelihood of harm			
Possible benefits			
Likelihood of benefits			

Case example 7.1   Balancing the risks of different care options for Danny

Danny came into care at the age of 4 following serious and prolonged physical and sexual abuse by his mother and stepfather, with whom he now has no contact. His experiences have affected him profoundly and his behaviour can be challenging and difficult to manage. He was placed initially with short-term foster-parents, and care proceedings were initiated. However they found him impossible to cope with, as did the second set of carers he was moved to. In the case of the second set of carers he had to be moved very quickly with no time for preparation. By the time care proceedings were completed, soon after his fifth birthday, he had experienced three different foster-homes. The care plan was for him to be placed with an adoptive family. Preparatory work was done with Danny, and a suitable adoptive family was sought for him. This took almost a year, taking him to his sixth birthday, by which time he had had to be moved to another set of short-term foster-carers, his fourth.

His placement with his adoptive family seemed to be going very well for six months. However at this point the adoptive parents suddenly announced that they felt unable to go through with the adoption. They said that they had been struggling for some time with the fact that they simply did not know how to love Danny. They did not think it was fair, either to themselves or to him, to go ahead with an adoption.

Danny was moved back temporarily to his previous set of foster-carers, the Thompsons, to give time for other long-term plans to be made. Imagine that you now take on the case as social worker. At this point he has been with the Thompsons for 10 months, and while efforts continue to be made to identify a permanent family for him, these have not so far been successful. The Thompsons had only ever taken him in as a short-term arrangement. They are both in their late fifties and had been making plans for retirement, when they had been looking forward to doing some travelling (something they both enjoy but had never had much time for). However they have grown fond of Danny, and are very concerned about unsettling him with a further move, and, though they do have some anxieties about how they will cope with him when he is a teenager, they have indicated that they would be willing to provide a permanent home for him. Danny seems to have grown more attached to them than any of his other carers and says he wants to stay with them. He is now approaching 7 and a half. Mr Thompson is 59, Mrs Thompson 58. Mr Thompson has been treated for a heart condition. The Thompsons are experienced short-term foster-parents, who have cared for many primary-school aged children, but never teenagers.

Should Danny remain with the Thompsons? Or should the agency increase its efforts to find another permanent placement for him?

COMMENTS

There are a number of risks in Danny remaining with the Thompsons. Their age and Mr Thompson's health suggest that there is a real chance that they may find it difficult to cope with the demands of caring for Danny through to adulthood. They also have no experience of fostering children in the teenage years, when a child with Danny's history is likely to present them with a lot of challenges. The fact that they have not chosen to foster teenagers before may also suggest that they may not feel confident about their abilities in this area (some people are good with little children but not so good with teenagers). I would also have some concerns about the fact that their offer to provide a permanent home for Danny may be being made with some reservations. They had not planned to carrying on fostering past retirement age and had been looking forward to a different and more relaxing scenario. Will this lead to resentment later? It is not hard to imagine a scenario in which they simply would not feel able to cope with him any more.

Yet there are obvious benefits too: continuity, the fact that there is affection on both sides, the fact that by remaining with them, Danny would avoid yet *another* move, after so many.

And what are the other alternatives? Are there other carers available for him? If not how long would he be likely to have to wait, and what would be the effect on him of another long wait, knowing that he was going to have to move again but not knowing when. How likely is it that another placement would not work out, as the previous one did not, so that Danny might experience a further wait, a move, and then yet another breakdown?

In such a situation you would need to explore very carefully the risks and benefits not only of the current situation but also of whatever alternative plans were realistic possibilities, tracking the implications of each, identifying possible advantages and difficulties and considering whether anything could be done to reduce the difficulties that each option presented. (Placement is after all only part of any plan. There are other kinds of service that could be built in as well, such as therapeutic work with Danny, additional support for carers, respite and so on.) This is emphatically a situation which requires a multi-context risk assessment. There is no risk-free option, and you are therefore not simply identifying and minimising risks but also weighing up risks and benefits.

CONFUSION ABOUT THE TYPE OF RISK ASSESSMENT

Suppose you have been having a problem with your health. Doctors have carried out various tests and examinations and they inform you that you have a condition which is likely to reduce your life expectancy and have increasing negative consequences for your general health. However the good news, the doctors tell you, is that there is a surgical procedure that will fix the problem.

This is being presented to you as a single-context risk assessment. The doctors have assessed the risks posed to you by your current condition and they have offered surgery as a way of reducing, or indeed eliminating those risks. The reality, though, is that any surgical intervention carries significant risks of its own, including a risk of fatality which, in the cases of some of the more intrusive surgical procedures, such as transplants, can be quite high. And surgery may not always solve the problem itself, or it may create new problems.

This means that the doctors should not have presented this to you as a single-context assessment at all, because surgery is not simply a way of reducing the risks in your present situation. It is something that creates a whole new context which carries risks, possibly quite considerable ones, in its own right. This is not always clearly explained by doctors. As Gerd Gigerenzer observes, 'many a physician confronts the patient with an apparent choice between *certainty* and *risk* rather than a choice between risks. Each alternative carries its own uncertain consequences, which need to be compared for an informed decision to be made' (Gigerenzer, 2002: 99).

There are many interventions carried out by social workers which, in a similar way, reduce one kind of risk while introducing new risks of their own, but this is not always acknowledged. I have sometimes encountered professionals in a child protection context who argued that a child should be removed from a family situation where there were some risks, because 'it is better to be safe than sorry'. Often it is non-social workers who will argue in this way, possibly because they are not as aware as social workers tend to be that being

Table 7.2   Unbalanced multi-context risk assessment

	Plan A	Plan B
Possible harm	▓▓▓▓▓▓	
Likelihood of harm	▓▓▓▓▓▓	
Possible benefits		▓▓▓▓▓▓
Likelihood of benefits		▓▓▓▓▓▓

Shaded boxes = areas being focused on
White boxes = areas being overlooked

in care carries its own risks. Some children are actually abused in care, others find it impossible to settle. Some fail to form attachments and end up going from one disrupted placement to another, with each one feeling like a new rejection, a new confirmation of worthlessness. Some simply cannot accept the separation from their own parents, however flawed their parents' care may have been. To look only at the benefits of taking children into care, and at the harm that might result from not doing so, is to miss out half the picture. It is not a fair comparison and will of course make taking children into care seem more attractive as an option. Table 7.2 represents this kind of unbalanced risk assessment, where the benefits of one option are compared with the risks of another option.

In the same way, people will sometimes argue that an old person should be 'made' to go into a residential home, even if she clearly states that she does not want to go, on the basis that it will be safer and she will receive better care there (see case example 6.1 in the previous chapter). Such demands do not always take into account the mental distress that independent old people often feel on giving up their own homes, and the deterioration in their mental, and even physical, state that can follow. When people are at some risk at home, whether they are children or vulnerable adults, removal from that home is not simply a method of reducing the risk in their present context, it is also a whole new context, with its own set of risks and benefits.

In such situations all of the available options carry risks as well as benefits. Indeed as we have seen it is impossible to avoid risk altogether, and often necessary to take a risk in order to obtain a benefit. So to decide the best course of action, we need to assess not only the risks but also the benefits of leaving things as they are, and we need to test each of the available alternative courses of action in exactly the same way, identifying the risks and benefits and then using these to make a choice.

Often of course this will not be our choice but our client's – our job is simply to ensure that he or she has the information needed to make it – but in some cases, where children are involved, or adults with a limited mental capacity, then we will have a key role in making the choice itself. In these situations, there may be a variety of pressures on us that might make us prone either to intervene too hastily or not to intervene hastily enough. We may be under pressure to do something quickly, or under pressure to back off. Cognitive dissonance and attribution bias (see Chapter 5) may give us an unrealistically optimistic view of the likely success of our own interventions; self-doubt may give us an unrealistically pessimistic view. A flavour of the pressures that exist in real-life situations is offered by the following personal account of a social worker's experience of 'sectioning' a middle-aged black woman (that is: having her compulsorily detained under mental health legislation) in spite of his own reservations:

> My strong suspicion was that this was not about mental illness, but about Mary's social and cultural situation … [and] it was my objective to give her the time to slowly resolve her 'crisis' in her own way. This type of crisis resolution work can be time consuming and for the other people engaged in the assessment, very frustrating. Also spending hours with a very disturbed person can be incredibly challenging and stressful … All of this in a time frame which although in principle can last for several days, in practice will only be given at best several hours. Despite my best efforts Mary showed no signs of 'coming down' from her heightened state of anxiety. I was unable to contact other family members or identify Mary's friends who may have been able to help. Now it was into the early afternoon and literally everybody, including Mary, was becoming increasingly frustrated and angry with me. Much to my regret, and yet another assessment from which the feelings of inadequacy haunted me for several days, I was unable to come to any alternative arrangement other than hospitalisation and Mary was placed on a Section 2 of the Mental Health Act 1983. (Kinney, 2009: 333–334)

These sorts of pressures make it even more important that we weigh up the risks and benefits of the various options in as systematic a way as we can manage. Risk assessment is not just a matter of identifying risks and eliminating them. We and our service users also have to live with risk if we are to live at all. We and they, and sometimes we *on their behalf*, cannot prevent all harmful outcomes, we can only hope to balance the risks and benefits in as realistic a way as possible.

PLACEMENT QUESTIONS 7.2   FLAWS IN THINKING ABOUT RISK

Having looked at the various ways in which our thinking about risk can be confused, or one-sided, consider your placement agency's practice again.

It is possible you may actually be able to spot instances of, say, the hindsight fallacy or the base-rate fallacy. But if not you could ask yourself questions such was 'how would the hindsight fallacy manifest itself in this context?' or 'what would the base-rate fallacy look like if it occurred here?'

Would you say your agency's practice in relation to risk management is balanced? Does it weigh up both the potential harm and potential benefits of the various options available? Or does it tend to weigh the hoped-for benefits of one option against the feared harmfulness of another?

CHAPTER SUMMARY

After discussing the debates about risk that take place in and around social work, I defined risk in terms of probability and harm and then went on to look at the ways in which we often get confused about probability. I then offered a simplified way of looking at the kinds of judgements we make about risks before moving on to note the positive aspects of risk-taking, and in fact the inevitability of risk-taking. Finally I discussed the principles involved in making a balanced risk assessment.

FURTHER READING

As was the case with 'harm', it is important when thinking about risk, you look at the specific issues in relation to the specific area in which you are working. The risk posed by sexual offenders, to give an instance, cannot be assessed just by using general principles, but must be informed by an awareness of the particular nature of that kind of behaviour. However the following book, while not that recent, is an excellent introduction to the issues involved in risk assessment across a whole range of different areas:

Parsloe, P. (ed.) (1999) *Risk Assessment in Social Care and Social Work*. London: Jessica Kingsley.

For those interested in thinking about risk and the ways in which we get confused about it, Gerd Gigerenzer's short book is recommended:

Gigerenzer, G. (2002) *Reckoning with Risk*. London: Penguin.

8 CHANGE

- Internal and external change
- Enforced and chosen change
- A change-conducive environment
- Power, empowerment and change
- Surface versus depth
- Resistance
- The cycle of change

Promoting or helping with change is, one would like to think, the point of social work (in other words the point is 'making a difference', which is what many social work students describe as their reason for going into this area of work). If it is to be called successful, a social work intervention must surely help bring about a positive change, prevent negative change, or, at the very minimum, help people to cope better with negative change which cannot be avoided (as might be the case, for instance, when working with people with terminal illness, when we may try to help people change the way they manage the illness, even if we can do nothing about the illness itself). Interventions which bring about no change, or negative change, as would happen, for instance, if the overall effect of an intervention was to undermine someone's confidence, are of course useless, or worse than useless, at least from the point of view of those they are supposed to benefit. (I add this last caveat because in reality there may be other beneficiaries: politicians who want to be able to demonstrate that 'something is being done' about a troubling social problem, members of the public who feel relieved to be able to leave their worries about their neighbours for someone else to deal with, and not least we ourselves, for whom social work provides a living. But I am making an assumption that social work which *only* served these other beneficiaries would not be seen by anyone as having very much real value.)

Hugely ambitious goals are given to social work by society, and by social workers themselves, in terms of the kinds of changes that it is supposed to bring about. Social workers are involved in trying to deflect people from offending and from substance abuse. They are involved in trying to help seriously mistreated children form new secure attachments, and help adults to cope with profound disabilities and mental health problems. They are involved in trying, often within very short periods of time, to change harmful patterns of parenting that may have a history that goes back for generations. (And all that is still not enough for those many writers on social work who urge the profession to transform the structure of society itself.)

It is all rather more easily said than done. Bringing about change of *some* kind in people's lives is not all that difficult, but it is much harder to know how to bring about *positive* changes and avoid negative ones. We need to think carefully about the ways we try to achieve change, and indeed at whether it is always wise to attempt it.

Case example 8.1   Deflecting Paul from offending

Paul is a 15-year-old who has been placed on a supervision order for several offences related to stealing cars and driving them dangerously (joy-riding). You are a member of a Youth Offending Team, and his case has been assigned to you. Your primary task is to try to deflect him from offending behaviour. What do you think you might usefully do now, both in terms of assessment and intervention, that would help to achieve this?

COMMENTS

Approaches akin to cognitive behavioural therapy are often used in the context of working with offenders. If you chose such an approach it would be a case of talking with Paul about the details of his offending behaviour, when it occurred, what triggered it, what was it that felt rewarding to him about it, and then working with him on recognising the trigger situations for offending in advance and finding other ways of behaving in such situations, so as to avoid going down the offending path.

It may occur to you, though, that such an approach would need to presuppose a certain amount of commitment on Paul's part to change. Paul did not choose to work with you, after all. (He is your supervisee whether he wants to be or not.) People are only likely to want to work on strategies to change their behaviour once they have decided that changing their behaviour is indeed a desirable objective. (You are not likely to go on a diet, for instance, if you are not worried about either your figure or your health: this is something I'll come back to later in the chapter when I talk about the stages of change:). For these kinds of reasons, Paul's feeling about his offending behaviour and his interest (if any) in changing it, are important questions that your assessment would need to address before you decide on your method of intervention. As I said in Chapter 3, the purpose of an assessment is to enable us to discriminate between one person and another, in order to deliver a service that is appropriate to the particular person in question, rather than a one-size-fits-all service which may be useful to some people but almost certainly won't be to others. A good assessment does not just identify areas where change might be desirable, it also looks at the resources of the person concerned and their current motivation and capacity for change.

In the event that Paul had little or no real desire to change his offending behaviour, there are several different angles that might be considered. You might think of trying some sort of conscious-raising approach, aimed at increasing Paul's awareness of the negative consequences of his actions, whether in terms of likely road accidents or in terms of increasingly unpleasant legal sanctions. (In a similar way, public health campaigns try to increase people's motivation to give up smoking or eat a healthy diet by confronting them with the consequences of not doing so.) But young people are often resistant to such messages (I can remember myself as a teenager leaving a luridly illustrated lecture on the health consequences of smoking, and promptly lighting up) and it could be that this approach will also not 'cut much ice' with Paul.

Another alternative might be not to focus on the offending behaviour at all, but to seek to address other areas in Paul's life that might be connected with his offending. Identifying what those other areas are would be something else that you would want to address in your assessment, but a couple of possibilities that occur to me are these:

a   Suppose that you discover that he is very bored. He hates school, perhaps. He is disruptive in classes because he has no idea what the teachers are talking about. He has no outside interests, and there are few affordable facilities for young people in the area where he lives. He has nothing going on his life to stimulate or challenge him, or to give him a sense of achievement. You might hypothesise that his joy-riding has been a way of filling that gap. You might concentrate your efforts on finding him alternative stimulating activities to get involved in, and perhaps getting him additional help at school

b   Alternatively you might discover that he is full of anger. Perhaps his father has left the family for a new partner and only keeps spasmodically in contact with him. Perhaps Paul is afraid to show his anger towards his father for fear of driving him still further away. You might hypothesise that his joy-riding – destructive and self-destructive as it is – is in part a way of expressing the rage inside him. In this case you might aim to provide him with opportunities to talk about his feelings and sort them out. Or you might look at trying to bring in his father, or both his parents together, and helping him to talk to them about his feelings and to negotiate some new living arrangement that would make him feel less rejected.

These are only a few thoughts, and one could go on. I hope the point has been made, though, that the business of finding the 'lever' that will facilitate change is complicated.

However, to make things more complicated still it is important to bear in mind the risk of making things worse. In this case, now that the supervision order has been made, you and Paul are, for a little while at least, stuck with each other. But in general there is a strong case for arguing that a professional involvement with youth offenders should be avoided where possible because of the risks associated with labelling (see Chapter 5). The very fact that Paul is now 'within the system' may serve to confirm to him and to others that he is indeed a young offender, and this may make it harder rather than easier for him to move on. (That this is a real danger of making things worse is illustrated by a study by Joan McCord [1978] which I will describe in the next chapter.)

INTERNAL AND EXTERNAL CHANGE

Many social work texts, drawing on literature from the fields of psychotherapy and counselling, focus a great deal on what I defined in Chapter 4 as 'direct work': face-to-face work aimed at facilitating personal change, whether that be change in a person's behaviour, change in a person's self-image or change in a person's relationship with others or with society. What a psychotherapist is aiming at is 'internal change': change within a person (though it may be that this will allow that person to make changes in their external circumstances that he or she might not otherwise have been able to make). Social workers too are often, though by no means always, aiming at internal change. For example a social worker may work towards increasing the confidence and independence of a person with learning disabilities, or helping a mother to respond more consistently to her child.

But social work is not all about 'direct work'. This is for two reasons. Firstly, social workers are not necessarily aiming at internal change at all. Mr Jones is having difficulty managing at home because he cannot physically get up and down the stairs. All he needs help with may be a practical change in his home (a stair lift perhaps, or his bed moved downstairs). He needs *external* change, a change in his environment, and quite probably would regard any form of 'therapeutic' intervention as intrusive and impertinent. Secondly, even if a social worker is trying to support internal change, she may still do this indirectly by changing a person's *environment* in some way, whether through advocacy, or by providing services, or by arranging, on a voluntary or involuntary basis, for a person to move from one environment to another. (In case example 8.1 above, the aim was certainly internal change – change in Paul's behaviour – but some of the means I suggested for doing it involved environmental changes rather than face-to-face work.)

Indeed strictly speaking, even if we are engaged in face-to-face direct work aimed at personal change, what we are in fact offering is still only a change in the service user's environment, for we have no direct access to the inside of a person's head. Psychotherapy or counselling constitute environmental changes, of a specialist kind, and usually for limited periods of time, which are intended to be conducive to internal change. Different schools of therapy differ from one another, essentially, in respect of the type of environment that they set out to create. (For example, solution-focused brief therapists offer a time-limited environment in which 'solution talk' is actively encouraged and 'problem talk' is as far as possible avoided, while Freudian analysts offer a much longer-lasting environment in which people are encouraged to uncover buried aspects of their lives.)

Ultimately all we can ever do is change, or offer to change, a person's environment. Sometimes we will do this purely to bring about practical changes in a person's life. (We help to arrange a stair lift for Mr Jones.) Sometimes we are hoping to support internal change. The rest of this chapter will be looking at internal change. But it is important to remember that making *any* significant changes in a person's environment inevitably brings about some internal change, even if that is not the primary intention. Being admitted to a residential home, for instance, is a major life event for an elderly person, and not just a change of address.

ENFORCED AND CHOSEN CHANGE

Another important difference between the work of therapists and counsellors and the work of social workers, is that social workers will sometimes *impose* changes on people: a mentally ill man is detained in a hospital, a child is removed from her parents, a young offender is required to attend supervision sessions. Not all service users are 'service requesters' (to return to the language I used in Chapter 2). Many are 'protectees' or 'supervisees'.

Even when acting in this 'control agent' capacity, though, the social worker still has no access to the inside of a person's head. People can be moved from A to B, they can be ordered to meet with social workers, they can be legally required to allow their activities to be monitored and supervised, but you cannot dictate how they will respond to these sorts of environmental changes, any more than a therapist can control how a client will respond to a therapeutic environment. (An analogy might be drawn here with attempts to bring about change on the international stage by the use of force. Force certainly makes a difference. If you invade a country it will never be quite the same again. But that does not mean that, with all the force in the world, you can turn that country into a particular type of society or make its citizens think in a particular kind of way.)

It is true that on occasion the use of legal powers provides a 'wake-up call', and creates a crisis in which a person will finally face up to the consequences of their behaviour and do something about it. 'The threat of statutory intervention' can indeed be a 'factor that tips the "decisional balance" scales towards action' (Corden and Somerton, 2004: 1041). Writing about the use of coercive instruments such as 'ASBOs' (anti-social behaviour orders) and 'ABCs' (acceptable behaviour contracts) in relation to homeless people, Suzanne Fitzpatrick and Sarah Johnsen observe that they can help some homeless people by acting as 'a "crisis point" prompting reflection and change' and by encouraging an 'engagement with support services, such as alcohol and drug treatment' (2009: 294). They quote the following two homeless people:

> I think it made me realise that I had to get out of that what I was in, that little rut because when you're on the street you're as low as it can be and you're basically giving up. So because I wanted to get away from getting arrested and that I've actually started to get a bit of an act together. When I was sleeping rough, it was just the same procedure. Wake up, make money, buy drugs, go to sleep, wake up, make money, buy drugs. At least now I've started eating and that again. ('Street user' cited by Fitzpatrick and Johnsen, 2009: 294)

> I'd lost interest in life really, I didn't want to know … It was get up in the morning, do what I had to do and spend the rest of the day using drugs … I think I am probably an ASBO success story … I had my first clean birthday as an adult about two weeks ago. ('Street user' cited by Fitzpatrick and Johnsen, 2009: 294)

But there is no guarantee that people will respond in this way. The use of statutory power may on the contrary alienate service users, making them more resistant to change; it may (unsurprisingly) increase their sense of powerlessness and inability to do anything; it may create an adversarial, them-and-us atmosphere in which it is increasingly difficult to communicate. In fact our use of coercive power can, paradoxically, result in us having less influence than we otherwise would have had.

I emphasise this point because the use of statutory powers can often seem like a tempting 'quick fix' and social workers may often find themselves under pressure to use them, even when they themselves have reservations. In the previous chapter I quoted an account by Malcolm Kinney of an occasion when he arranged for a service user to be detained under the 1983 Mental Health Act, against his own better judgement. Here is a further extract:

> What Mary needed most was sleep and somebody she trusted to be near by when she work up. Unfortunately, even such a seemingly simple plan was not possible to organise – the risks were considered too high. The police would give me no more time as they wanted to move on to 'more important cases', the doctor was unwilling to prescribe temazepam (sleeping tablets), I could not insist that the husband leave the home to de-escalate the crisis … and home-based crisis services would not become involved as the risks were deemed too high … For Mary this meant that she was escorted, forcibly, to the ambulance by the police, with a gaggle of neighbours looking on. For the police, the doctors and the managers this for them, was, I'm sure, a job well done. For me it was another personal and professional failure. For Mary it was an intensely traumatic, shameful and stigmatizing experience. (Kinney, 2009: 334)

The use of coercive power is not necessarily inappropriate – it can be life-saving and it can be life-changing in a positive way – but we should still be wary of its use, and should not imagine that the changes it allows us to bring about will necessarily be positive ones, for we cannot command people to think or feel what we want them to think or feel. This means that social workers do need on occasion to stand up to others who pressure them, in the ways that Kinney describes, to use coercive power when, in their own judgement, the use of such power will not help the situation. This can be difficult but, as Hazel Davies puts it, we really should not be in the business of exercising control over others unless we ourselves are 'in submission' to a coherent set of values (Davies, 2009: 324). For otherwise we will indeed be likely to follow the easiest path, or politically the most expedient one.

A CHANGE-CONDUCIVE ENVIRONMENT

We cannot directly bring about positive 'internal change' in other people, but only, at best, create environments in which such change is supported. What, then, might be the characteristics of such an environment? In relation to 'direct work' environments a common finding of researchers is that the nature of the working relationship may be a more important factor than the specific technique that is used. Lambert and Barley (2002) for instance, based on their own research and an overview of other research studies, conclude that 'process factors' (factors to do with the quality of the interaction) account for 30 per cent of variance in the outcome of psychotherapy, as against 15 per cent which is due to the technique used (or what in social work we might refer to as the theoretical model or method).

The other factors they identify are 'expectancy', which they estimate accounts for 15 per cent, and 'extratherapeutic change', which accounts for 40 per cent. ('Expectancy' really means the placebo effect: the change that results simply from our expectation that change will occur. 'Extratherapeutic change' refers to changes made by clients outside of the therapeutic process.)

Relationship variables associated with successful outcomes (see Norcross, 2002) include 'goal consensus and collaboration' (agreement between client and professional about what is being worked on and how), empathy and the 'therapeutic alliance', a term that includes both collaborative working and an 'affective' connection, by which is meant a connection at the level of feelings such as 'mutual trust, liking, respect and caring' (Horvath and Bedi, 2002: 41). The word 'mutual' is important here. Successful outcomes do depend a great deal on what the service user is able to contribute, as well as the professional. Indeed Norcross (2002: 5) suggests that client-related factors such as motivation to change are the *most* important predictors of change. (We really should not be surprised that people have got to want to change for change to be likely to occur, but it does sometimes seem to be forgotten in social work, with the result that direct work can end up as a kind of futile nagging.) But it is not *all* down to the client. 'Therapeutic alliance' and 'collaboration' do of course also involve a contribution by the professional.

As I have already noted, a social worker's job is different from that of a therapist, not least because a substantial proportion of social work clients are involuntary clients ('supervisees' or 'protectees' in my terms). Given the importance of the client's own motivation to change for successful outcomes, we are setting ourselves a difficult task when we try to support internal change in people who did not choose to work with us in the first place. However, the following are factors which research cited by Chris Trotter (2007) has identified as being linked with successful work with involuntary clients, listed with my own commentary after each.

- *Role clarification.* This involves being both clear and honest about your role and in particular about the dual nature of that role (as helper and controller). Achieving this requires that we set out the ground rules in respect of confidentiality and the nature of the work to be undertaken, and be completely clear about the areas for negotiation and the areas that are not negotiable. Trotter cites a range of studies in support of the position that role clarification improves outcomes, and argues that the most effective workers are those who are able to convey *both* sides of their role to those they work with.
- *Reinforcing and modelling pro-social values.* If you are working with an involuntary client there will be some aspect of their behaviour which is thought likely either to harm others or harm the client him or herself, and which you are trying to get the client to change. Reinforcing and modelling pro-social behaviour involves being consistent about what is being aimed for, and not giving mixed messages, either through the feedback you give to the service user, or through your own behaviour. With Paul in case example 8.1, you would be needing to ensure that you were giving an absolutely consistent message that joy-riding was unacceptable, and not inadvertently giving him the message that you were in any way amused or impressed by it. Young social workers, who may have not so very long ago been through a phase of adolescent rebellion themselves (and perhaps still have some of an adolescent's fear

of seeming 'uncool') may occasionally find it particularly hard to hold the line here, but older social workers can find it difficult too, and are not immune to similar pressures. It should be clear though that you really should not be in youth offending work if you are not prepared or able to hold these sorts of line, for you will simply undermine yourself and confuse your clients.

- *Collaborative problem-solving.* Although, of necessity, there are some non-negotiable areas when working with involuntary clients, your work is likely to be more effective if, as far as possible, you show yourself willing to work on problems agreed with the service user. We have seen above that collaboration is associated with success in therapeutic relationships generally, and there is no reason why things should be any different in respect of involuntary clients. Indeed, since with involuntary clients there are some aspects which are indeed non-negotiable (including the existence of the working relationship itself), it may be *particularly* important here to ensure that the client is able to have some say on what is worked on, in order to restore to them some sense of control and agency.

POWER, EMPOWERMENT AND CHANGE

Power and change are closely intertwined. One could define power, in fact, as the ability to influence or control events, and powerlessness as the lack of ability to do so. People *have* to experience themselves as having some power if they are to bring about changes for themselves, whether those changes are internal or external. Many of the people whom social workers encounter have been given the message pretty consistently that they do not have much power. Indeed anyone who has lived for any length of time in adverse conditions which they have not been able to change has, even if only implicitly, been given this message (this is what is meant by 'learned helplessness' [Peterson et al., 1995]). If the effect of the social work intervention is to further reinforce that message, then it is not likely to be of much help, and could quite easily make things even worse.

The word 'empowerment' is one of those annoying buzzwords (like 'partnership') which are used very freely in social work, sometimes without much thought as to what it really means. But we could define empowerment as *helping people to experience themselves as having power.* And if we do define it in these terms it is easy to see that *empowering* people (whether or not we choose to use that word) really is not some politically correct optional extra, but an essential component of any effort to support or encourage personal change, while actions which disempower people will inevitably *diminish* people's ability to make changes for themselves:

> Service users who are not empowered become passive consumers whose competence is undermined. In other words, if service users are not empowered they become more dependent rather than independent. (Neville, 2004: 27)

Empowerment is not necessarily the same thing as being 'nice' to people, though, and disempowerment is not necessarily the same thing as being unpleasant to them. You can disempower people very effectively by sorting out all their problems for them, or by exonerating them from the responsibility for their own actions, and they may well be very grateful to you and think you a very nice person, without noticing that you have actually undermined their sense of their own agency. (The word 'agency', as used here, means 'the capacity to influence events', which of course is also how I defined 'power'.) Conversely you can sometimes empower people by confronting them and giving them a 'reality check', though this may involve you saying things to them which they would rather not hear, and they may experience you as being negative and unkind, even if you have in fact done them the favour of treating them like responsible human beings who are able to make choices.

Empowerment is not a straightforward matter and what is empowering in one particular context could well be disempowering in another. But what *is* clear and straightforward is that you cannot undermine people's sense of their own power, their own ability to influence events, and then ask of them that they make changes in their lives. As Albert Bandura observes:

> Unless people believe that they can produce desired results by their actions, they have little incentive to act, or to persevere in the face of difficulties. Whatever other factors serve as guides and motivators, they are rooted in the core belief that one has the power to effect changes by one's actions. (Bandura, 2006: 170)

Power of course has a political and structural dimension as well as a personal one. A familiar radical critique of social work interventions, as well as of psychiatric and psychological ones, is that they have the effect of concealing and bolstering up oppression by making the results of structural injustice look like personal problems, so that it becomes the victim of injustice who is seen as having a problem and needing to change rather than the unjust society itself. A perennial debate in the social work literature has therefore been about the appropriate level at which efforts towards change should be targeted. To give a simple example: an unemployed disabled man is suffering from depression. Should the focus of intervention be his depression and/or his disability? Or should it be the fact that he is discriminated against in the job market because he is disabled? Does he require 'therapy' or advocacy?

But the fact is that both advocacy *and* therapy have the potential to undermine an individual's sense of agency. Although it is certainly important to think carefully about the 'system level' (individual, family, community, society) upon which efforts towards change should be focused, it is probably even more important to consider the net effect of any intervention, at any system level, on its recipient's sense of his or her ability to act and to influence events.

PLACEMENT QUESTIONS 8.1   CHANGE AND EMPOWERMENT

- What kinds of changes does your placement agency aim to bring about in the lives of service users?
- What are the principle means it uses to bring about change? (In other words: what sorts of intervention does it offer, and how are these interventions supposed to work?)

- How well does your placement agency do at empowering, as opposed to disempowering its service users? (You could address this by listing things that the agency and its staff do that you think a service user would find encouraging and empowering, and then listing things that you think a service user would find discouraging, undermining and disempowering.)
- If you were a service user of your placement agency, would you feel like a subject (a free agent, who the agency listened to, and supported in taking action) or an object (someone that the agency does things to and for)?

SURFACE VERSUS DEPTH

Whether to focus on the observable surface or the hidden depths is another perennial argument, exemplified in the mid-twentieth century by the debate between behaviourism and psychodynamic psychology: the former concentrating on achieving observable changes in a person's actual behaviour, the second trying to achieve deep change in a person's understanding of, and relationship with, themselves and others. However, that debate is much wider than the one existing between these two schools of psychology. Proponents of solution-focused brief therapy, for instance, are also interested in changes of behaviour rather than changes in deep understanding (see, for instance, de Shazer, 1985: 7).

There is a natural tendency to invoke the idea of deeper, 'underlying' problems in order to explain the fact that people are resistant to change – or are unable to sustain it – even when change is what they say they want, and even when it seems very clearly in their own interests. Ideas such as the 'Internal Working Model' in Attachment Theory (Bowlby, 1998) or the 'Life Script' in Transactional Analysis (Byng-Hall, 1995) help us to make sense of this fact by postulating some inner structure that also requires modification, in addition to mere behavioural change, if the latter is to become permanent. The construction of problem behaviours like drug use or eating problems as *illnesses* or *diseases* or *disorders* is another way in which we try to make sense of the fact that people persist in doing things that seem to go against their own interests. By making an analogy with physical illness we move away from looking at such behaviour as a series of choices (which one might call a 'surface' view) and look instead as at some inner malformation.

But perhaps such ideas can themselves at times be obstacles to change? If we believe ourselves to be suffering from an incurable illness called 'addiction' perhaps this makes it harder, rather than easier, to realise that to change a problem behaviour we simply have to make up our minds to stop doing it. Writers who apply 'postmodernist' and social constructionist insights to the business of social work intervention often make this kind of point. (See for example Parton and O'Byrne [2000]. See also Davies [1997] for a challenge to conventional notions about 'addiction'. Or look at Kroll and Taylor [2003: 57–84] for a discussion on different ways of conceptualising substance misuse and the pros and cons of viewing it as an 'illness' on the one hand, or as an act of choice on the other.)

RESISTANCE

However we explain it, though, people *do* often resist changes which would seem to be obviously in their own best interests. And people also resist making changes which they themselves agree would be to their advantage. Consider changes such as giving up smoking, or going on a diet, changes of the kind which most of us have decided at some point or other to make, but which most of us find hard to make and stick to. There is a reason for this of course: going on a diet or giving up smoking are things that we feel ambivalent about. Yes, we want the benefits (a trimmer figure, better health), but we do not want to give up the pleasure and comfort that we get from our present eating or smoking habits, and we do not want to have to deal with the cravings that we know we will feel if we change them. What makes these decisions hard, in other words, is the fact that we really are *in two minds about them.*

And typically the negative side of our ambivalence – the *resistance* – increases as the moment of change approaches. Going to the gym three times a week may seem a great New Year resolution in advance, but come January, the idea of going out in the cold and working out for an hour may seem a lot less appealing than staying in and watching TV. Ambivalence, wanting the benefits of change but not wanting to give up what is comforting about the way things are, is the thing that makes change of any kind difficult.

So how do we help people to overcome their own resistance to change? Miller and Rollnick (2002) developed a widely used counselling technique known as 'motivational interviewing' which aims to help with this. Central to their approach is the view that, if the worker attempts to overcome resistance by arguing in favour of change, this merely encourages the client to take the polar opposite position of arguing *against* change and finding more and more reasons for why that change isn't possible. The worker should therefore avoid arguing directly for change, and should not directly challenge resistance. By 'rolling with resistance', they argue, (the phrase comes from boxing, where a fighter tries to 'roll with' his opponent's punches) rather than attempting to challenge it, the counsellor avoids falling into the trap of becoming the advocate for change and thus encouraging the client to develop still more arguments against it:

> In everyday language, we can literally talk ourselves into (or out of) things. If A [the client] is caused to take up the opposite side of the ambivalence dilemma, and to point out the down side of the course of action for which R [the helper] is arguing, then that course of action becomes less likely to occur. In effect A is inadvertently talked out of it. (Miller and Rollnick, 2002: 21)

I suspect that most of us have had direct experience of this which confirmed the sense of this position. You can probably think of occasions when a friend tried to persuade you to take a course of action which you had told them you were thinking about. ('Oh yes, that is a brilliant idea! You really must do it!') If the friend tried too hard, you may well have noticed yourself feeling pushed, irritated and even bullied. You may well have started to feel that your friend was skating over all the difficulties and problems as if they were nothing. 'It's all very well for you,' you may have found yourself thinking, 'you're not the one who is going to have to deal with any of this.' In order to redress the imbalance, you may well have ended up arguing *against* your friend, and against the course of action which you yourself had almost persuaded yourself to take. Miller and Rollnick suggest that, to support change, we need to encourage the client to develop the arguments for change for herself.

THE CYCLE OF CHANGE

A final, very important point to make about change, one which I alluded to in my discussion of the case example earlier, is that people can be in different stages of readiness for change. The best way to work with someone on change will depend on what stage they are at. There is no point in working out a detailed plan of action, for instance, with a person who is not seriously interested in making a change at all.

James Prochaska, Carlo DiClemente and various colleagues are associated with a well-known stage model of change (see Prochaska et al., 1992) that was developed particularly in relation to changes such as giving up smoking, but which they propose is quite generally applicable. They claim also that it applies both to people receiving professional help and to people working on change without professional help, as of course most of us do most of the time. (I like the way this demystifies the business of change, and reminds us that professional therapists did not invent personal change, and are really only refining techniques that everyone uses to some degree.) This model has been influential in the UK not only in the field of addictive behaviours but also in the field of child and family work, partly as the result of the model being taken up by Horwath and Morrison (2000) and incorporated in government guidance (Department of Health, 2000). There are some criticisms of the model, and in particular questions about its applicability outside of the fields in which it originated (see Corden and Somerton, 2004), but I think it contains important messages about change which are worth assimilating.

The basis of the model is that, in respect of changes in their life, people will be at one of the following stages:

- *Precontemplation:* People at the precontemplation stage do not see themselves as having a real problem. If they seek for, or go along with, some kind of therapeutic intervention at this stage it will be because of pressure from others.
- *Contemplation:* People 'are aware that a problem exists and are seriously thinking about overcoming it, but have not yet made a commitment to take action' (Prochaska et al., 1992: 1103).
- *Preparation:* People are intending to take action and have made 'some small behavioural changes, such as smoking five cigarettes less' (Prochaska et al., 1992: 1104).
- *Action:* The 'stage in which individuals modify their behaviour, experiences or environment in order to overcome their problems' (Prochaska et al., 1992: 1104). Prochaska et al. note that 'people, including professionals, often erroneously equate action with change' rather than seeing it as a stage in a change process that in reality may have been going on for some time, *and which is still not complete.*'As a consequence, they overlook the requisite work that prepares changers for action and the important efforts necessary to maintain the changes following action' (ibid.: 1104).

- *Maintenance:* 'The stage at which people work to prevent relapse and consolidate the gains attained during action' (ibid.: 1104). The maintenance stage, as ex-smokers and dieters will attest, is in many ways the most challenging part, and it may be here that the most support is needed. It is worth bearing this in mind, because in social work there is often pressure to close cases and move on to new ones very quickly, and it can happen that this occurs precisely at the moment that the will power of their service users is most in need of support.

The process is not necessarily linear. People may reach the maintenance stage and then relapse to an earlier stage. 'With smoking, for example, successful self-changers make an average of from three to four action attempts before they become long-term maintainers' (ibid.: 1104). The model can therefore be presented as a circle (see Figure 8.1), which we enter, and typically go round more than once before eventually exiting. (Alternatively it can be seen as a spiral, because 'most relapsers do not revolve endlessly in circles and … do not regress all the way back to where they started' (ibid.: 1105.)

IMPLICATIONS FOR INTERVENTION

Prochaska et al. suggest that attempts to work with people on change often offer a one-size-fits-all approach, when in fact effective working needs to be tailored to the stage that a

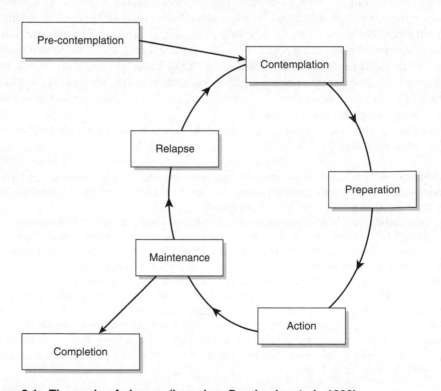

Figure 8.1 The cycle of change (based on Prochaska et al., 1992)

person is at: 'To treat all of these smokers as if they were the same would be naïve. And yet, that is what we traditionally have done in many treatment programmes' (Prochaska et al., 1992: 1105). It seems to me that social work agencies may sometimes make similar mistakes when trying to work with people on personal change. Are all the parents who attend parenting skills groups, for instance, at the same stage in respect of change, or have they all been lumped together simply because they have 'parenting problems' and without much regard for their readiness for change? If a parent has not really accepted there is even a problem with the way he parents, he is unlikely to be responsive to work that will involve making difficult behavioural changes, even though he may be prepared to go along with attending sessions in order to get the professionals 'off his back'.

PLACEMENT QUESTIONS 8.2   RECOGNITION OF STAGES OF CHANGE

If your placement agency is involved in trying to support internal change, then you might like to consider how sophisticated the agency's understanding of the process of change is, as demonstrated by its actual actions.

- Does it offer one-size-fits-all interventions? Or is there some recognition of the fact that people may be at different stages?
- Does the agency's assessment practice encourage workers to look at readiness for change? To what extent does the agency explore the level of insight people have about their own behaviour?

Prochaska et al. also suggest that, regardless of precise theoretical labels, we can identify a range of different processes which are involved *both* in professional therapeutic interventions *and* in people's own attempts to bring about change for themselves. These are summarised in Table 8.1 below.

You can see that the earlier processes in the list are associated more with insight-based interventions, while lower down the list appear processes associated with behaviour and action. In other words, some are 'depth' and some are 'surface' approaches, in the terms used earlier in this chapter, but Prochaska et al.'s approach to the surface versus depth question is a novel one: they suggest that different processes are appropriate to different stages. Action-based behavioural approaches are unlikely to work in the early stages of pre-contemplation and contemplation because the individual lacks the insight or motivation to be prepared to see things through ('overt action without insight is likely to lead to temporary change': Prochaska et al., 1992: 1111). On the other hand, practical, behavioural approaches such as 'counter-conditioning', 'stimulus control' and 'reinforcement management' are necessary at the later stages of action and maintenance, rather than purely insight-based approaches, because 'insight alone does not necessarily bring about behaviour change' (ibid.: 1110). Prochaska et al. conclude:

Competing systems of psychotherapy have promulgated apparently rival processes of change. However, ostensibly contradictory processes can become complementary when embedded in the stages of change. (1992: 1112)

Table 8.1 Titles, definitions and representative interventions of the processes of change

Process	Definitions: Interventions
Consciousness raising	Increasing information about self and problem: observations, confrontations, interpretations, bibliotherapy
Self-reevaluation	Assessing how one feels and thinks about oneself with respect to a problem: value clarification, imagery, corrective emotional experience
Self-liberation	Choosing and commitment to act or belief in ability to change: decision-making therapy, New Year's resolutions, logotherapy techniques, commitment enhancing techniques
Counterconditioning	Substituting alternatives for problem behaviors: relaxation, desensitisation, assertion, positive self-statements
Stimulus control	Avoiding or countering stimuli that elicit problem behaviors: restructuring one's environment (e.g., removing alcohol or fattening foods), avoiding high risk cues, fading techniques
Reinforcement management	Rewarding one's self or being rewarded by others for making changes: contingency contracts, overt and covert reinforcement, self-reward
Helping relationships	Being open and trusting about problems with someone who cares: therapeutic alliance, social support, self-help groups
Dramatic relief	Experiencing and expressing feelings about one's problems and solutions: psychodrama, grieving losses, role playing
Environmental reevaluation	Assessing how one's problem affects physical environment: empathy training, documentaries
Social liberation	Increasing alternatives for nonproblem behaviors available in society: advocating for rights of repressed, empowering, policy interventions

(Reprinted with permission from Prochaska, J., DiClemente, C. and Norcross, J. (1992) 'In search of how people change: applications to addictive behaviours', *American Psychologist*, 47(9): 1102–14. Published by the American Psychological Association.)

IMPLICATIONS FOR ASSESSMENT

Social workers are often involved in trying to assess people's ability to change, or in trying to determine whether the changes made are likely to last. This might be the case, for instance, when working with offenders, working with people with substance abuse problems, or working on parenting problems. How do we judge whether past patterns will repeat themselves or not? This can be a fairly important question when we are, for instance, working with a violent offender or a paedophile.

The implication of the Prochaska model is that we should be looking for insight if we want some indication that a person is approaching a readiness for change, for this would suggest that a person has at least reached the contemplation stage. Of course many people, in moments of pressure, will express a vague intention to change, but this should not be taken as evidence of contemplation in itself. More convincing would be evidence that the person has thought for him or herself about his or her behaviour, its consequences and why it happens. Peter Reder (2003), writing about assessment of parents, suggests that a crucial element of this is the ability to reflect on the past:

> The ability to undergo transitions in personal functioning and move on from adverse experiences seems to be crucially linked to a capacity to reflect on the past. It is necessary to be able to recall past experiences, with the appropriate affect, and to acknowledge the continuity between past and present ....

> At assessment, parents with limited psychological mindedness give superficial accounts of their history, with significant gaps and minimal affective content. Answers are given in a matter-of-fact way and they may become irritated when the interviewer focuses on emotional issues. (Reder, 2003: 238–239)

However, as we've seen, the Prochaska model makes clear that insight in itself is not enough. Again this is something that most of us probably know from personal experience. Most of us, it seems to me, have habits – eating, drinking, smoking, prevaricating – which we do know are not really good for us, and which we do have some understanding of, but which we do not in fact end up doing anything about. Lasting change does not occur until we move on from contemplation through preparation and action to maintenance. I know for example that I am prone to eat snacks as a way of distracting myself when I am a little anxious, or when I want to delay getting on with something that seems onerous, and I know too that snacks are not particularly good for me, but at the time of writing, this insight has never quite been enough. (Indeed this chapter alone has involved several biscuit breaks at moments when I was struggling to find precisely the words I wanted to write.)

This brings me to another point from the model which I think is relevant to social work. This is that changes, even when made, are not necessarily permanent. As we've seen, relapse is common and, in respect of some behaviours like smoking, occurs more often than not. But in the case of high-risk behaviours, where relapse might pose an immediate threat to the well-being of others, we cannot afford to be relaxed about the possibility that people may have to go through the whole cycle again. And this means that we need to look not only for insight and action, but also for evidence that the change has been maintained for a significant period of time. In respect of changes in parenting, Reder suggests the following:

> Transitions in personal identity and relationship patterns take time to be negotiated and consolidated .... If the parent who is the subject of the assessment is claiming that a personality adaptation has occurred, then it seems to be important to have the evidence of at least a year's alternative functioning to underpin their assertion. (Reder, 2003: 241)

A positive message to take from the model, though, is that, as Corden and Somerton put it, 'we are all pre-contemplators first!' (2004: 1041). The fact that someone is not seriously thinking about a given change does not mean that they are incapable of making that change. But what the model does tell us is that we should not expect them to be able to leap straight from this pre-contemplative state into preparation and action, and we should not expect them to be able to respond to interventions geared towards preparation and action. People are subjects, agents in their own right, and we cannot expect to move them around like pieces on a chessboard, however much that busy social workers might sometimes wish that bringing about change could indeed be that simple.

CHAPTER SUMMARY

In this chapter I have considered the kinds of change that social workers are expected to make. I made a distinction between 'internal' change (changes in a person's thinking, feelings or behaviour) and 'external' change (changes in a person's environment), while pointing out that since we do not have direct access to other people's minds, even 'internal' change can only be supported by making changes in a person's environment. I discussed the differences between changes which a service user chooses, and those which are imposed on service users by the use of legal powers, and I pointed out the limits to what such powers can be expected to achieve. I looked at the factors which, in a working relationship, are likely to be conducive to change, and pointed out the connections with the idea of 'empowerment': no one can make changes if they have no sense of having power. I touched briefly on old debates about whether we should aim for personal or structural change, and whether we should be happy to work with changes in behaviour or whether we should aim for 'depth'. I discussed the idea of 'resistance' and the fact that we are almost inevitably ambivalent about significant change. Finally I introduced the important idea of the 'cycle of change'. We need to take account of people's readiness to change if we are to choose what kind of intervention to offer.

FURTHER READING

The issues regarding 'change' are different in different contexts, and you should seek out books about the particular issues that arise in the context of your placement. However for an overview of some of the general issues discussed in this chapter about what does and what does not support personal change, the following book is useful:

Norcross, J. (ed.) (2002) *Psychotherapy Relationships That Work: Therapist Contributions and Responsiveness to Patients*. Oxford: Oxford University Press.

In a field of work where (unlike in psychotherapy) a large number of service users are involuntary ones, it is very important to think about the particularly difficult and complex issues that are involved when working with people who did not choose to work with you. A starting point here is Chris Trotter's book:

Trotter, C. (2007) *Working With Involuntary Clients: A Guide to Practice* (2nd edn). London: Sage.

9 EVALUATION

- Criteria of success
- Objectivity
- Methodological complications
- Evidence and social work

As I observed in the previous chapter, the point of any kind of social work is to make a difference in a positive way for those on the receiving end of its services – or at least one would hope so. But how do we know what kind of difference we have made? How do we know whether we have made things better or worse? How can we separate out the changes that have occurred as the result of our interventions from the changes that would have occurred anyway? How do we know in advance which interventions are likely to be helpful in a given situation?

These are all questions which you will no doubt be asking yourself as you attempt to evaluate both the work done by your placement agency, and the work you are doing yourself. They are questions which one would expect any social worker or social work manager to be concerned with, and they are certainly questions which any service user would reasonably expect to have been considered (just as we would expect our doctors to have some basis for thinking that the medicine they prescribed us would do us good). They are also questions which one would expect those who *fund* social work to be interested in. (When there are so many different calls on public money, why spend money on something unless you can be reasonably confident that it will serve a useful purpose?) But although these questions might seem like quite basic ones they are surprisingly hard to answer. This final chapter will consider some of the issues involved.

CRITERIA OF SUCCESS

If we are going to measure the success of anything, we need to consider the criteria we would use. What would be evidence that we had made things better? What do we mean by 'better'? The following are some possibilities.

SERVICE USER VIEWS

An obvious way of finding out whether a service is doing any good is to ask the recipients of that service. Indeed it would be extraordinarily arrogant to deliver a service *without* seeking feedback of this kind. But we should be wary of assuming that this is the only kind of information we need, for a number of reasons. Firstly, service users may not always be completely frank about what they think about the service. The real or perceived power of social workers can mean that service users are hesitant to be too critical (just as students are sometimes hesitant to be overly critical of practice teachers who are marking their work). Service users are often also kind people who may also be hesitant about being critical if they like the social worker and feel she has done her best. (If a lecturer who you personally like and believe to work very hard, were to deliver a course which you found dull and irrelevant, but which the lecturer had clearly put his heart and soul into, you might be tempted, if asked for your opinion, to err on the generous side.) On the other hand some service users may be overly negative, perhaps as a way of 'getting their own back' on a social worker who acted in a way they did not like, or which made them feel uncomfortable. And people who felt embarrassed about asking for help, or about not being able to cope on their own, may wish to minimise the amount of help they have actually received. Finally, but importantly, many service users, notably small children, really do not have the capacity to understand all the implications of a question about the service being delivered.

Secondly, the question 'Who is the service user?' is not always a straightforward one, and services are not always intended solely for the benefit of those to whom they are delivered. If you are working with parents, for instance, under the 1989 Children Act, your primary concern is supposed to be the welfare of the children. Parents are not intended to be the primary recipients of the service. If you were working with a family where abuse was suspected, it is obvious that the views of the suspected abuser should not be the sole criterion you use to judge the success of your intervention. Indeed to deal effectively with abuse, it is frequently necessary to act *against* the wishes of the adults involved. This is one of the ways in which work with 'supervisees' (as I used this term in Chapter 2), differs from work with 'service requesters'.

What is more, even if they are entirely voluntary clients, service users are not necessarily in a good position to know what the overall effect of an intervention has been. A striking illustration of this is provided by a study by Joan McCord (1978). McCord's work is a follow-up of a large-scale programme carried out thirty years previously which aimed to prevent boys from getting involved in offending behaviour. The programme had provided a range of services including the input of counsellors who visited families roughly twice monthly over a five-year period, along with a variety of other inputs including extra academic tuition, summer camps and medical or psychiatric help. The programme had been delivered to 253 boys and their families (the 'treatment group'), while another 253 boys had been in a matched 'control group' and had not received these services. (At the time of the original programme, boys had been matched in pairs for similar characteristics, and then one member of each pair had been assigned to the control group, and one to the treatment group, through the toss of a coin.) McCord was able to find the majority of those involved, who were of course now grown men, both in the control group and in the 'treatment' groups. She sent them questionnaires which were returned by 113 members of the treatment group (54 per cent) and 122 members of the control group (60 per cent). Two-thirds of the men who had been in the treatment group said that the programme had been helpful to them. Comments made included 'I was put on the right road' and some said that, without the support of their counsellors, 'I would probably have ended up in a life of crime' or 'I would probably be in jail' (McCord, 1978: 287). Of the one-third of the treatment group who did not comment positively, 11 did not comment at all, 13 said they could not remember the project, and 13 said the project had not been helpful, though some of these had 'fond memories' of aspects of it (ibid.: 287).

In other words service user feedback on the programme was broadly positive. But when McCord came to look at what had actually happened in the lives of the members of the treatment group, she found a surprisingly different story. There was no evidence that men in the treatment group had been deflected from offending behaviour as boys. On the contrary, while the incidence of first offences was similar between the two groups, men in the treatment group were *more* likely to have committed more than one offence than those in the control group, and they also scored less well than the control group on a number of other measures. For example they were slightly more likely to evidence signs of alcoholism and/or mental illness, more likely to have a lower status job, and more likely to report being unsatisfied with their work. It seems that, *even though it scored well in terms of service user satisfaction*, the project actually had had on average a slightly negative effect in terms of the offending behaviour which it was supposed to prevent, and in terms of other measures too. This is worrying because, on the face of it, what the project offered is not so different from what many might still regard as good preventative work.

We can only speculate on why this negative effect might occur. McCord wondered whether 'interaction with adults whose values are different from the family milieu may produce later internal conflicts' (ibid.: 288). Perhaps, too, the treatment group boys might have felt 'labelled' as a result of their involvement in the project, in the way discussed in Chapter 5. It must have struck these boys as odd, after all, that they were having all this input when most of their friends and schoolmates were not and perhaps this made them think that there must be something different about them. Edwin Schur's (1973) argument for 'radical non-intervention' (referred to in Chapter 4) was based on his view that interventions aimed at reducing youth offending were likely to make things worse by having just this sort of labelling effect. Or perhaps the high level of intervention over a long period created 'dependency on outside help' (McCord, 1978: 288) which undermined the boys' and parents' sense of their own agency (in which case this would illustrate the point made in the previous chapter that being nice and supportive to people is not necessarily the same thing as empowering them).

Whatever the reason, though, this study demonstrates that service user satisfaction does not necessarily equate with positive outcomes. While this at first seems surprising, it is actually not difficult to see how this might occur. If I had received medical treatment and was asked to rate the performance of the doctor, I can see how it could come about that I would rate my doctor highly if she was sympathetic, helpful and willing to listen, even if in fact she was not really any good at curing illnesses. After all, just like the men in McCord's study I am not in a good position to know whether my doctor is actually any good at changing things for the better, because I do not know how I would have been if I had never been to my doctor, or if I had never had any treatment from her. I would guess that millions of us probably do regularly take pills and other cures, whether these are prescribed by doctors or alternative therapists, or recommended by friends, on the basis that we trust the advice we are given, or like and respect those who give it to us. We might well believe the pills are helping, even if they are not, for how do we know how we would be feeling if we were not taking the pills?

None of which is to say that service user feedback is not important or not relevant, but simply to point out that it is not the whole story.

WORKER INTUITION

Leaving aside certain very practical interventions whose utility is indeed obvious (Mr Jones could not go up the stairs before but now he can), very few social workers, I would guess, could point to entirely objective evidence that their interventions have been successful, bearing in mind that a change for the better is not in itself conclusive evidence, unless it is clear that it would not have occurred in any case. (Many young offenders grow out of offending behaviour, for instance, with or without intervention.) As a rule social workers tend to rely on their own intuitions as a guide to whether their interventions have been successful or not, informed by a combination of service user feedback and their own observations.

But in fact the kinds of reasons which I gave above for arguing that service user feedback is not on its own a reliable way of measuring success, apply equally well to social workers. The professionals in the McCord study cited above, for instance, probably had no more information to go on than did the boys they were working with and would most likely have come to similar conclusions about the benefits of the programme for similar reasons.

What is more, we as professionals have a vested interest in believing that our interventions are productive. Our livelihoods, our self-esteem and our sense of purpose are all wrapped up in the idea that we are making a positive difference, and there is a range of cognitive manoeuvres (as discussed in Chapter 5) which allow us to discount evidence to the contrary. Cognitive dissonance, for instance, allows us to reframe failure as success. Attribution bias allows us to claim positive outcomes as our own achievements, while blaming others for negative outcomes. To make things even more complicated, in moments of doubt or uncertainty, we may even *underestimate* our own ability to bring about change (attribution bias, as we have seen, can go in two directions) or fail to recognise positive changes as indeed being in part due to our own efforts.

SERVICE OUTPUTS

Since there are real problems with purely subjective evaluations of services, whether by workers or service users, there are obvious attractions in trying to find more objective measures. As we will see shortly, it can be quite difficult to objectively measure the actual *outcomes* of services (the actual effects that they have had on people's lives) so performance is often measured in terms of '*outputs*' or actions performed. The success of an agency is measured against performance targets that it has set itself, or has had set for it by government. For instance, in child and family social work, agencies are supposed to complete 'initial assessments' within seven working days. Their performance is, in part, measured by their success in meeting this target. If your placement is in a statutory agency, you will almost certainly become aware of targets of this kind that its staff are expected to meet.

There are at least two difficulties with using these sorts of service outputs as measures of success. The first is that such service outputs do not necessarily equate with better outcomes for service users. Whether or not initial assessments are completed in seven days, for instance, may well be irrelevant to service use outcomes. What is more likely to be relevant to actual outcomes is (a) the quality of assessments and (b) the extent to which the agency is able to provide services that meet the needs that an assessment identifies. Some output measures may indeed correlate well with good outcomes for service users, but unless this connection has actually been established in a systematic way, then there is no reason to think that measures based on service outputs (however precise and statistical they may seem to be) are a reliable way of telling whether a service is really making a difference. If measures based on service outputs are simply dreamed up by politicians or civil servants, then they may be completely irrelevant to actual outcomes. To give an example, I mentioned in Chapter 2 that there is a widespread assumption among policy makers that closer inter-agency working is a 'good thing'. If one assumes that it is necessarily a good thing then one might be tempted to devise performance measures that focused on the degree to which an agency worked closely with other agencies. However, I also mentioned in Chapter 2 a study which suggested that, in at least one context, increased service co-ordination actually reduced the quality of the service, as measured by outcomes for service users (Glisson and Hemmelgarn, 1998). If we just measure service outputs as a way of deciding how good a service is, then we never get to look at whether those outputs themselves are actually useful. This may be politically convenient but it does not make sense if we want to know if the service delivers real benefits.

The second problem with a focus on specific service outputs as opposed to measuring service user outcomes is that pursuing targets defined in terms of specific outputs may result in changes to an organisation's practice and priorities that actually have negative consequences for service users. I discussed in Chapter 2, the study by Broadhurst et al. (2010) on initial assessments, which showed that pressure to complete within seven days can lead to serious flaws in the depth and reliability of these documents. The target is about the time taken to sign off the assessment, not about its quality, and therefore attention is focused on the former not the latter. Bridget McKeigue and I (2010) have argued that, in a similar way, the UK government's focus on reducing delays in care proceedings (desirable though that is) could easily have the unintended consequence of increasing delays *before* court. Some children in our study had been accommodated in foster homes for a year, without any clear long-term plan, before care proceedings were commenced, but that time would not be counted as court delay.

SERVICE USER OUTCOMES

As we have seen, there are problems with using service user views, worker intuitions or service outputs as measures of the success of the a service, because none of these necessarily relate in a straightforward way to outcomes for service users. If we want to know whether a service is making a positive difference, it therefore makes sense to try to find a way of measuring, not just how much of a service has been delivered or how quickly, nor what people *think* the benefits of a service have been (useful though all this information might be in its own right), but the *actual changes* the service has brought about. The McCord study, cited earlier, is an example of an attempt to do this. It looked at offending rate, a measure of the actual behaviour that the original project had been intended to reduce. Not all service user outcomes can be so easily measured of course. But without any such measure it is difficult to be really sure about the efficacy of the service being offered (whether it actually does what it is supposed to do), or about its efficiency (whether resources are being deployed to the best possible effect).

PLACEMENT QUESTIONS 9.1   HOW DOES YOUR AGENCY KNOW WHAT WORKS?

- How does your agency know whether it is doing any good or not?
- What kinds of service user outcomes does your agency aim to promote? Does the agency have any way of measuring them?
- Is it possible that some of the agency's interventions might, on balance, have the effect of making things worse, and if so is there any means by which the agency might become aware of this fact?
- What performance measures or targets seem to preoccupy the agency? How do these relate to service user outcomes?
- If you were to try to systematically evaluate the service that your placement agency offers, how would you go about it in a way that would get beyond subjective impressions, and would, so far as possible, eliminate the kinds of biases that creep in when those involved have a vested interest in coming to a particular conclusion?

OBJECTIVITY

I mentioned above that if I went to a doctor and she prescribed pills for me, I would expect that medication to have been properly tested. I would assume that there was some evidence that the pills would do me more good than harm. Drugs are typically tested using some form of randomised control trial. Basically, the drug is tested on people who have been randomly assigned to at least two groups. The people in one group are given the drug. The people in the other group are not. At the beginning of the group, the health of the people in both groups is assessed in some quantifiable way. At the end of the trial their health is assessed again to determine firstly whether there have been measurable improvements, and secondly whether or not those improvements have been greater for the treatment group than for the control group.

By comparing the treatment group with the control group (rather than by comparing people before and after treatment) the researchers ensure that they are looking at the effect of the drug rather than just the effects of time passing. (Almost any cure for the common cold would seem to be effective, if we measured its effects just by administering the drug and seeing if people got better, because in due course everyone does anyway.) Since people have been assigned randomly to the control and treatment groups, it follows that significant differences that emerge are likely to be due to the medication rather than to other factors. I say *significant* differences because of course it is always possible that any difference between the two groups is a purely chance occurrence. For this reason tests of statistical significance are applied to the data. This means basically that a mathematical calculation is made as to how likely it is that the difference has occurred by chance. If a finding is said to be significant at the 1 per cent level ($p = 0.01$) it means there is a 1 per cent chance that the result could have occurred by chance ($p > 0.01$ means that there is a less than 1 per cent chance). For the non-mathematical, like myself, this can all seem rather daunting, but the calculation is based on the same laws of probability that we discussed in Chapter 7: the same laws that allow us to calculate, say, that the chance of throwing a dice and getting two sixes in a row is 1 in 36. Statistical difference is easier to achieve if larger groups are used. (This is obvious when you think about it. If you stopped two people in a high street and asked them if they planned to vote Labour, and they both said yes, you would not conclude from that that most people in the town supported Labour. If you stopped a thousand people and they all said they were Labour voters, you would probably feel more confident in saying that this place was indeed a Labour stronghold.)

Actually the randomised drug trial I described above could still be rather prone to bias, so a number of refinements are usually added to the basic design. First of all, rather than just comparing the treatment group with a group who are not given any treatment at all, the treatment group may be compared to a control group who are given similar pills, but without the active ingredient, and the patients themselves are not told which group they are in (a 'blind trial'). The advantage of this is that it controls for the 'placebo effect'. (Some improvement often occurs, or is imagined, simply as the result of believing that treatment is being given, and this can make a drug look effective even when it is not.) Secondly, the researchers who assess the patient's health may themselves not be told which group each patient in is (a 'double-blind' trial) to avoid any conscious or unconscious bias that could creep in as a result of their preconceptions about the effectiveness of the drug, or the personal stake they may have in the outcome.

I am going to look shortly at the extent to which this sort of objective trial can be carried out in the social care field, but first I want to deal with a possible objection to the sort of methodology discussed above. A lot of people – and I am one of them – are more interested in stories than they are in numbers (to borrow a way of describing it used by Newman et al., 2005). That being so, why do we have to bother with measurable outcomes, statistical significance and all the rest? Isn't that stuff rather dry and boring? Why not just go with stories? The answer is that relying on stories, while very human, can easily deceive us precisely *because* they are more appealing:

> Quantitative studies largely deal with impersonal numbers. An emotional account of how a particular procedure saved someone's life may carry more persuasive weight than a statistical table suggesting that, overall, the procedure causes more harm than good. (Newman et al., 2005: 18)

We have already seen an example of this in the McCord study cited above. Individual stories suggest that the project studied was a success, but the statistics suggest that on balance the project actually made things worse. The author reports 7 different comparisons, out of 57 comparisons made in total, where the control group outperformed the treatment group to a degree that was significant at the $p < 0.05$ level, while there were no comparisons at all that went the other way. She calculates 'the probability that by chance, 7 out of 57 comparisons would favor the control group is 1 in 10,000' (McCord, 1978: 288). I suggest that the virtue of properly conducted double-blind trials does not lie in the numbers *per se* (numbers have no particular virtues), but in the fact that they are designed to avoid the biases that are otherwise almost inevitably caused by wishful thinking, self-interest, and cognitive illusions.

As we will now see, it is not always easy or even possible to do this kind of trial in social work, but rather than just shrug this off, we need to be aware of the consequences. Unless we can demonstrate in a reasonably objective way that we are making things better, then we have to face the possibility that in fact we are not, and we need to have the humility to admit that and deal with its implications.

METHODOLOGICAL COMPLICATIONS

It is sometimes possible to use randomised control trials in relation to social interventions, the study by Joan McCord being an example. As we've seen, boys were randomly assigned to treatment and control groups, and outcomes compared (in this case after thirty years). But this sort of comparison is not normally going to be possible in social work for ethical reasons. You cannot, for instance, take two groups of elderly people and do nothing at all for one group, but provide a range of home care services for the other.

There has been a lot of concern recently about the poor outcomes of the British care system for children. Children leave public care scoring much worse than other children on many measures including educational attainment, health and offending behaviour (Department for Education and Skills, 2006a). This does not necessarily mean, though, that public care causes all these problems, because children who come into care have more problems at the outset than children in the general population, since they are not taken into care unless there are significant problems. Children in the general population, in other words, are not a valid 'control' against which to measure the effect of care. (We would not conclude that hospitals cause cancer, after all, on the basis that there are more people with cancer in hospitals than there are in the general population!) A proper controlled trial of the care system, a trial to tease out the positive and negative effects that care on average has on children, would involve identifying a group of children with problems and assigning them to two groups, one of which was taken into care, while the other was left alone. But of course it is not acceptable to simply refuse a service to one group of children for experimental purposes.

Another difficulty that is much greater when it comes to evaluating social work interventions lies in defining precisely what it is that is being evaluated. If you are evaluating a medicine, you are looking at the effect of a particular dosage of a particular chemical compound, and it is possible to be quite precise both about the dosage and about the composition of the compound. But suppose you want to evaluate, say, solution-focused work. You are immediately faced with the questions such as what has to happen in a therapeutic session for it to 'count' as solution focused, given that the content of every single therapy session will be different from every other? Suppose you carry out an evaluation of solution-focused therapy by comparing a treatment group which has received it, with a control group which has not, how can you be sure that any differences between the two groups are due to the solution-focused method, rather than to some other factor present in the therapeutic session (notably the personality of the therapist and the quality of the working relationship between therapist and professional, which, as we saw in the last chapter, often turn out to be more powerful predictors of outcome than the method used). In order to really get a handle on the power of the solution-focused approach, you would need to find some way of teasing out the effect of these other variables.

If we look at the McCord study, interesting as it is, we can see that what is being evaluated is not very specific. What the study does is compare those who participated in the programme with a matched group who did not, and what it suggests is that the programme as a whole was unsuccessful, and indeed harmful, when measured against its own objectives. We know that the core of the programme consisted of regular visits to families by 'counsellors', but the data described in McCord's paper, and discussed earlier in this chapter, do not allow us to compare the work of different counsellors or indeed the different approaches that individual counsellors may have tried at different times. It could be that some of the counsellors, or some of the approaches, really were effective at deflecting boys from crime, even if the programme, taken as a whole, was not.

In fact the situation is even more complicated than that, because it might be that some approaches worked for some counsellors but did not work for others. (I have a certain personality and you have a different personality: my way of doing things may not work for you and vice versa.) Nor do the complications stop there, for the boys and families are factors in the outcome too, and not just the counsellors. It could be that certain counsellors, using certain techniques, really were effective with *some* boys and families but not with others, and that different counsellors and/or different techniques, really were effective with other boys and families. As Helen Dickinson observes, the kind of service that is delivered by social workers differs from many other kinds of 'product' in that 'it cannot be quality controlled prior to its delivery; each action of delivery is unique and to some degree is co-produced between the deliverer and the receiver' (2008: 9). If you are planning to visit a service user and do some direct work, you cannot pre-plan in advance *precisely* what you are going to say, or how you are going to say it, because the service user's own responses and reactions will inevitably (and quite rightly) affect what you do and say when you are actually there.

PLACEMENT QUESTIONS 9.2   EVALUATING YOUR AGENCY'S WORK

Before going further, you might like to consider how you could design a study that would evaluate the service provided by your placement agency.

What kind of service user outcomes would you measure, and how could you measure them in a way that would, as far as possible, eliminate bias and wishful thinking, so that you could be satisfied that you really were getting a fair measure of the success or otherwise of the service?

EVIDENCE AND SOCIAL WORK

The business of pinpointing what works in social work, and what does not, turns out to be a very complicated matter, and this relates to the fact that social workers tend to operate in Donald Schön's 'swampy lowland where situations are confusing "messes" incapable of technical solution' (1991: 42, as discussed in Chapter 5). This has led some commentators to argue that there is no point in even trying to ask these sorts of questions, or even to suggest that a preoccupation with such questions is likely to be harmful (see for example Webb, 2001). Certainly these matters are complicated, and certainly some of the statements made in support of evidence-based social work can seem unrealistic and even a little absurd, a point that Stephen Webb makes by quoting the following from two enthusiastic proponents of evidence-based practice:

> Evidence-based professionals pose specific answerable questions regarding decisions in their practice, search electronically for the answer, critically appraise what they find, carefully consider whether findings apply to a particular client, and together with the client, select an option to try and evaluate the results. (Gibbs and Gambrill, 2002: 453)

It does indeed seem unrealistic to imagine that social workers could ever pinpoint solutions to problems in such a mechanical and straightforward way, given that each situation encountered by social workers is unique, but I am not sure that this gives us the right to simply shrug off the whole question of evidence, as Webb seems to be suggesting.

Webb is not on his own. There is considerable resistance in the social work literature to any attempt to systemise or contain social work: resistance not only to evidence-based practice, but also to managerialism, to a 'planned rational order' (Webb, 2001: 76) and to any perceived threat to professional autonomy. There are valid reasons for this. We feel uneasy about reducing our work with individual human beings on their individual problems to some sort of mechanical process. As Zygmunt Bauman observes, drawing on the work of the philosopher Knud Løgstrup:

> If the demand for responsibility and care 'could be spelled out in detail', as – tired of perpetual uncertainty – we so often dream, 'the demand would be purely an external matter', 'without any investment of our own humanity, imagination, or insight'. (2000: 10)

And indeed, as Webb argues, it is probably the case that if we attempted to shoehorn all of our work into a few procedures tried and tested in controlled trials, it would almost certainly reduce our overall efficiency, rather than increase it, for it would reduce our ability to respond flexibly to new situations and draw on our own experience.

These are all important points. But there is a more unattractive side to social work's resistance to rules and evidence and containment, and it is to do with clinging jealously, as all professions do, to status and power. As I observed at the very beginning of this book, social work intrudes into people's lives, often whether they want it to or not. (This last point, in particular, is so often brushed aside when social workers call for more autonomy and less regulation: the fact that *we ourselves are involved in regulating others!*) I think we owe it to those whose lives we intrude into to have at least some basis for thinking that our interventions are likely to change things for the better, not for the worse. For on what basis, otherwise, do we have the right to insist that they let us through their doors?

CHAPTER SUMMARY AND CONCLUDING THOUGHTS

This chapter has looked at the question of evaluating social work, something that you will be wanting to do on your placement as you consider your own work and the work of the agency in which you are placed. How do we know whether we are doing any good? The chapter has scratched the surface of a big subject by looking at the criteria we might use for success, the difficulty in achieving objectivity, and some of the methodological challenges that face us if we attempt to evaluate the effectiveness of social work. Finally I have very briefly touched on a debate about the relevance of evidence in social work, concluding with some thoughts about social work as a profession.

FURTHER READING

I can recommend the following book as a helpful and readable introduction to the issues involved in trying to gather evidence about what works in social work. It was this book which drew my attention to the study by Joan McCord which I have used in this chapter as an example of the dangers of relying on subjective impressions.

Newman, T., Moseley, A., Tierney, S. and Ellis, A. (2005) *Evidence-Based Social Work: A Guide for the Perplexed*. Lyme Regis: Russell House.

But, as ever, I do also suggest that you look for articles and books which review the evidence about what works in relation to the specific service area in which you are placed.

REFERENCES

Alaszewski, A. and Alaszewski, H. (2002) 'Towards the Creative Management of Risk: perceptions, practices and policies', *British Journal of Learning Disabilities*, 30 (2), 56–62.

Argyle, M. (1994) *The Psychology of Interpersonal Behaviour* (5th edn). London: Penguin

Association for Improvements in Mental Health Services (AIMS) (2004) 'Press Release – 1 October 2004: Health visitors are now the health police – and the government's campaign to stop aggression against NHS staff is backfiring, says maternity pressure group', www.aims.org.uk (accessed Nov 2009).

Bandura, A. (2006) 'Toward a Psychology of Human Agency', *Perspectives on Psychological Science*, 1 (2), 164–180.

Bateman, N. (2000) *Advocacy Skills for Health and Social Care Professionals*. London: Jessica Kingsley.

Bauman, Z. (2000) 'Am I my brother's keeper?', *European Journal of Social Work*, 3 (1), 5–11.

Becker, H. (1997 [1963]) *Outsiders: Studies in the Sociology of Deviance*. New York: Free Press.

Beckett, C. (2003) 'The Language of Siege: military metaphors in the spoken language of social work', *British Journal of Social Work*, 33 (5), 625–639.

Beckett, C. (2006) *Essential Theory for Social Work Practice*. London: Sage.

Beckett, C. (2007a) *Child Protection: An Introduction* (2nd edn). London: Sage.

Beckett, C. (2007b) 'The Reality Principle: realism as an ethical obligation', *Ethics and Social Welfare*, 1 (3), 269–281.

Beckett, C. (2008) 'Risk, Uncertainty and Thresholds', in M. Calder (ed.), *Contemporary Risk Assessment in Child Protection*. Lyme Regis: Russell House, pp. 40–51.

Beckett, C. and Maynard, A. (2005) *Values and Ethics in Social Work: An Introduction*. London: Sage.

Beckett, C. and McKeigue, B. (2003) 'Children in Limbo: cases where care proceedings have taken two years or more', *Adoption and Fostering*, 27 (3), 31–40.

Beckett, C. and Taylor, H. (2010) *Human Growth and Development* (2nd edn). London: Sage.

Beckett, C., McKeigue, B. and Taylor, H. (2007) 'Coming to Conclusions: social work perceptions of the decision-making process in care proceedings', *Child and Family Social Work*, 12 (1), 54–63.

Blaine, B. (2007) *Understanding the Psychology of Diversity*. London: Sage.

Bordo, S. (2003) *Unbearable Weight: Feminism, Western Culture and the Body*. Berkeley: University of California Press.

Bowlby, J. (1998) *Separation*. London: Pimlico.

Bradshaw, J. (1972) 'The Concept of Social Need', *New Society*, March, 640–643.

Brandon, D. and Brandon, T. (2001) *Advocacy in Social Work*. Birmingham: Venture Press.

Broadhurst, K., Wastell, D., White, S., Hall, C., Peckover, K., Pithouse, A. and Davey, D. (2010) 'Performing "Initial Assessment": identifying the latent conditions for error at the front-door of local authority children's services', *British Journal of Social Work*, 40(2): 352–370.

Brooker, C. and Repper, J. (2009) *Mental Health: From Policy to Practice*. London: Elsevier.

Brown, D. (2007) *Tricks of the Mind*. London: Channel 4 Books.

Byng-Hall, J. (1995) *Rewriting Family Scripts: Improvisation and Systems Change*. New York: Guilford Press.

Campbell, D. (2008) 'Scandal of patients left for hours outside A&E', *The Observer*, 17 Feb, p 1. Available at: http://www.guardian.co.uk/society/2008/feb/17/health.nhs1?gusrc=rss&feed=networkfront (accessed Jan 2009).

Clinnard, M. and Meier, R. (2008) *Sociology of Deviant Behaviour*. Belmont, CA: Wadsworth.

Cobb, R. and Ross, M. (1997) 'Denying Agenda Access: strategic considerations', in R. Cobb and M. Ross (eds), *Cultural Strategies of Agenda Denial*. Kansas: University of Kansas Press, pp. 25–48.

Corden, J. and Somerton, J. (2004) 'The Trans-Theoretical Model of Change: a reliable blueprint for assessment in work with children and families?', *British Journal of Social Work*, 34 (7), 1025–1044.

Cowden, S. and Singh, G. (2007) 'The "User": friend, foe or fetish? A critical exploration of user involvement in health and social care', *Critical Social Policy*, 27 (1), 5–23.

Croydon, H. (2009) 'Is sex for the disabled the last taboo?', Times Online, 12 Nov, at http://women.timesonline.co.uk/tol/life_and_style/women/relationships/article6912760.ece (accessed Nov 2009).

Dalrymple, J. and Burke, B. (2006) *Anti-Oppressive Practice: Social Care and the Law* (2nd edn). Maidenhead: Open University Press.

Davies, H. (2009) 'Ethics and Practice in Child Protection', *Ethics and Social Welfare*, 3 (3), 322–328.

Davies, J. (1997) *The Myth of Addiction* (2nd edn). Amsterdam: Harwood.

Davies, L. (2008) 'Reclaiming the Language of Child Protection: mind the gap. Family support versus child protection: exposing the myth', in M. Calder (ed.), *Contemporary Risk Assessment in Child Protection*. Lyme Regis: Russell House, pp. 25–39.

Davies, M. (1991) *The Essential Social Worker* (3rd edn). Aldershot: Arena.

de Shazer, S. (1985) *Keys to Solution in Brief Therapy*. New York: WW Norton.

Dean, H. (2010) *Understanding Human Need*. Bristol: Policy Press.

Department for Education and Skills (DfES) (2003) *Every Child Matters* [Green Paper]. London: The Stationery Office.

Department for Education and Skills (DfES) (2006a) *Care Matters: Transforming the Lives of Children and Young People in Care*. London: The Stationery Office.

Department for Education and Skills (DfES) (2006b) *Working Together to Safeguard Children*. London: The Stationery Office.

Department of Health (2000) *Framework for the Assessment of Children in Need and their Families*. London: The Stationery Office. (Also at http://www.dh.gov.uk/en/Publicationsandstatistics/Publications/PublicationsPolicyandGuidance/DH_4003256 [accessed Nov 2009].)

Department of Health (2001) *The Children Act Now: Messages from Research*. London: The Stationery Office.

Department of Health (2003) 'Fair Access to Care Services: Guidance on Eligibility Criteria for Adult Social Care'. Available at http://www.dh.gov.uk/en/Publicationsandstatistics/Publications/Publications PolicyandGuidance/DH_4009653 (accessed Nov 2009).

Department of Health (2009) 'Individual Budgets', at http://www.dh.gov.uk/en/SocialCare/Socialcarereform/Personalisation/Individualbudgets/DH_4125774 (accessed April 2009).

Dickinson, H. (2008) *Evaluating Outcomes in Health and Social Care*. Bristol: Policy Press.

Dominelli, L. (2002) *Anti-Oppressive Social Work: Theory and Practice*. Basingstoke: Palgrave.

Dominelli, L. (2004) *Social Work: Theory and Practice for a Changing Profession*. Cambridge: Polity.

Duncan, B. (1976) 'Differential social perception an attribution of inter-group violence: testing the lower limits of stereotyping of blacks', *Journal of Personality and Social Psychology*, 34 (4): 390–398.

Early, T. and GlenMaye, L. (2000) 'Valuing Families: social work practice with families from a strengths perspective', *Social Work*, 45 (2), 118–130.

Edelman, M. (1985) *The Symbolic Uses of Politics*. Chicago: University of Illinois Press.

Eisenberg, M. and Resnick, M. (2006) 'Suicidality among Gay, Lesbian and Bisexual Youth: the role of protective factors', *Journal of Adolescent Health*, 39 (5), 662–668.

Elster, J. (1989) *Solomonic Judgements: Studies in the Limitations of Rationality*. Cambridge: Cambridge University Press.

Evans, T. and Harris, J. (2004) 'Street-Level Bureaucracy: social work and the (exaggerated) death of discretion', *British Journal of Social Work*, 34 (6), 871–895.

Fahlberg, V. (1981) *Helping Children When They Must Move*. London: British Association for Adoption and Fostering.

Fahlberg, V. (1994) *A Child's Journey Through Placement*. London: BAAF.

Farmer, E. and Owen, M. (1995) *Child Protection Practice: Private Risks and Public Remedies*. London: The Stationery Office.

Festinger, L. (1962) *A Theory of Cognitive Dissonance*. Stanford, CA: Stanford University Press.

Fitzpatrick, S. and Johnsen, S. (2009) 'The Use of Enforcement to Combat "Street Culture" in England: an ethical approach?', *Ethics and Social Welfare*, 3 (3), 284–302.

Gibbs, L. and Gambrill, E. (2002) 'Evidence-Based Practice: counterarguments to objections', *Research on Social Work Practice*, 12 (3), 452–476.

Gigerenzer, G. (2002) *Reckoning with Risk*. London: Penguin.

Gill, T. (2007) *No Fear: Growing Up in a Risk Averse Society*. London: Calouse Gilbenkian Foundation.

Glasby, J. (2003) *Hospital Discharge: Integrating Health and Social Care*. Abingdon: Radcliffe.

Glendinning, C., Challis, D., Fernández, J., Jacobs, S., Jones, K., Knapp, M., Manthorpe, J., Moran, N., Netten, A., Stevens, M. and Wilberforce, M. (2008) *Evaluation of the Individual Budgets Pilot Programme: Final Report*. York: Social Policy Research Unit, University of York. Available at: http://www.dh.gov.uk/en/Publicationsandstatistics/Publications/PublicationsPolicyAndGuidance/DH_089505 (accessed April 2009).

Glendinning, L. and Jones, S. (2008) 'Baby P death sparks national child protection review', *The Guardian*, 11 Nov, at http://www.guardian.co.uk/society/2008/nov/11/childprotection-ukcrime3 (accessed April 2009).

Glisson, G. and Hemmelgarn, A. (1998) 'The Effects of Organizational Climate and Interorganizational Coordination on the Quality and Outcomes of Children's Service Systems', *Child Abuse and Neglect*, 22 (5), 401–425.

Goldacre, B. (2006) 'Prosecuting and defending by numbers', *The Guardian*, 28 Oct. Available at http://www.guardian.co.uk/science/2006/oct/28/uknews1 (accessed Dec 2009).

Greenland, C. (1987) *Preventing CAN Deaths: An International Study of Deaths due to Child Abuse and Neglect*. London: Tavistock.

Gupta, A. and Blewett, J. (2005) 'Involving Families Living in Poverty in Social Work Education', Unpublished conference paper: Joint Universities Social Work Education Conference (JUSWEC), Loughborough (cited by Cowden and Singh [2007]).

Guterman, N. (2001) *Stopping Child Maltreatment before it Starts: Emerging Horizons in Early Home Visitation*. Thousand Oaks, CA: Sage.

Harlow, H. (1963) 'The Maternal Affectional System', in B.M. Foss (ed.), *Determinants of Human Behaviour*. London: Methuen, pp. 3–29.

Harne, L. and Radford, J. (2008) *Tackling Domestic Violence: Theories, Policies and Practice*. Maidenhead: Open University Press.

Healy, K. (2005) *Social Work Theories in Context: Creating Frameworks for Practice*. Basingstoke: Palgrave.

Herring, R. and Thom, B. (1997) 'The Right to Take Risks: alcohol and older people', *Social Policy and Administration*, 31 (3), 233–246.

Horvath, A. and Bedi, R. (2002) 'The Alliance', in J. Norcross (ed.), *Psychotherapy Relationships That Work: Therapist Contributions and Responsiveness to Patients*. Oxford: Oxford University Press, pp. 37–70.

Horwath, J. and Morrison, T. (2000) 'Assessment of Parental Motivation to Change', in J. Howarth (ed.), *The Child's World: Assessing Children in Need*. London; Department of Health, pp. 77–90.

Humphreys, C. and Thiara, R. (2003) 'Mental Health and Domestic Violence: "I call it symptoms of abuse"', *British Journal of Social Work*, 33 (2), 209–226.

International Federation of Social Workers(IFSW) (2000) 'Definition of Social Work', at http.//www.ifsw.org/en/f38000138.html (accessed Jan 2009).

Iskedjian, M. Bereza, B. Gordon, A. Charles Piwko, C. and Einarson, T. (2007) 'Meta-analysis of cannabis based treatments for neuropathic and multiple sclerosis-related pain', *Current Medical Research and Opinion*, 23 (1), 17–24.

Janis, I. (1982) *Groupthink: Psychological Studies of Policy Decisions and Fiascos*. Boston, MA: Houghton Mifflin.

Johnson, H. and Thompson, A. (2008) 'The Development and Maintenance of Post-Traumatic Stress Disorder (PTSD) in Civilian Adult Survivors of War Trauma and Torture: a review', *Clinical Psychology Review*, 28 (1), 26–47.

Kinney, M. (2009) 'Being Assessed Under the 1983 Mental Health Act – can it ever be ethical?', *Ethics and Social Welfare*, 3 (3), 329–336.

Kroll, B. and Taylor, A. (2003) *Parental Substance Abuse and Child Welfare*. London: Jessica Kingsley Publishers.

Lambert, M. and Barley, D. (2002) 'Research Summary on the Therapeutic Relationship and Psychotherapy', in J. Norcross (ed.), *Psychotherapy Relationships That Work: Therapist Contributions and Responsiveness to Patients*. Oxford: Oxford University Press, pp. 17–32.

Laming, Lord H. (2003) *The Victoria Climbié Inquiry: Report Of An Inquiry*. London: The Stationery Office.

Laming, Lord H. (2009) *The Protection of Children in England: A Progress Report*. London: The Stationery Office.

Lesseliers, J. and Van Hove, G. (2002) 'Barriers to the Development of Intimate Relationships and the Expression of Sexuality Among People with Developmental Disabilities: their perceptions', *Research and Practice for Persons with Severe Disabilities*, 27 (1), 69–81.

Lipsky, M. (1980) *Street-Level Bureaucracy: Dilemmas of the Individual in Public Services*. New York: Russell Sage.

Lishman, J. (2009) *Communication in Social Work* (2nd edn). Basingstoke: Palgrave.

Loftus, E. (1977) 'Shifting Human Color Memory', *Memory and Cognition*, 5 (6), 696–699.

Loftus, E. and Palmer, J. (1974) 'Reconstruction of Automobile Destruction: an example of the interaction between language and memory', *Journal of Verbal Learning and Verbal Behavior*, 13, 585–589.

Marsh, P. and Doel, M. (2005) *The Task-Centred Book*. London: Routledge.

Maslow, A. (1970) *Motivation and Personality* (2nd edn). New York: Harper & Row.

McClaren, H. (2007) 'Exploring the Ethics of Forewarning: social workers, confidentiality and potential child abuse disclosures', *Ethics and Social Welfare*, 1 (1), 22–40.

McCord, J. (1978) 'A Thirty-year Follow-up of Treatment Effects', *American Psychologist*, 33 (3), 284–289.

McKeigue, B. and Beckett, C. (2010) 'Squeezing the Toothpaste Tube: will tackling court delay result in pre-court delay in its place?', *British Journal of Social Work*, 40 (1), 154–169.

McLaughlin, H. (2009) 'What's in a Name: "client", "patient", "customer", "consumer", "expert by experience", "service user" – what's next?', *British Journal of Social Work*, 39 (6), 1101–1117.

Menzies, I. Lyth (1988) 'The Functions of Social Systems as a Defence Against Anxiety: a report on a study of the nursing service of a general hospital', in I. Menzies, *Containing Anxiety in Institutions: Selected Essays*, vol. 1. London: Free Association Books, pp. 43–88.

Mezulis, A., Abramson, L., Hyde, J. and Hankin, B. (2004) 'Is There a Universal Positivity Bias in Attributions? A meta-analytic review of individual, developmental, and cultural differences in the self-serving attributional bias', *Psychological Bulletin*, 130 (5), 711–747.

Miller, W. and Rollnick, S. (2002) *Motivational Interviewing: Preparing People for Change*. New York: Guilford Press.

Milner, J. and O'Byrne, P. (2009) *Assessment in Social Work* (3rd edn). Basingstoke: Palgrave.

Morris, G. (2006) *Mental Health Issues and the Media: An Introduction for Health Professionals*. London: Routledge.

Munro, E. (2002) *Effective Child Protection*. London: Sage.

Neville, D. (2004) *Putting Empowerment into Practice: Turning Rhetoric into Reality*. London: Whiting and Birch.

Newman, T., Moseley, A., Tierney, S. and Ellis, A. (2005) *Evidence-Based Social Work: A Guide for the Perplexed*. Lyme Regis: Russell House.

Norcross, J. (2002) 'Empirically Supported Therapy Relationships', in J. Norcross (ed.), *Psychotherapy Relationships That Work: Therapist Contributions and Responsiveness to Patients*. Oxford: Oxford University Press, pp. 3–16.

NSPCC (2009) *About the NSPCC*. At: http://www.nspcc.org.uk/whatwedo/aboutthenspcc/about thenspcc_wda36522.html (accessed April 2009).

Parry-Jones, B. and Soulsby, J. (2001) 'Needs-Led Assessment: the challenges and the reality', *Health and Social Care in the Community*, 9 (6), 414–428.

Parton, N. and O'Byrne, P. (2000) *Constructive Social Work*. Basingstoke: Palgrave.

Penny, L. (2009) 'Case Study: "I never went anywhere without this slogan written on my hand. It was my mantra"', *The Guardian*, 21 Nov, p 11. Accessible online at http://www.guardian.co.uk/lifeandstyle/2009/nov/20/kate-moss-motto-pro-anorexic (accessed Nov 2009).

Peterson, C., Maier, S. and Seligman, M. (1995) *Learned Helplessness: A Theory for the Age of Personal Control* (new edn). New York: Oxford University Press.

Plant, E. and Peruche, M. (2005) 'The Consequences of Race for Police Officers' Response to Criminal Suspects', *Psychological Science*, 16 (3), 180–183.

Pohl, R. (2004a) 'Effects of Labelling', in R. Pohl (ed.), *Cognitive Illusions*. Hove: Psychology Press, pp. 327–344.

Pohl, R. (2004b) 'Introduction: Cognitive Illusions', in R. Pohl (ed.), *Cognitive Illusions*. Hove: Psychology Press, pp. 1–20.

Pohl, R. (2004c) 'Hindsight Bias', in R. Pohl (ed.), *Cognitive Illusions*. Hove: Psychology Press, pp. 363–378.

Prochaska, J., DiClemente, C. and Norcross, J. (1992) 'In Search of How People Change: applications to addictive behaviours', *American Psychologist*, 47 (9), 1102–1114.

Reder, P. (2003) 'Does the Past Predict the Future?', in P. Reder, S. Duncan and C. Lucey (eds), *Studies in the Assessment of Parenting*. Hove: Brunner-Routledge, pp. 229–246.

Reid, L and Epstein, W. (1972) *Task-Centered Casework*. New York: Columbia University Press.

Rooney, R. (1992) *Strategies for Work with Involuntary Clients*. New York: Columbia.

Rose, R. and Philpot, T. (2005) *The Child's Own Story: Life Story Work with Traumatized Children*. London: Jessica Kingsley.

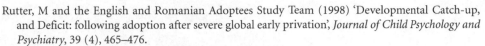

Rutter, M and the English and Romanian Adoptees Study Team (1998) 'Developmental Catch-up, and Deficit: following adoption after severe global early privation', *Journal of Child Psychology and Psychiatry*, 39 (4), 465–476.

Saleebey, D. (2006) 'The Strengths Perspective: philosophy, concepts and principles', in D. Saleebey (ed.), *The Strengths Perspective in Social Work Practice* (4th edn). Boston, MA: Allyn and Bacon, pp. 7–9.

Schön, D. (1991) *The Reflective Practitioner: How Professionals Think in Action.* Aldershot: Arena.

Schur, E. (1973) *Radical Non-Intervention: Rethinking the Delinquency Problem.* Englewood Cliffs, NJ: Prentice-Hall.

Scourfield, P. (2007) 'Social Care and the Modern Citizen: client, consumer, service user, manager and entrepreneur', *British Journal of Social Work*, 37 (1), 107–122.

Seden, J. (2005) *Counselling Skills in Social Work Practice* (2nd edn). Maidenhead: Open University Press.

Shakespeare, T. (2006) *Disability Rights and Wrongs.* London: Routledge.

Sim, R. (2003) *Reminiscence: Social and Creative Activities with Older People in Care.* Bicester: Speechmark.

Smale, G. and Tuson, G. with Brehal, N. and Marsh, P. (1993) *Empowerment, Assessment, Case Management and the Skilled Worker.* London: National Institute for Social Work.

Stanley, J. and Goddard, C. (2002) *In the Firing Line: Violence and Power in Child Protection Work.* Chichester: Wiley.

Stovall-McClough, K. and Cloitre, M. (2006) 'Unresolved Attachment, PTSD, and Dissociation in Women with Childhood Abuse Histories', *Journal of Consulting and Clinical Psychology*, 74 (2), 219–228.

Taylor, H., Beckett, C. and McKeigue, M. (2008) 'Judgements of Solomon: anxiety and defences for social workers involved in care proceedings', *Child and Family Social Work*, 13 (1), 23–31.

Thompson, N. (2006) *Anti-Discriminatory Practice* (4th edn). Basingstoke: Palgrave.

Trotter, C. (2004) *Helping Abused Children and their Families: Towards an Evidence-Based Practice Model.* London: Sage.

Trotter, C. (2007) *Working with Involuntary Clients: A Guide to Practice* (2nd edn). London: Sage.

Walshe, C., Todd, C., Caress, A.-L. and Chew-Graham, C. (2008) 'Judgements Made About Fellow-Professionals and the Management of Patients Receiving Palliative Care in Primary Care: a qualitative study', *British Journal of General Practice*, 58 (549), 264–272.

Ware, A. and Goodin, R. (1990) 'Introduction', to A. Ware and R. Goodin (eds), *Needs and Welfare.* London: Sage, pp. 1–11.

Warren, J. (2007) *Service User and Carer Participation in Social Work.* Exeter: Learning Matters.

Weale, A. (1983) *Political Theory and Social Policy.* London: Macmillan

Webb, S. (2001) 'Some Considerations on the Validity of Evidence-Based Practice in Social Work', *British Journal of Social Work*, 31 (1), 51–79.

Whittaker, J. (1989) *Social Treatment: An Introduction to Interpersonal Helping in Social Work Practice* (2nd edn). New York: De Gruyter.

Williams, I. and Young, J. (2003) 'Managing the Transient Workforce: Thinking, Knowledge Sharing and Transfer in the Social Services Arena', Conference paper: 3rd European Knowledge Management Summer School, 7–12 Sept 2003, San Sebastian, Spain. At: https://secure.knowledge-board.com/cgi-bin/item.cgi?id=2233 (accessed April 2009).

Wilson, A. and Beresford, P. (2000) '"Anti-Oppressive Practice": Emancipation or Appropriation?', *British Journal of Social Work*, 30 (5), 553–573.

Youth Justice Board (2009) *Youth Offending Teams – Who are they? What do they do?* At: http://www.yjb.gov.uk/en-gb/yjs/YouthOffendingTeams (accessed April 2009).

INDEX

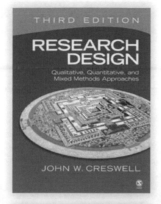

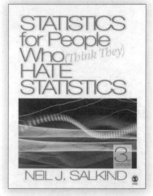

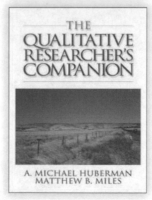

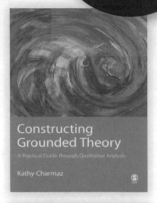
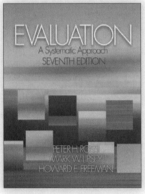
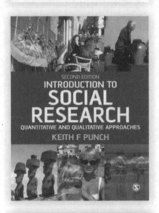
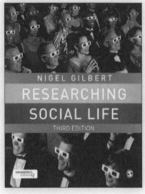